Dry Shave

(a comic strip)

by Rod Filbrandt

T-Bone Maverick Monkey-Man Earl Lipschitz Velvet

Anvil Press Publishers
(Vancouver)

CANADIAN CATALOGUING IN PUBLICATION DATA

Filbrandt, Rod
Dry Shave (a comic strip)

ISBN 1-895636-21-3
I. Title
PN6734.D79F54 1998   C741.5'971   C98-910738-8

PUBLISHED BY
Anvil Press
Suite 204-A – 175 East Broadway,
Vancouver, BC V5T 1W2 CANADA

FIRST EDITION
COVER DESIGN: Rod Filbrandt

The publisher gratefully acknowledges the assistance of the B.C. Arts Council and the Canada Council for the Arts.

THE CANADA COUNCIL | LE CONSEIL DES ARTS
FOR THE ARTS | DU CANADA
SINCE 1957 | DEPUIS 1957

Represented in Canada by the Literary Press Group
Distributed by General Distribution Services.

PRINTED AND BOUND IN CANADA

For Tanya

Special Thanks To

The Lava Lounge, Jean Lafitte's Blacksmith Shop,
Sammibar, The Nitelite, The Original Oak, Hunter Bar,
The Rendezvous, Englehardt's, The Pharmacy, Vito's,
The Marine Club, Giovanni's Sequels, The White Horse,
The Tonga Room, Toranado, The Dungeon, The Skyrack,
Port-of-Call, The Mauna Loa, Tipitina's, The Gay '90s,
Vesuvio's, Two Bells, The Old Nickel, Spec's, Snug
Harbor, Pepe's, Three Legs, and The Funky Butt.

Velvet and Lipschitz. T-Bone and Monkey-Man. Maverick and Nutpants. A superhero named Ashtray Boy whose mission is to seek and destroy unsightly collections of cigarette butts. A big-nosed rube named Flappy with an overwhelming sexual fixation involving pancakes. A bullet-headed bully named Earl humping a three-legged bar stool and yelling "Ruth Buzzi!"

These are not characters from *The Family Circus*.

In fact, when *Dry Shave*'s prototypical travelling salesman promises a man with a shiv "a more sociopathic you in 10 easy lessons", he could well have been writing the parental guidance advisory for the slim volume you now hold in your hands.

From this, you might think that *Dry Shave* is just gratuitous sex, violence, and degradation played for cheap laughs. Well, yeah. But *Dry Shave* is also about the collision of the punk flotsam of the 1980s (which its precursor *Wombat* deftly nailed) and the lounge-noir jetsam of the 1950s. It's a tribute to everything that's grade-B, from Ernest Borgnine and Ennio Morricone to pretentious loft-snob would-be artists and fancy-ass French cigarettes.

Have you got that, Chowderheads? It's about culture, but don't let the thought of it drive you to Sunnygrove. It's time for a martooni at the Lava Lounge.

Charles Campbell,
Former Editor of *The Georgia Straight*

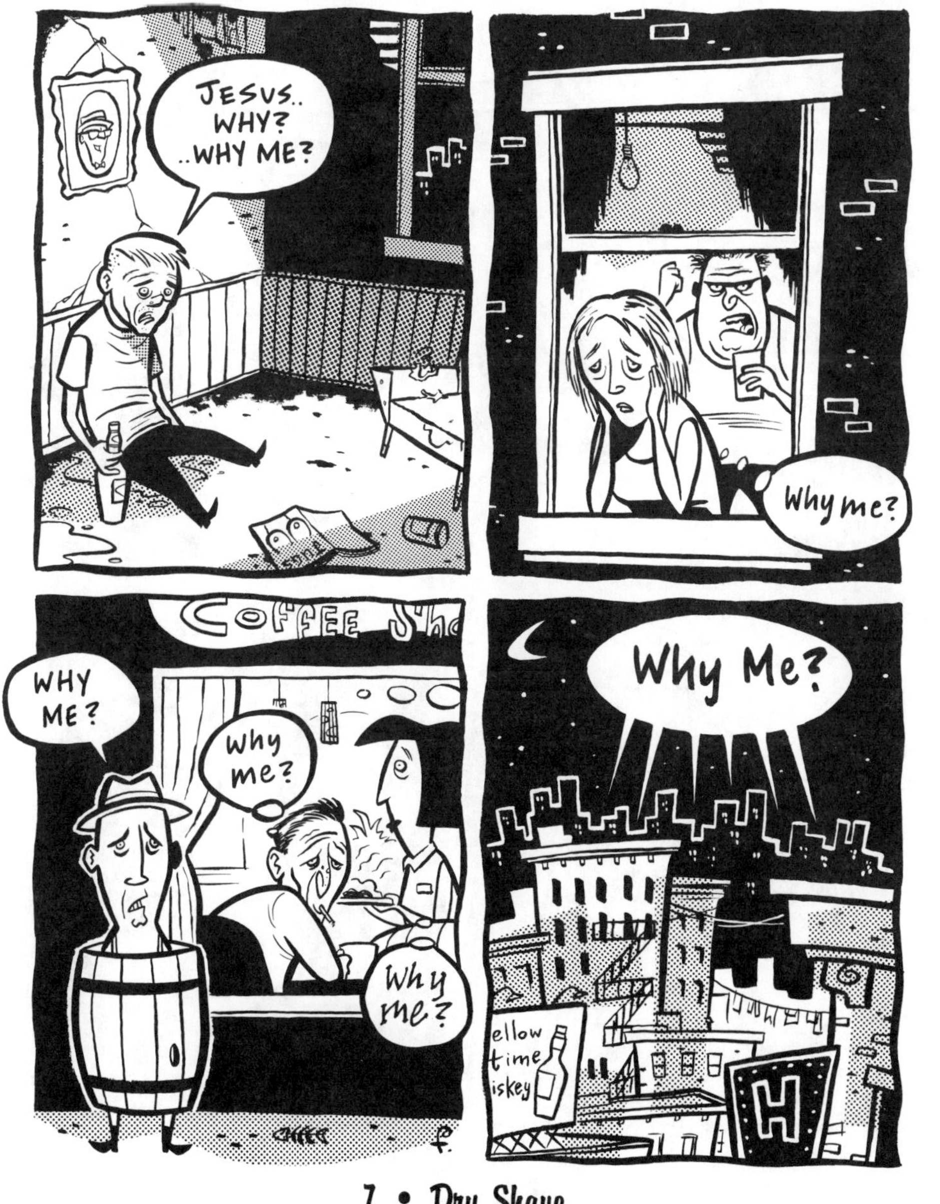
JESUS..
WHY?
..WHY ME?
Why me?
Coffee Sho
WHY ME?
Why me?
Why me?
Why Me?
ellow
time
iskey
H

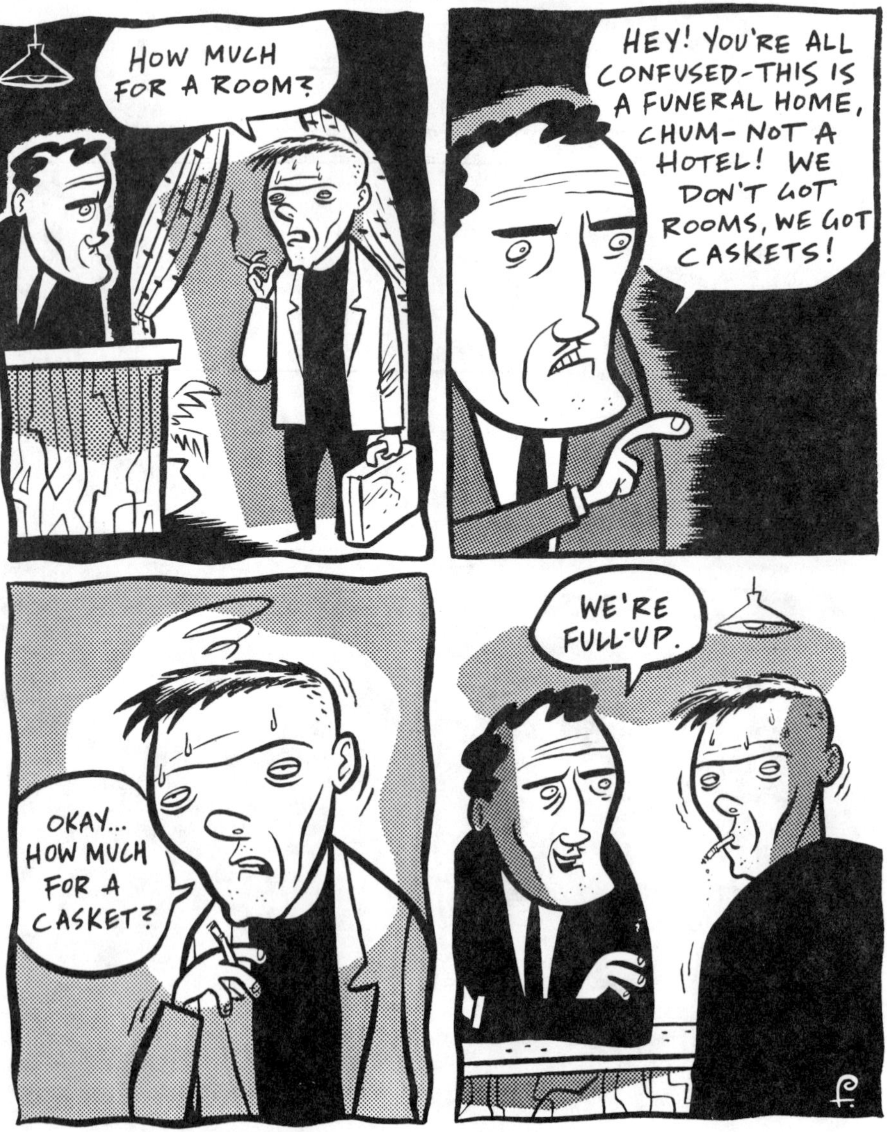
HOW MUCH FOR A ROOM?
HEY! YOU'RE ALL CONFUSED-THIS IS A FUNERAL HOME, CHUM-NOT A HOTEL! WE DON'T GOT ROOMS, WE GOT CASKETS!
OKAY... HOW MUCH FOR A CASKET?
WE'RE FULL-UP.

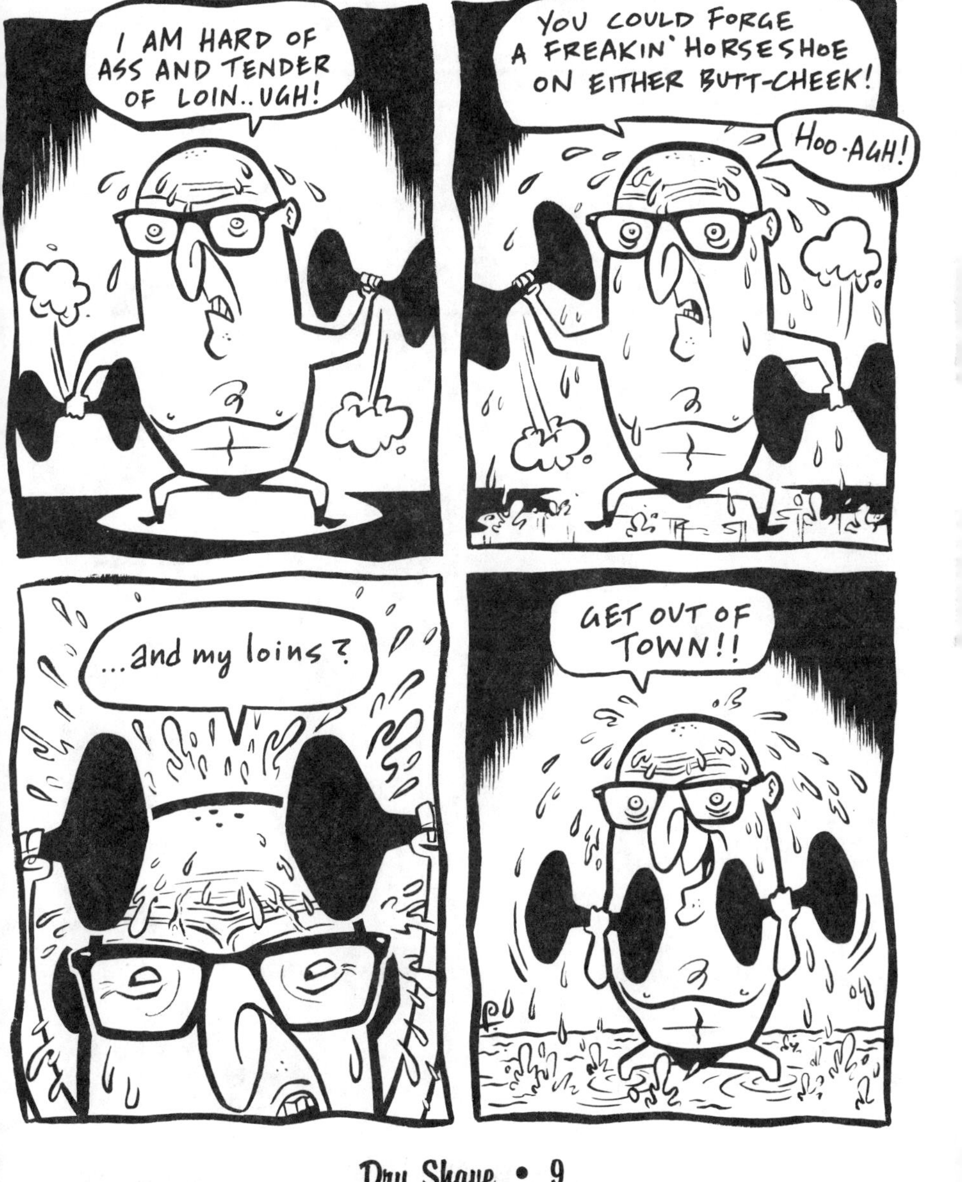
I AM HARD OF ASS AND TENDER OF LOIN..UGH!
YOU COULD FORGE A FREAKIN' HORSESHOE ON EITHER BUTT-CHEEK!
HOO-AGH!
...and my loins?
GET OUT OF TOWN!!

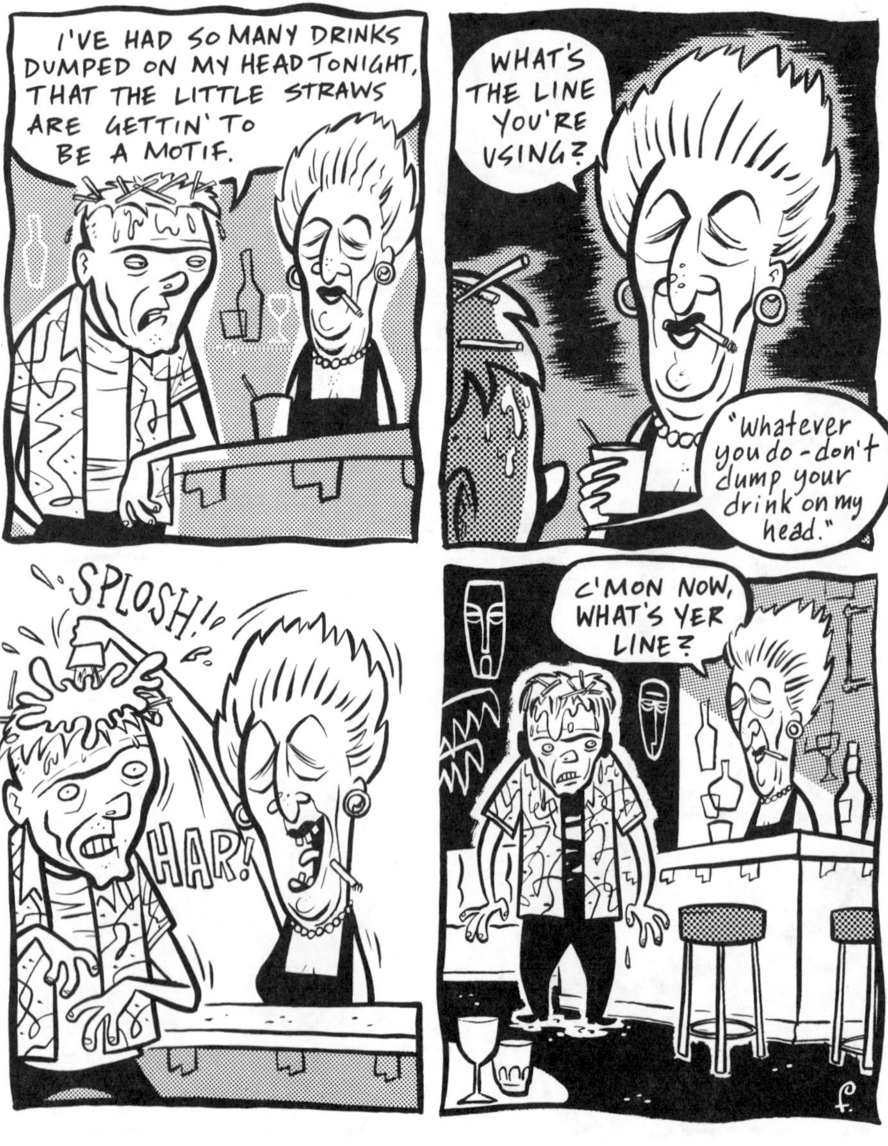
I'VE HAD SO MANY DRINKS DUMPED ON MY HEAD TONIGHT, THAT THE LITTLE STRAWS ARE GETTIN' TO BE A MOTIF.
WHAT'S THE LINE YOU'RE USING?
"whatever you do - don't dump your drink on my head."
SPLOSH!
HAR!
C'MON NOW, WHAT'S YER LINE?
f.

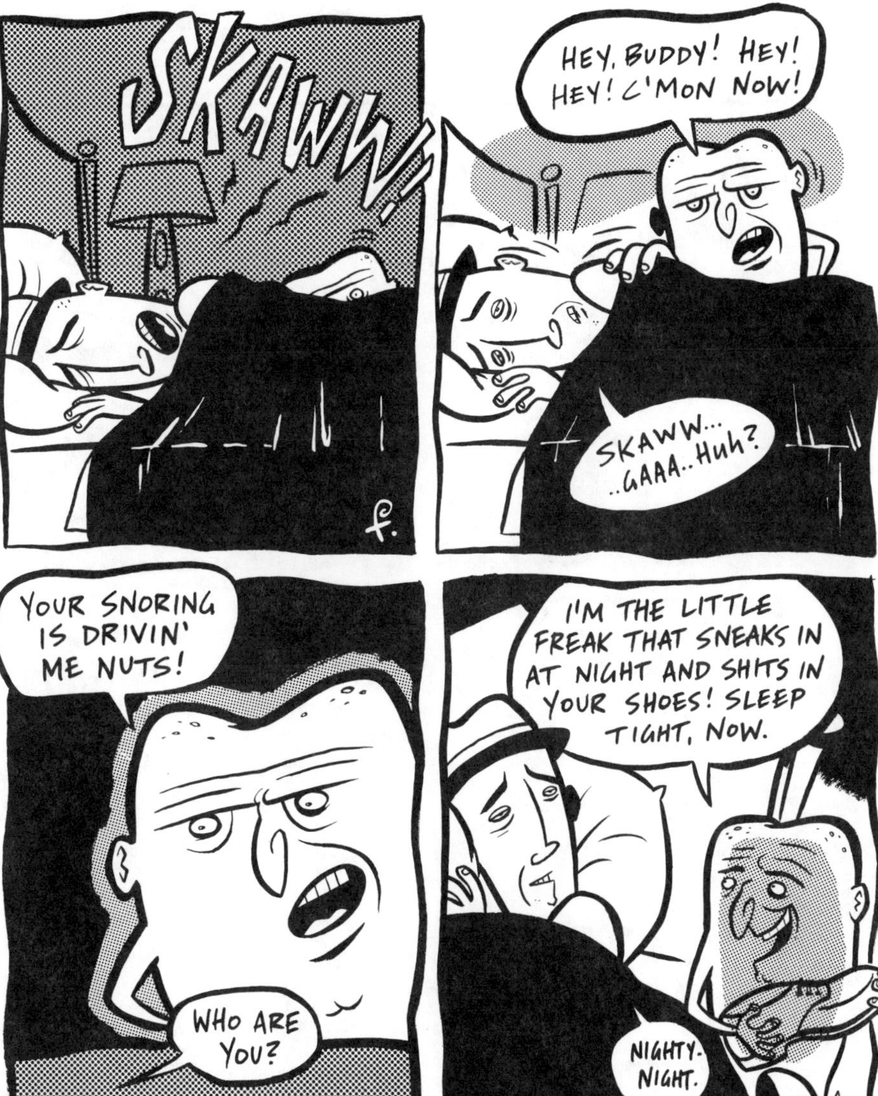
SKAWW!!
HEY, BUDDY! HEY! HEY! C'MON NOW!
SKAWW... ..GAAA..Huh?
YOUR SNORING IS DRIVIN' ME NUTS!
WHO ARE YOU?
I'M THE LITTLE FREAK THAT SNEAKS IN AT NIGHT AND SHITS IN YOUR SHOES! SLEEP TIGHT, NOW.
NIGHTY-NIGHT.

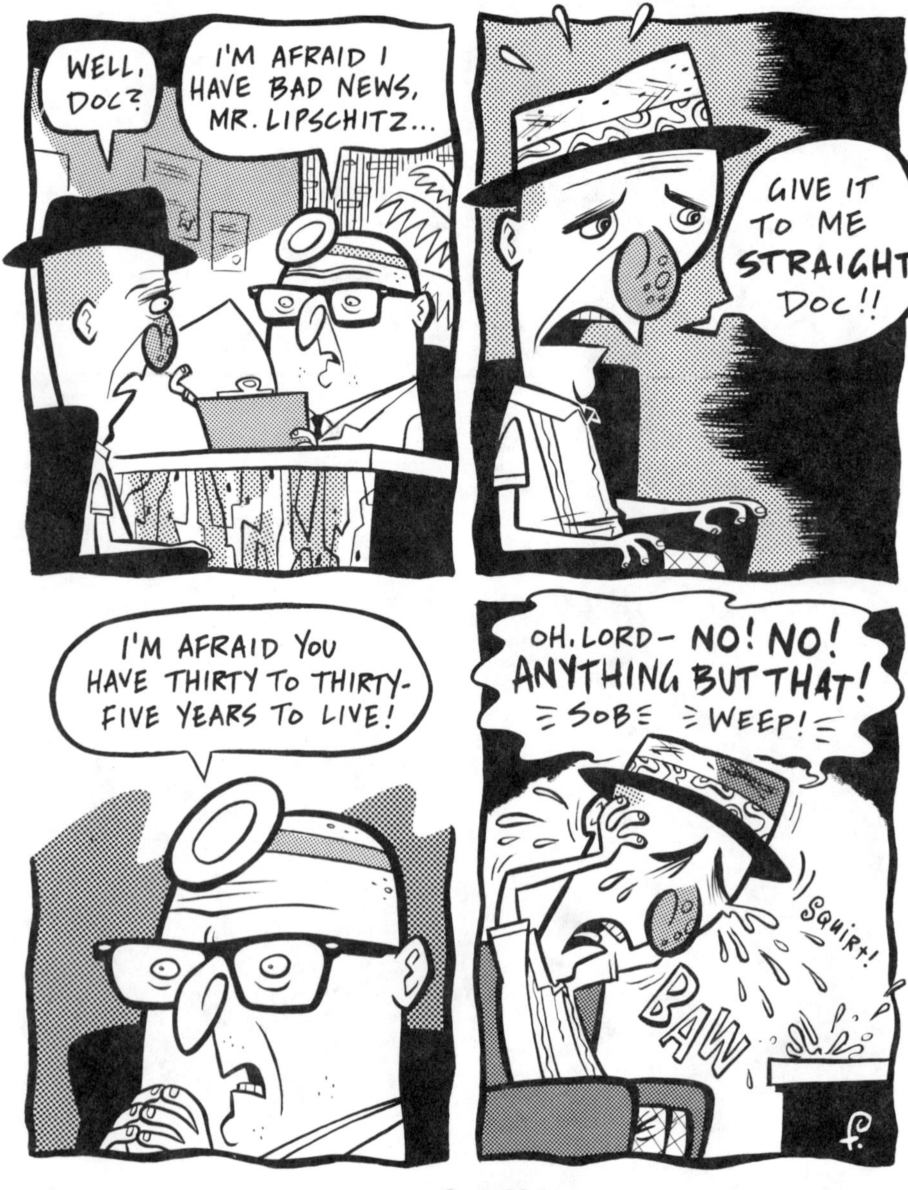
WELL, DOC?
I'M AFRAID I HAVE BAD NEWS, MR. LIPSCHITZ...
GIVE IT TO ME STRAIGHT, DOC!!
I'M AFRAID YOU HAVE THIRTY TO THIRTY-FIVE YEARS TO LIVE!
OH, LORD- NO! NO! ANYTHING BUT THAT!
SOB WEEP!
SQUIRT!
BAW

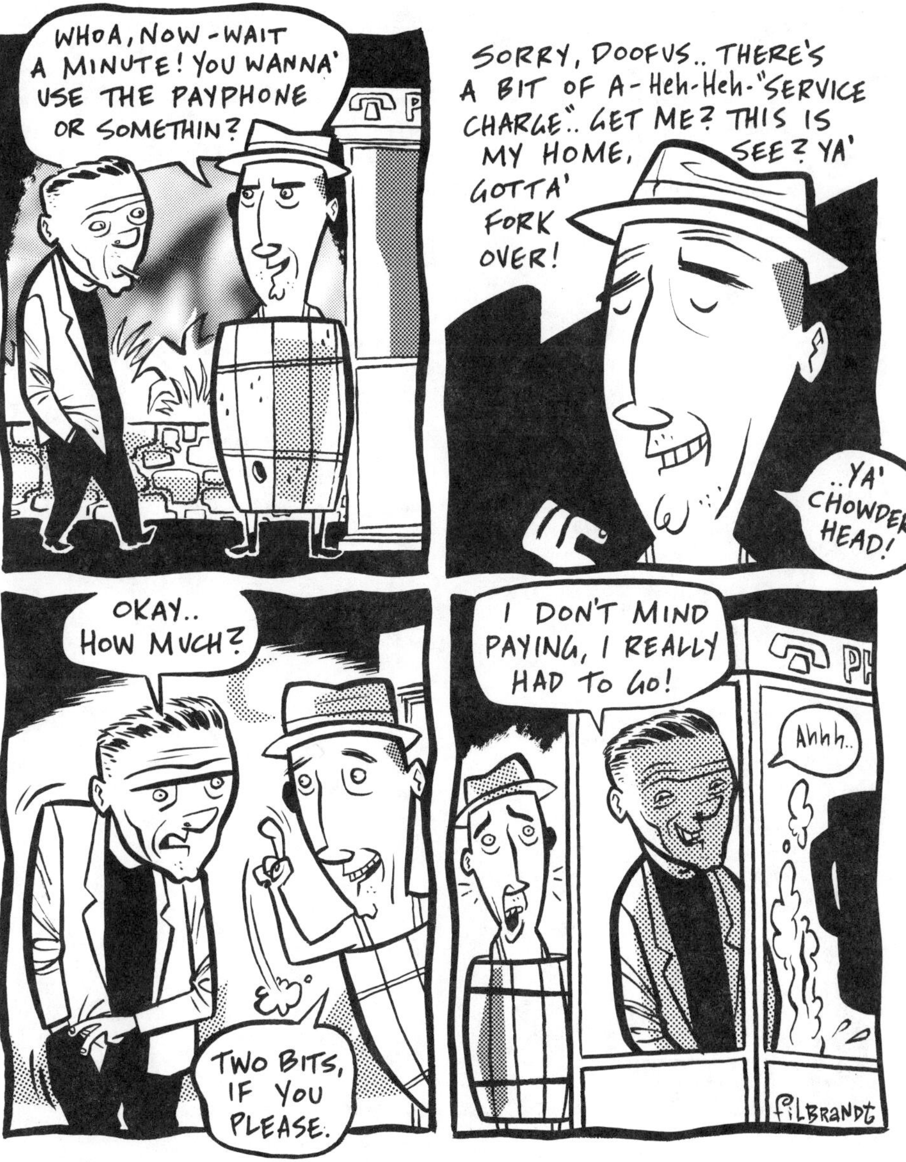
WHOA, NOW-WAIT A MINUTE! YOU WANNA' USE THE PAYPHONE OR SOMETHIN?
SORRY, DOOFUS.. THERE'S A BIT OF A-Heh-Heh-"SERVICE CHARGE".. GET ME? THIS IS MY HOME, SEE? YA' GOTTA' FORK OVER!
..YA' CHOWDER-HEAD!
OKAY.. HOW MUCH?
TWO BITS, IF YOU PLEASE.
I DON'T MIND PAYING, I REALLY HAD TO GO!
Ahhh..
FILBRANDT

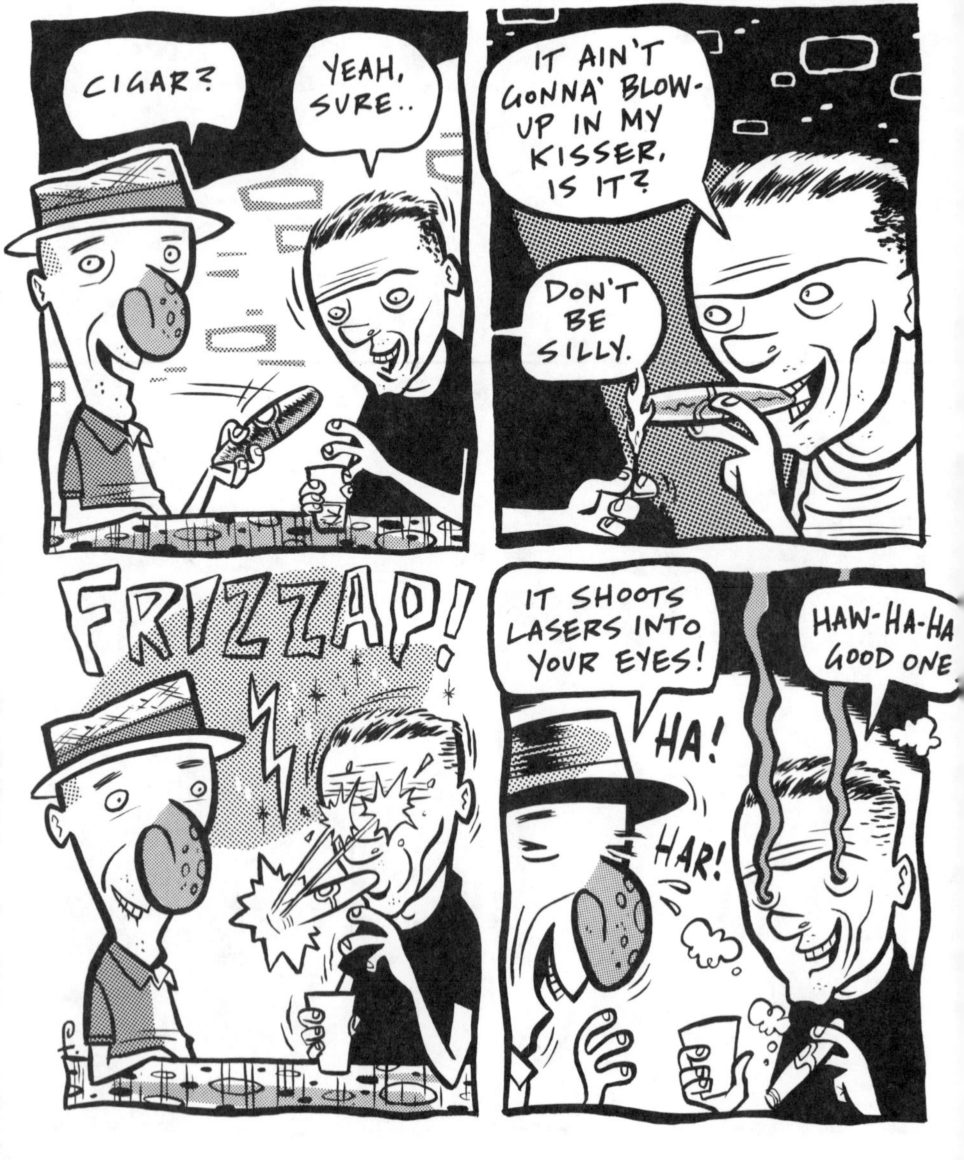
CIGAR?
YEAH, SURE..
IT AIN'T GONNA' BLOW-UP IN MY KISSER, IS IT?
DON'T BE SILLY.
FRIZZAP!
IT SHOOTS LASERS INTO YOUR EYES!
HA!
HAR!
HAW-HA-HA GOOD ONE

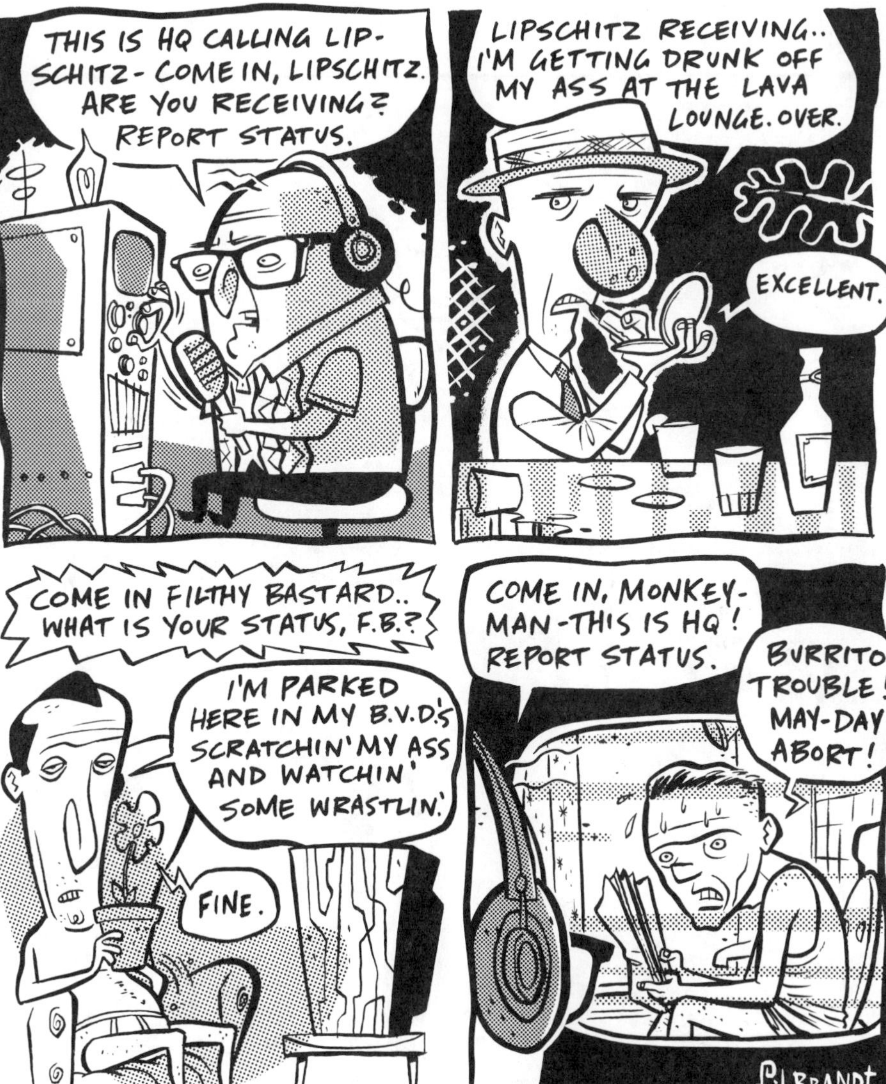
THIS IS HQ CALLING LIP-SCHITZ- COME IN, LIPSCHITZ. ARE YOU RECEIVING? REPORT STATUS.
LIPSCHITZ RECEIVING.. I'M GETTING DRUNK OFF MY ASS AT THE LAVA LOUNGE. OVER.
EXCELLENT.
COME IN FILTHY BASTARD.. WHAT IS YOUR STATUS, F.B.?
I'M PARKED HERE IN MY B.V.D.'S SCRATCHIN' MY ASS AND WATCHIN' SOME WRASTLIN'.
FINE.
COME IN, MONKEY-MAN-THIS IS HQ! REPORT STATUS.
BURRITO TROUBLE! MAY-DAY! ABORT!
FILBRANDT

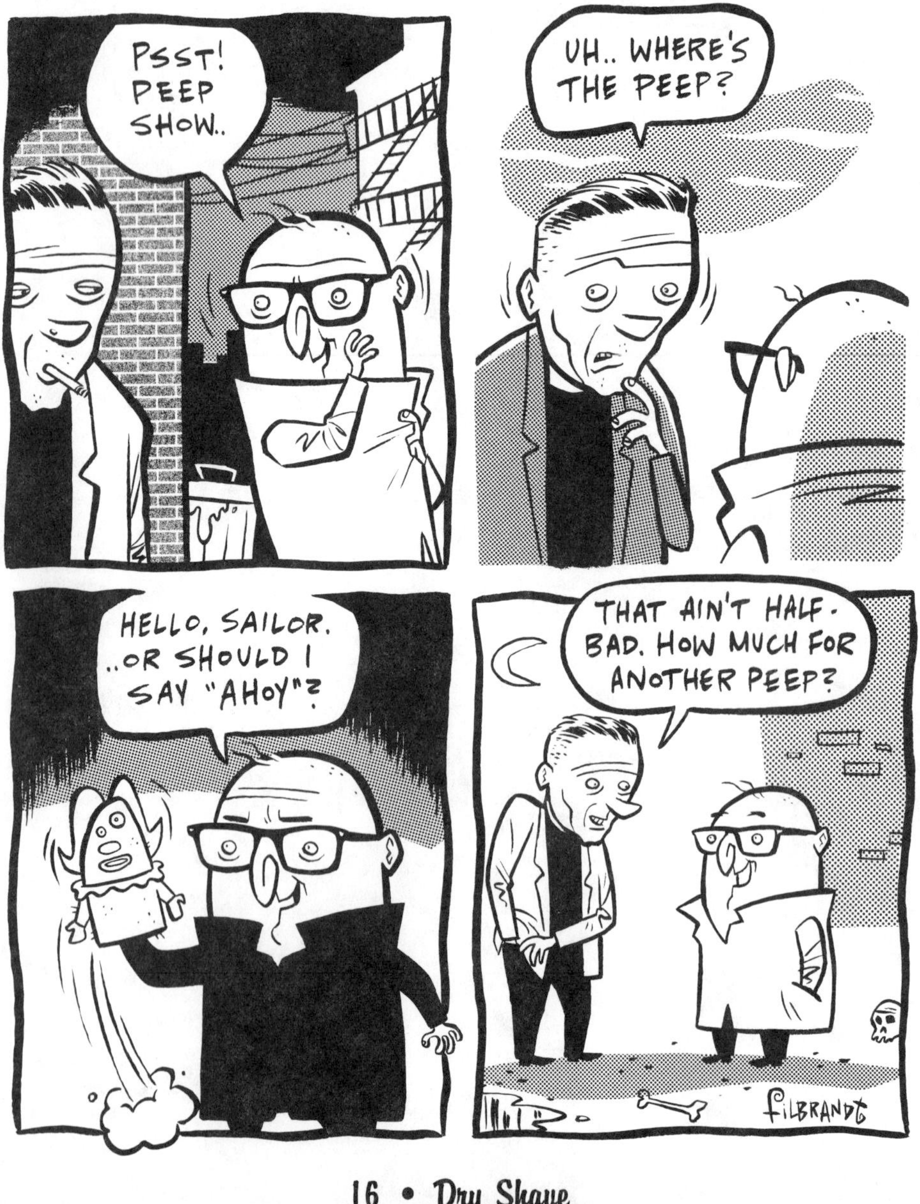
PSST! PEEP SHOW..
UH.. WHERE'S THE PEEP?
HELLO, SAILOR. ..OR SHOULD I SAY "AHOY"?
THAT AIN'T HALF-BAD. HOW MUCH FOR ANOTHER PEEP?
FILBRANDT

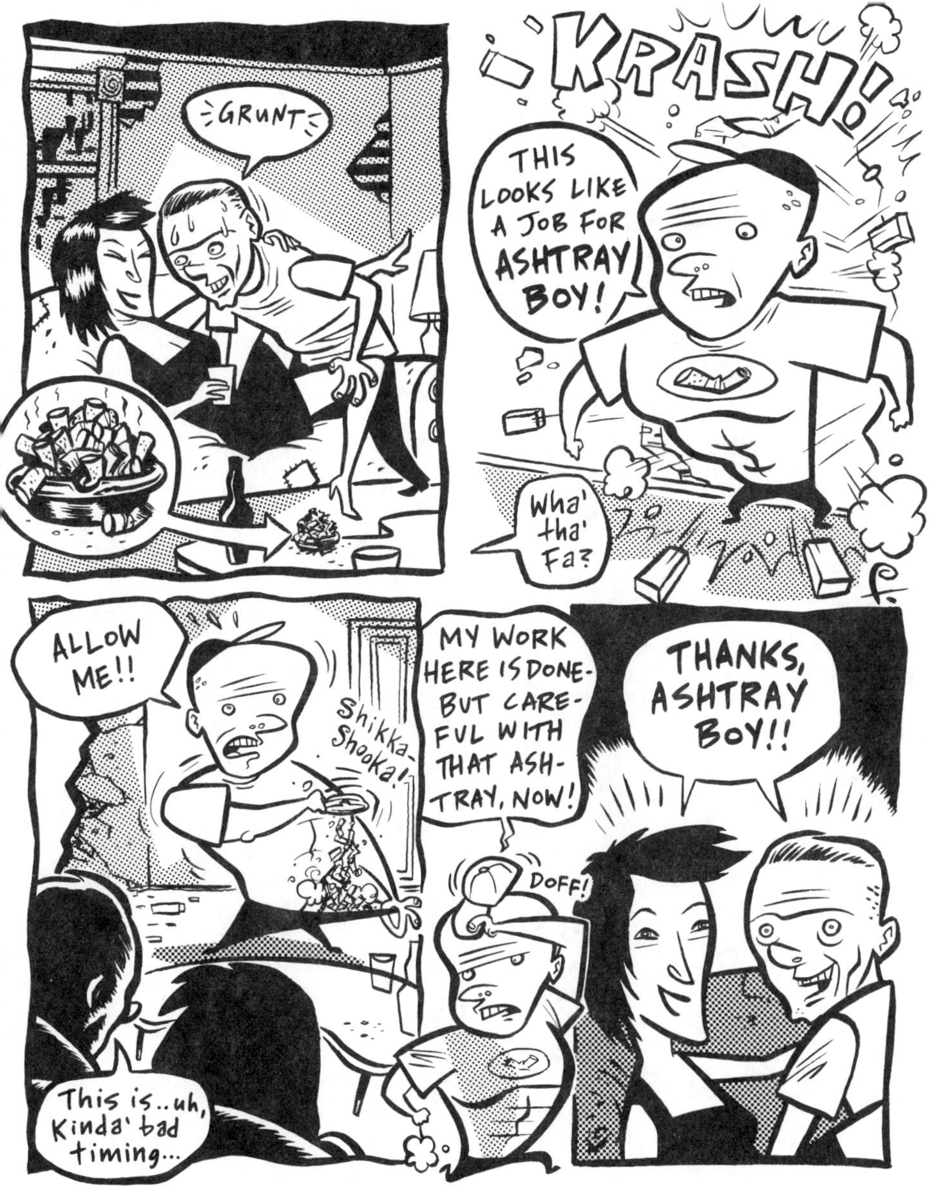
GRUNT
KRASH!
THIS LOOKS LIKE A JOB FOR ASHTRAY BOY!
Wha' tha' Fa?
ALLOW ME!!
Shikka-Shooka!
This is..uh, Kinda' bad timing...
MY WORK HERE IS DONE- BUT CAREFUL WITH THAT ASHTRAY, NOW!
DOFF!
THANKS, ASHTRAY BOY!!

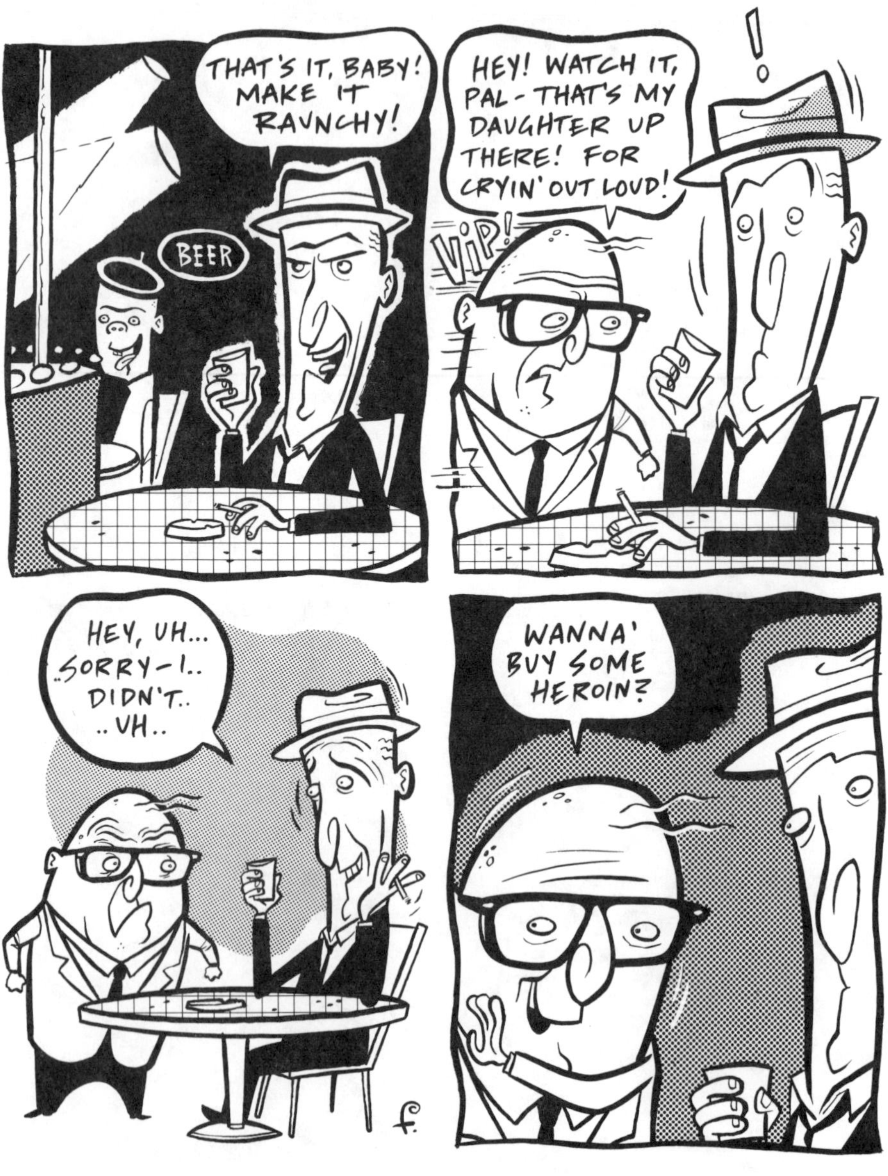
THAT'S IT, BABY! MAKE IT RAUNCHY!
BEER
HEY! WATCH IT, PAL - THAT'S MY DAUGHTER UP THERE! FOR CRYIN' OUT LOUD!
VIP!
!
HEY, UH... ..SORRY-I.. DIDN'T.. ..UH..
WANNA' BUY SOME HEROIN?

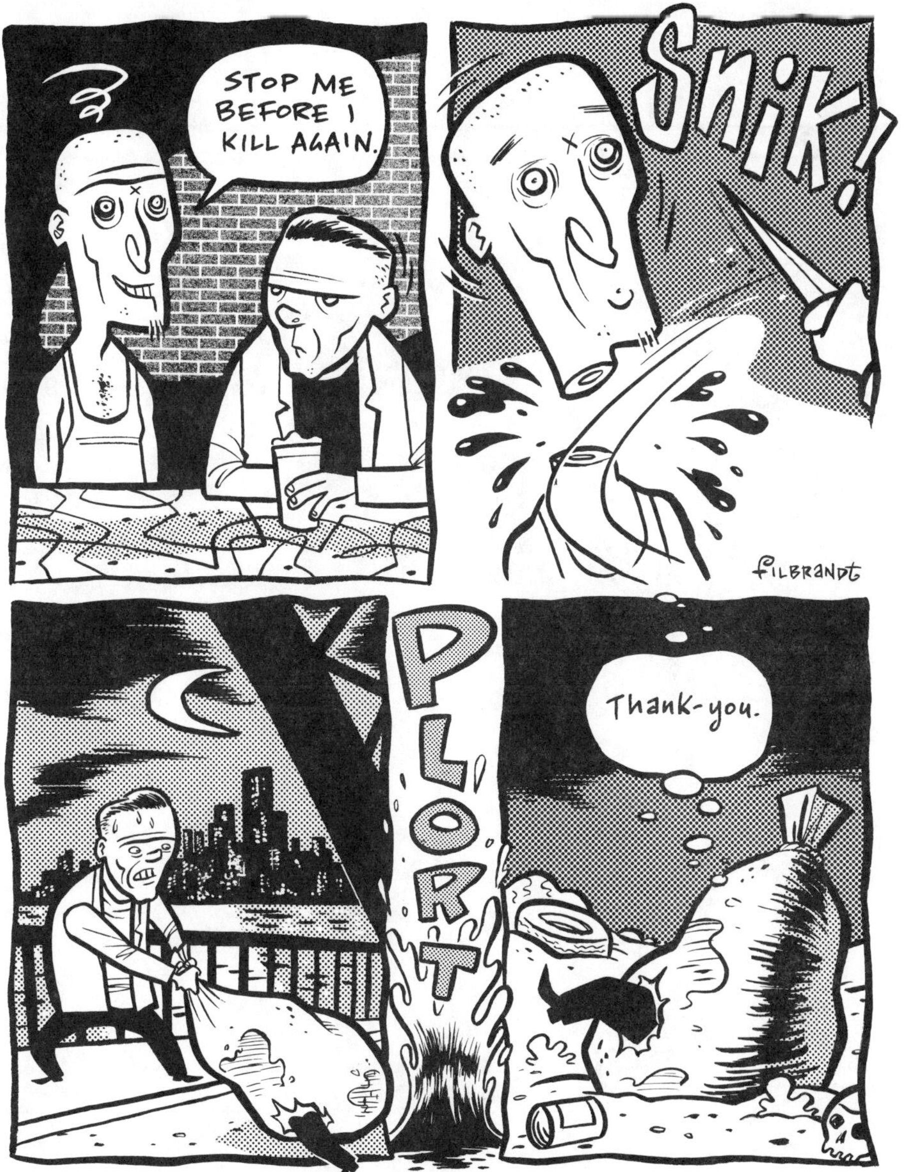
STOP ME BEFORE I KILL AGAIN.
SNIK!!
FILBRANDT
PLLORT
Thank-you.

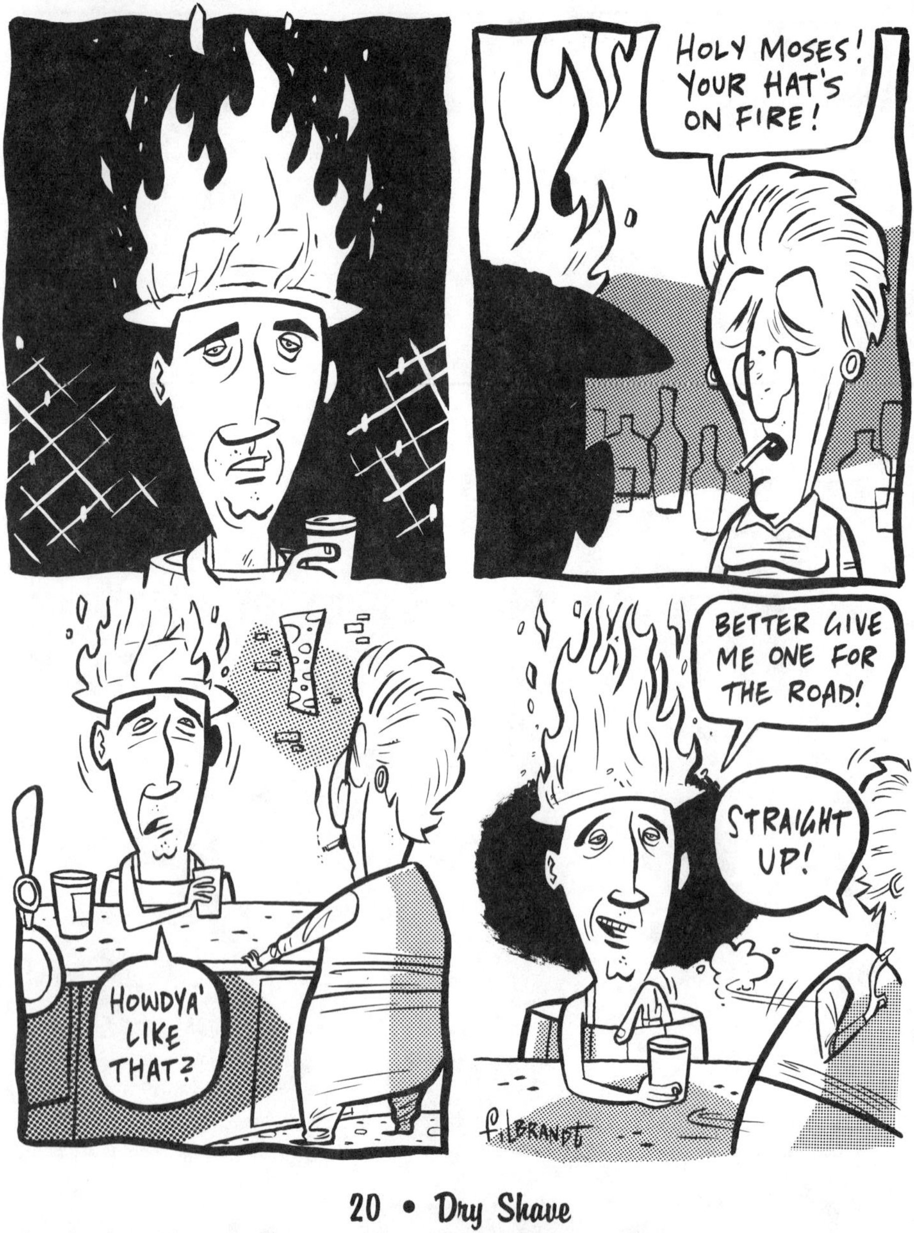
HOLY MOSES! YOUR HAT'S ON FIRE!
HOWDYA' LIKE THAT?
BETTER GIVE ME ONE FOR THE ROAD!
STRAIGHT UP!
FILBRANDT

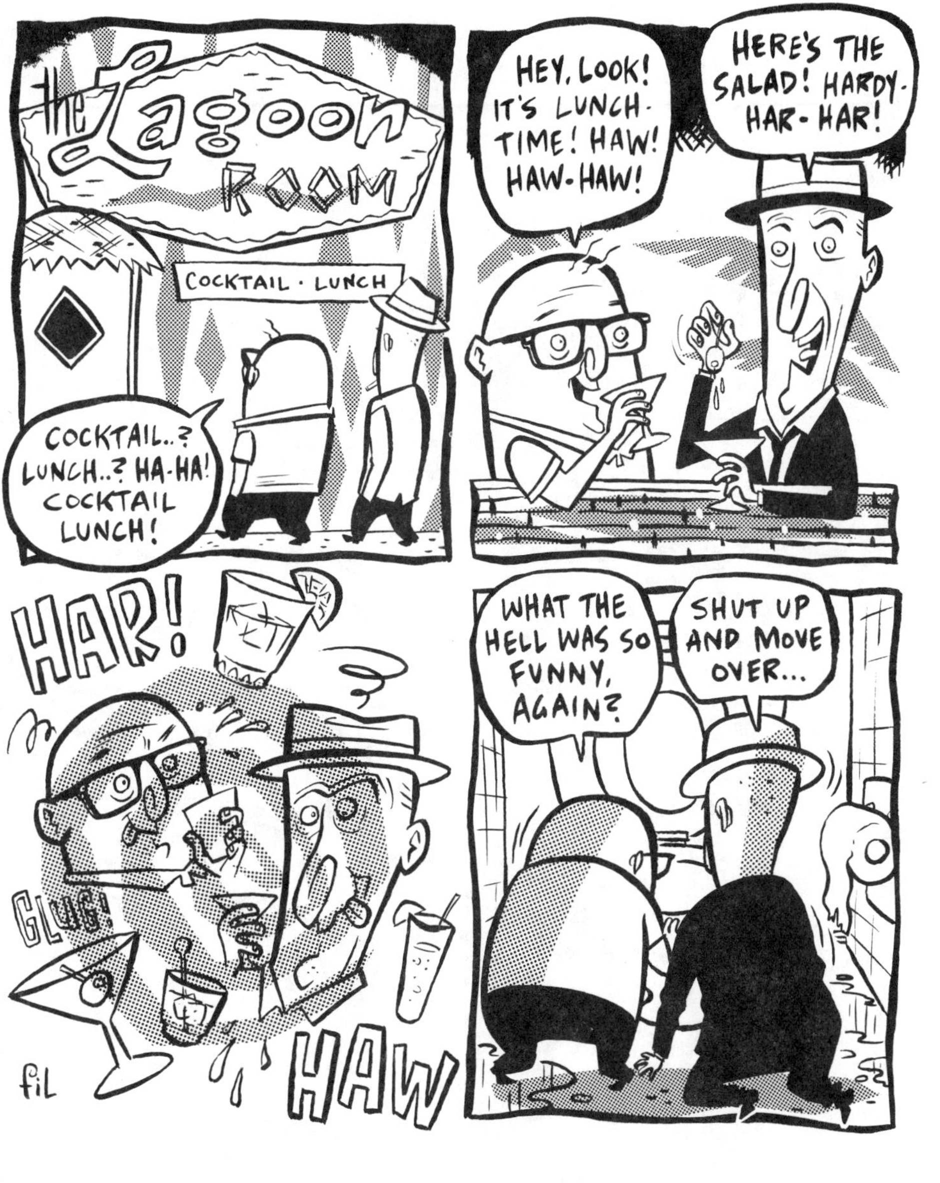
The Lagoon Room
COCKTAIL · LUNCH
COCKTAIL..? LUNCH..? HA-HA! COCKTAIL LUNCH!
HEY, LOOK! IT'S LUNCH-TIME! HAW! HAW-HAW!
HERE'S THE SALAD! HARDY-HAR-HAR!
HAR!
GLUG!
HAW
fiL
WHAT THE HELL WAS SO FUNNY, AGAIN?
SHUT UP AND MOVE OVER...

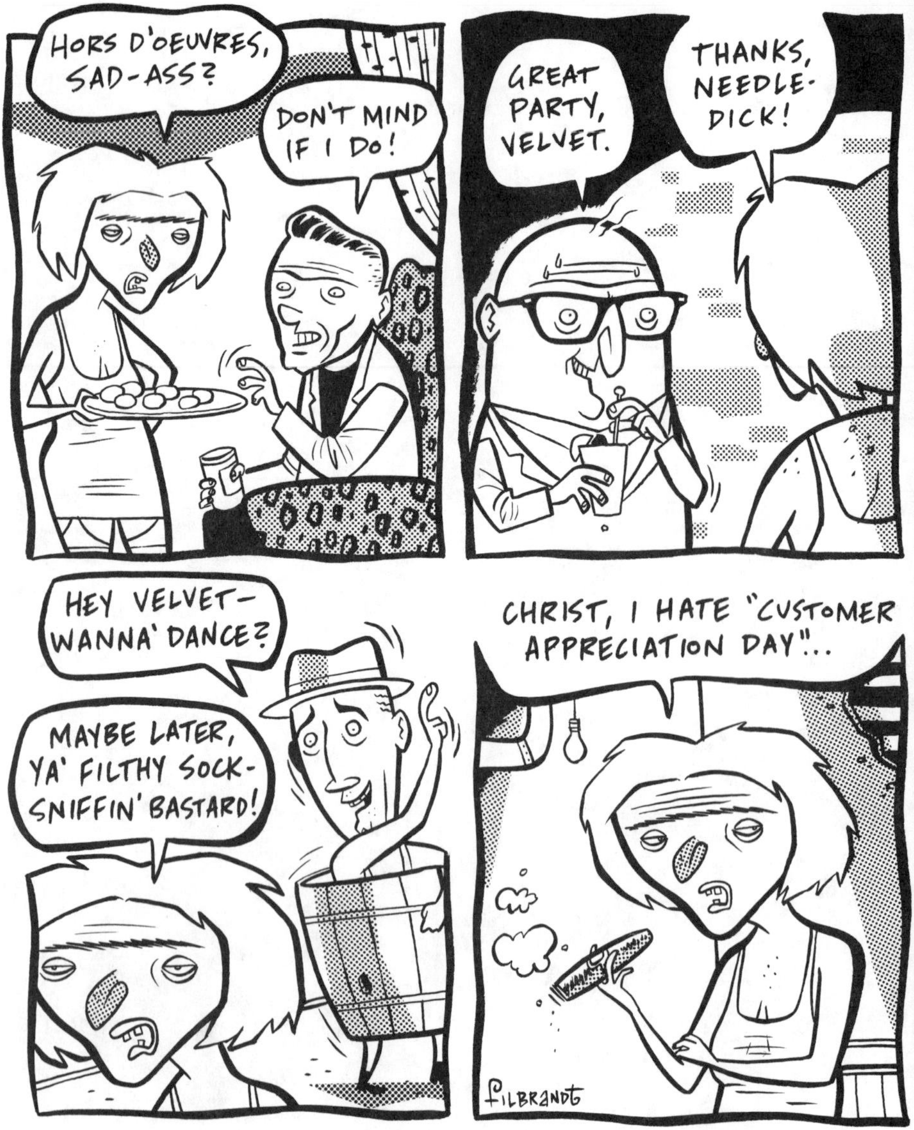

HORS D'OEUVRES, SAD-ASS?
DON'T MIND IF I DO!
GREAT PARTY, VELVET.
THANKS, NEEDLE-DICK!
HEY VELVET— WANNA' DANCE?
MAYBE LATER, YA' FILTHY SOCK-SNIFFIN' BASTARD!
CHRIST, I HATE "CUSTOMER APPRECIATION DAY"...
FILBRANDT

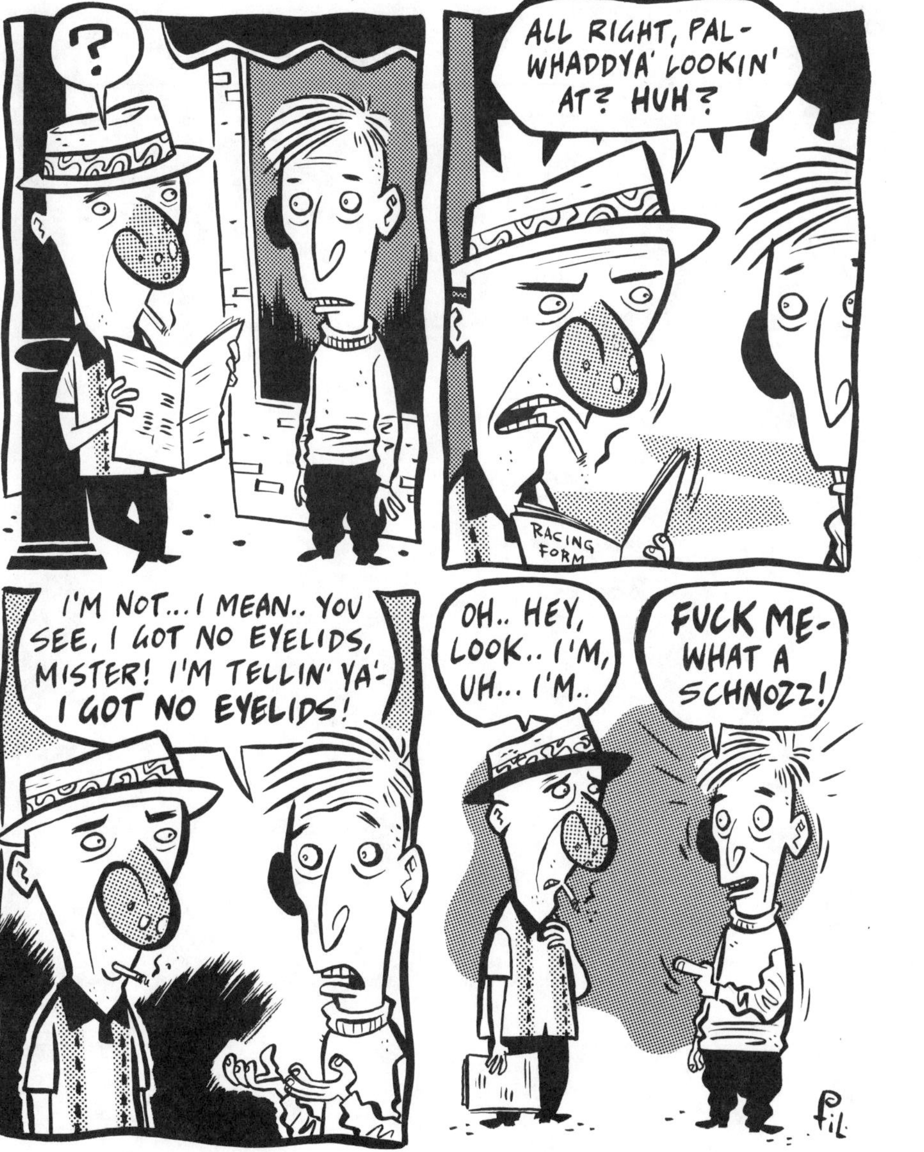
?
ALL RIGHT, PAL- WHADDYA' LOOKIN' AT? HUH?
RACING FORM
I'M NOT... I MEAN.. YOU SEE, I GOT NO EYELIDS, MISTER! I'M TELLIN' YA'- I GOT NO EYELIDS!
OH.. HEY, LOOK.. I'M, UH... I'M..
FUCK ME- WHAT A SCHNOZZ!
fil

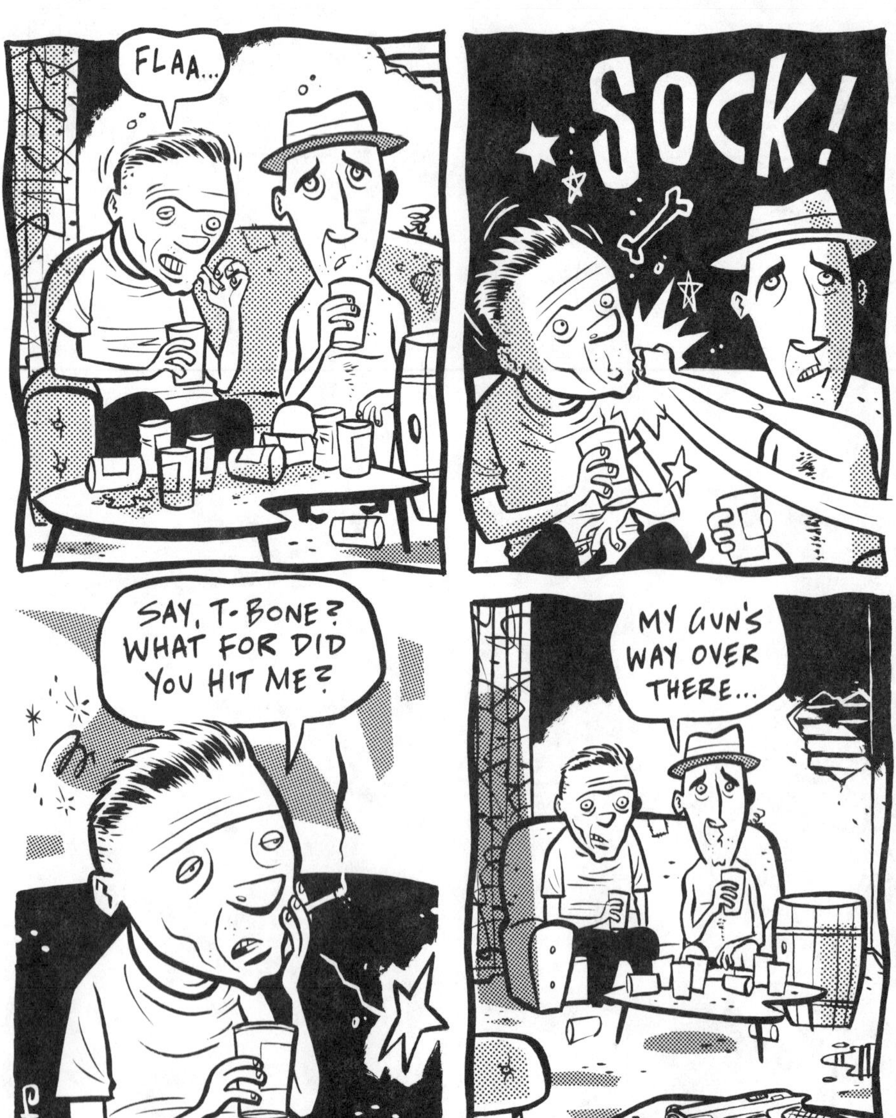
FLAA...
SOCK!
SAY, T-BONE? WHAT FOR DID YOU HIT ME?
MY GUN'S WAY OVER THERE...

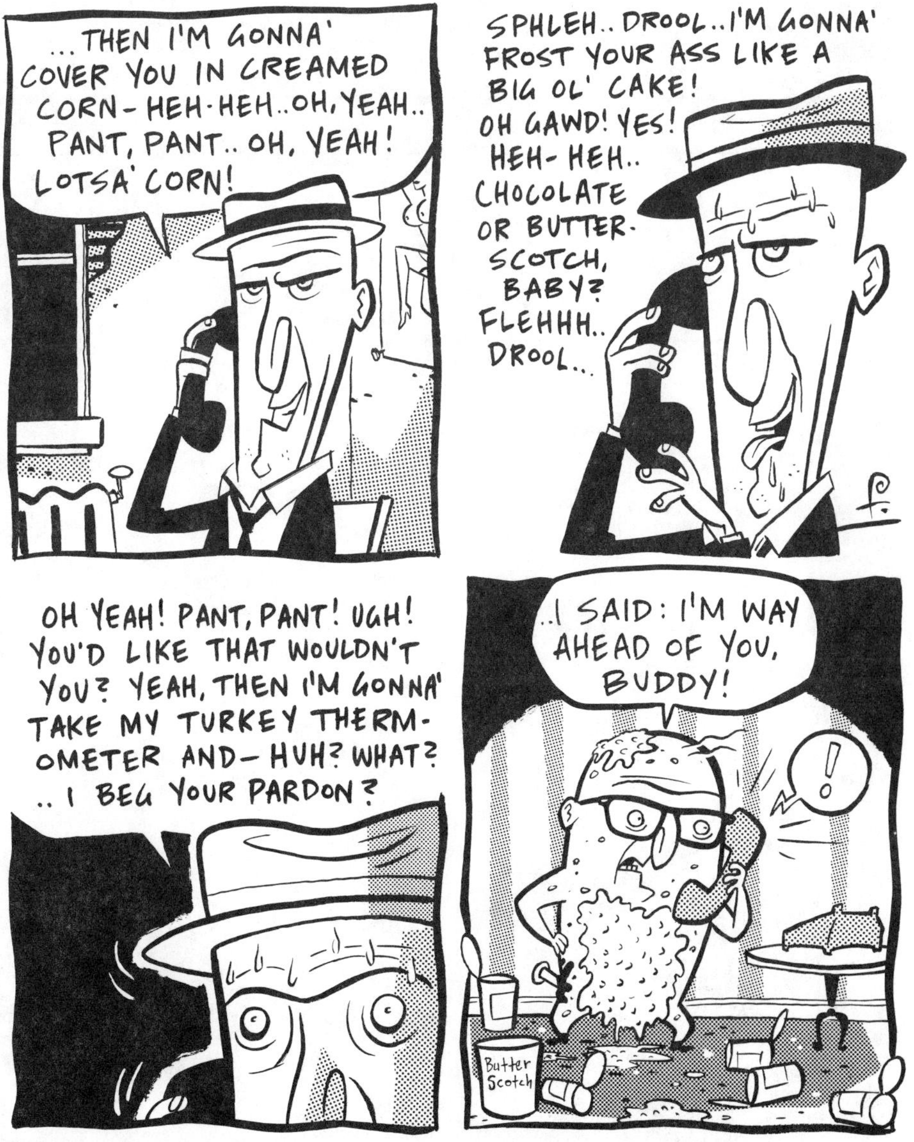

...THEN I'M GONNA' COVER YOU IN CREAMED CORN-HEH-HEH..OH, YEAH.. PANT, PANT.. OH, YEAH! LOTSA' CORN!
SPHLEH.. DROOL..I'M GONNA' FROST YOUR ASS LIKE A BIG OL' CAKE! OH GAWD! YES! HEH-HEH.. CHOCOLATE OR BUTTER-SCOTCH, BABY? FLEHHH.. DROOL...
OH YEAH! PANT, PANT! UGH! YOU'D LIKE THAT WOULDN'T YOU? YEAH, THEN I'M GONNA' TAKE MY TURKEY THERM-OMETER AND-HUH? WHAT? ..I BEG YOUR PARDON?
..I SAID: I'M WAY AHEAD OF YOU, BUDDY!
!
Butter Scotch

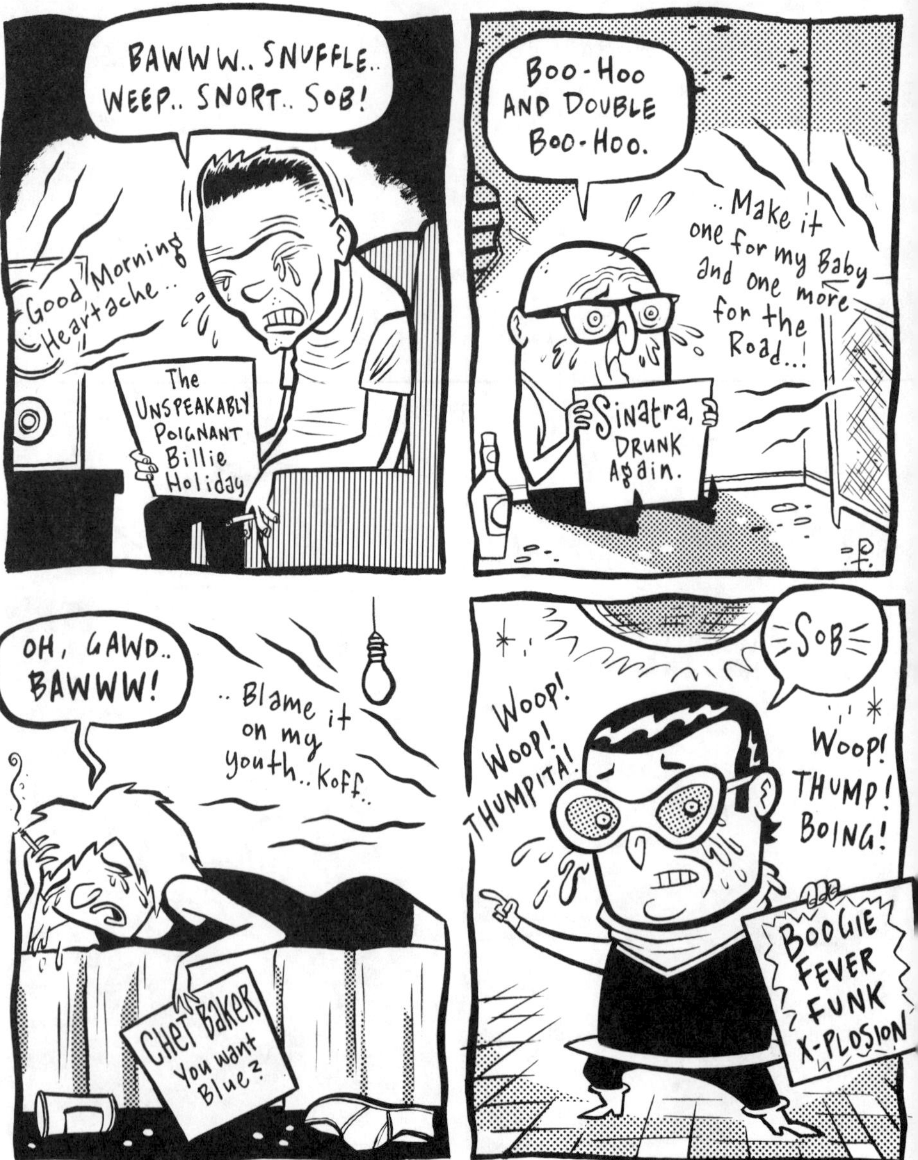

BAWWW.. SNUFFLE.. WEEP.. SNORT.. SOB!
Good Morning Heartache..
The UNSPEAKABLY POIGNANT Billie Holiday
Boo-Hoo AND DOUBLE Boo-Hoo.
..Make it one for my Baby and one more for the Road..!
Sinatra, DRUNK Again.
OH, GAWD.. BAWWW!
..Blame it on my youth..koff..
CHET BAKER You want Blue?
SOB
Woop! Woop! THUMPITA!
Woop! THUMP! BOING!
BOOGIE FEVER FUNK X-PLOSION

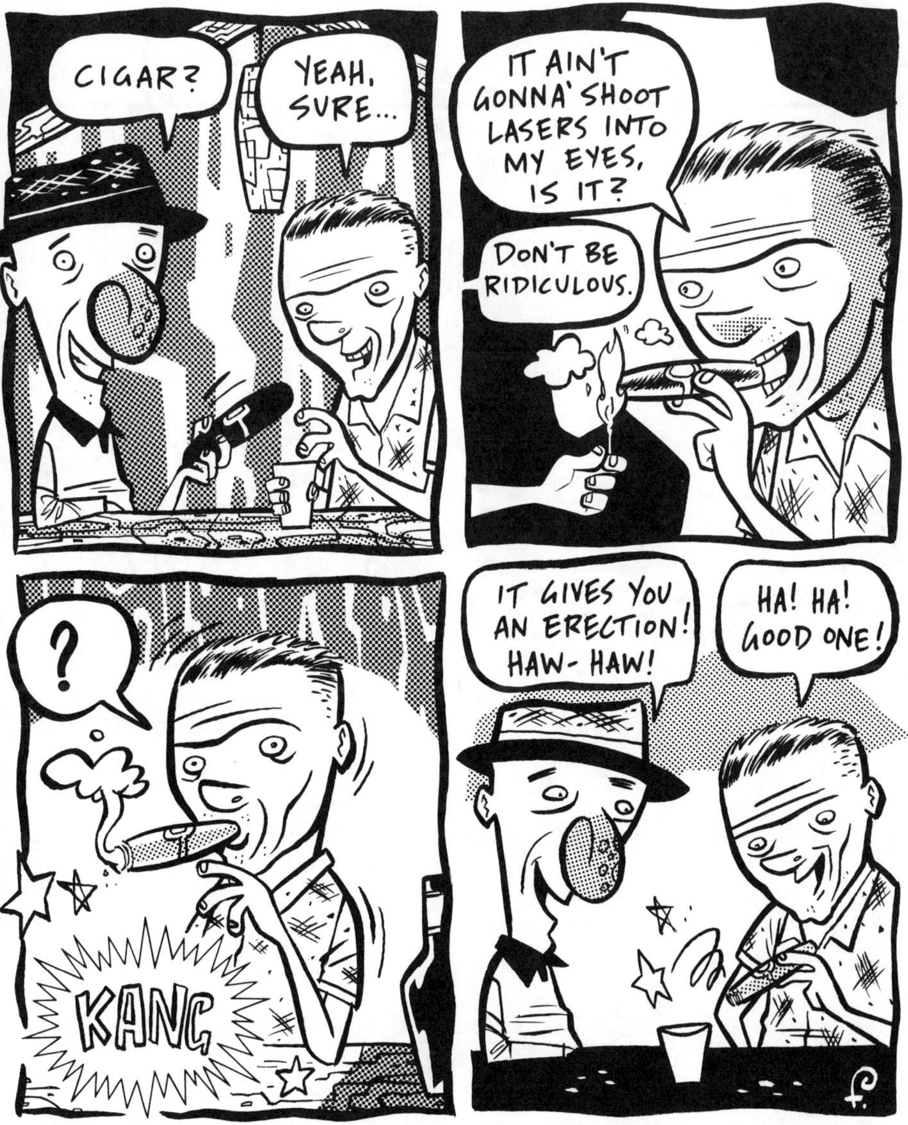
CIGAR?
YEAH, SURE...
IT AIN'T GONNA' SHOOT LASERS INTO MY EYES, IS IT?
DON'T BE RIDICULOUS.
?
KANG
IT GIVES YOU AN ERECTION! HAW-HAW!
HA! HA! GOOD ONE!

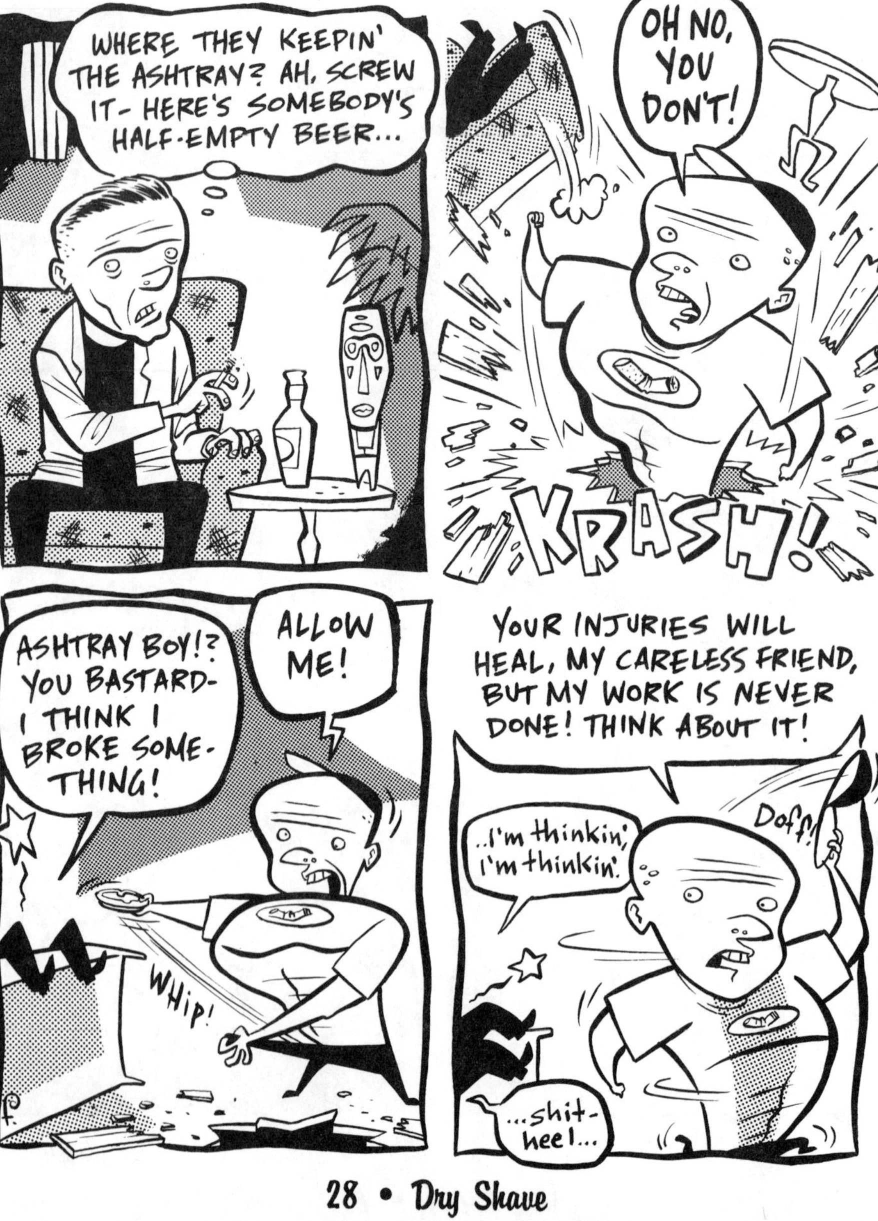
WHERE THEY KEEPIN' THE ASHTRAY? AH, SCREW IT- HERE'S SOMEBODY'S HALF-EMPTY BEER...
OH NO, YOU DON'T!
KRASH!
ASHTRAY BOY!? YOU BASTARD- I THINK I BROKE SOME-THING!
ALLOW ME!
WHIP!
YOUR INJURIES WILL HEAL, MY CARELESS FRIEND, BUT MY WORK IS NEVER DONE! THINK ABOUT IT!
Doff!
..I'm thinkin', I'm thinkin'.
...shit-hee!...

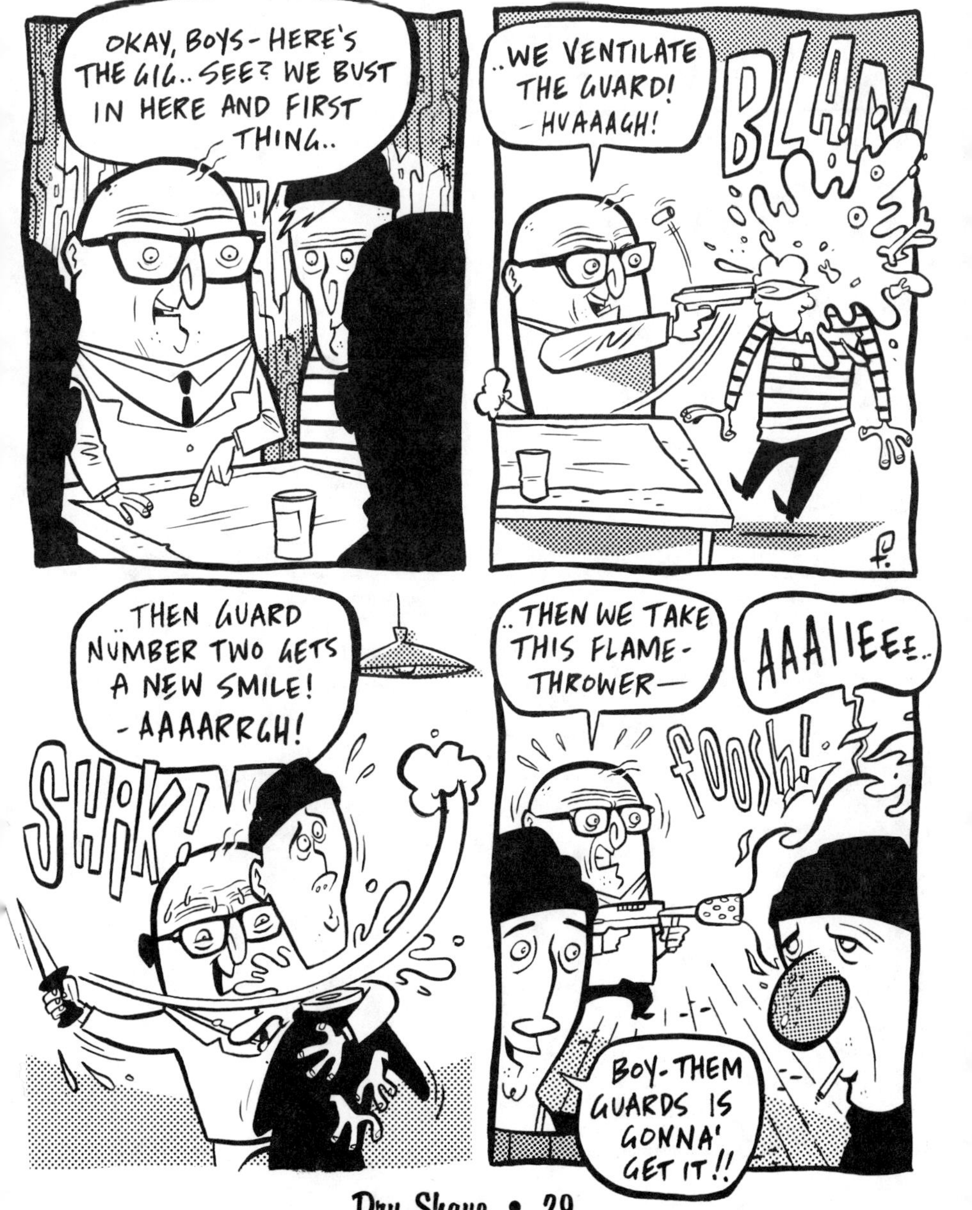
OKAY, BOYS-HERE'S THE GIG.. SEE? WE BUST IN HERE AND FIRST THING..
..WE VENTILATE THE GUARD! -HUAAAGH!
BLAM
..THEN GUARD NUMBER TWO GETS A NEW SMILE! -AAAARRGH!
SHIK!
..THEN WE TAKE THIS FLAME-THROWER—
AAAIIEEE..
FOOSH!
BOY-THEM GUARDS IS GONNA' GET IT!!

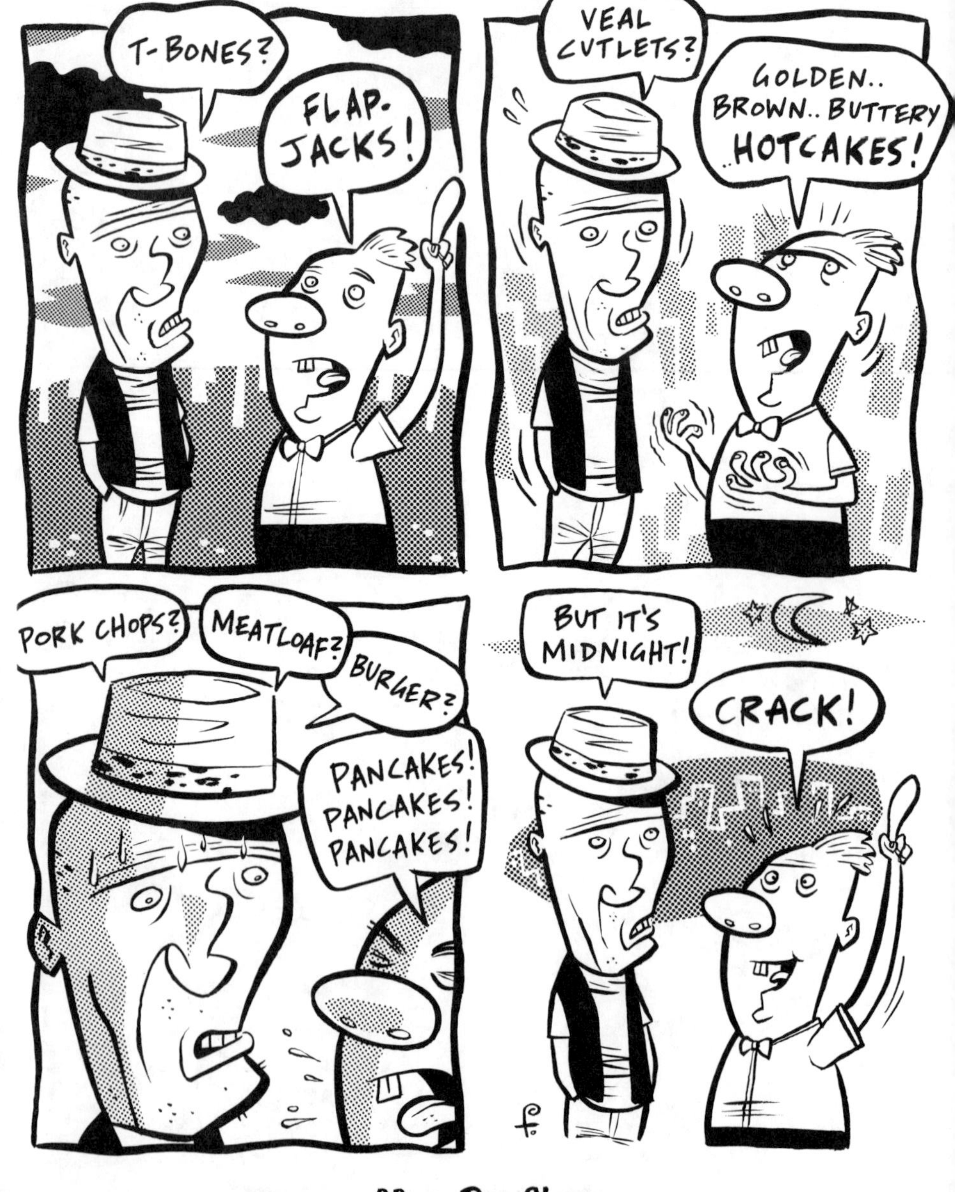
T-BONES?
FLAP-JACKS!
VEAL CUTLETS?
GOLDEN.. BROWN.. BUTTERY ..HOTCAKES!
PORK CHOPS?
MEATLOAF?
BURGER?
PANCAKES! PANCAKES! PANCAKES!
BUT IT'S MIDNIGHT!
CRACK!

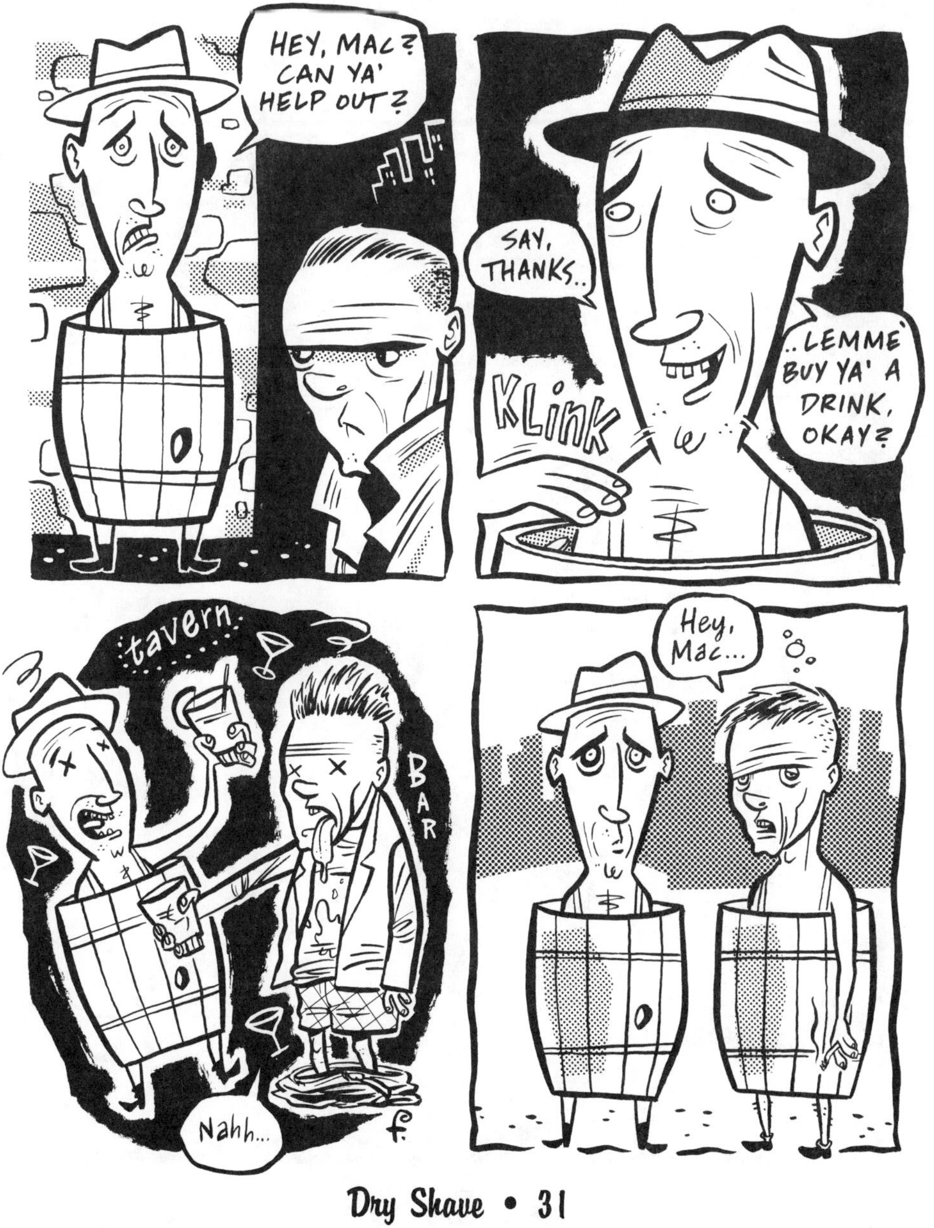
HEY, MAC? CAN YA' HELP OUT?
SAY, THANKS..
KLink
..LEMME BUY YA' A DRINK, OKAY?
tavern
BAR
Nahh...
Hey, Mac...

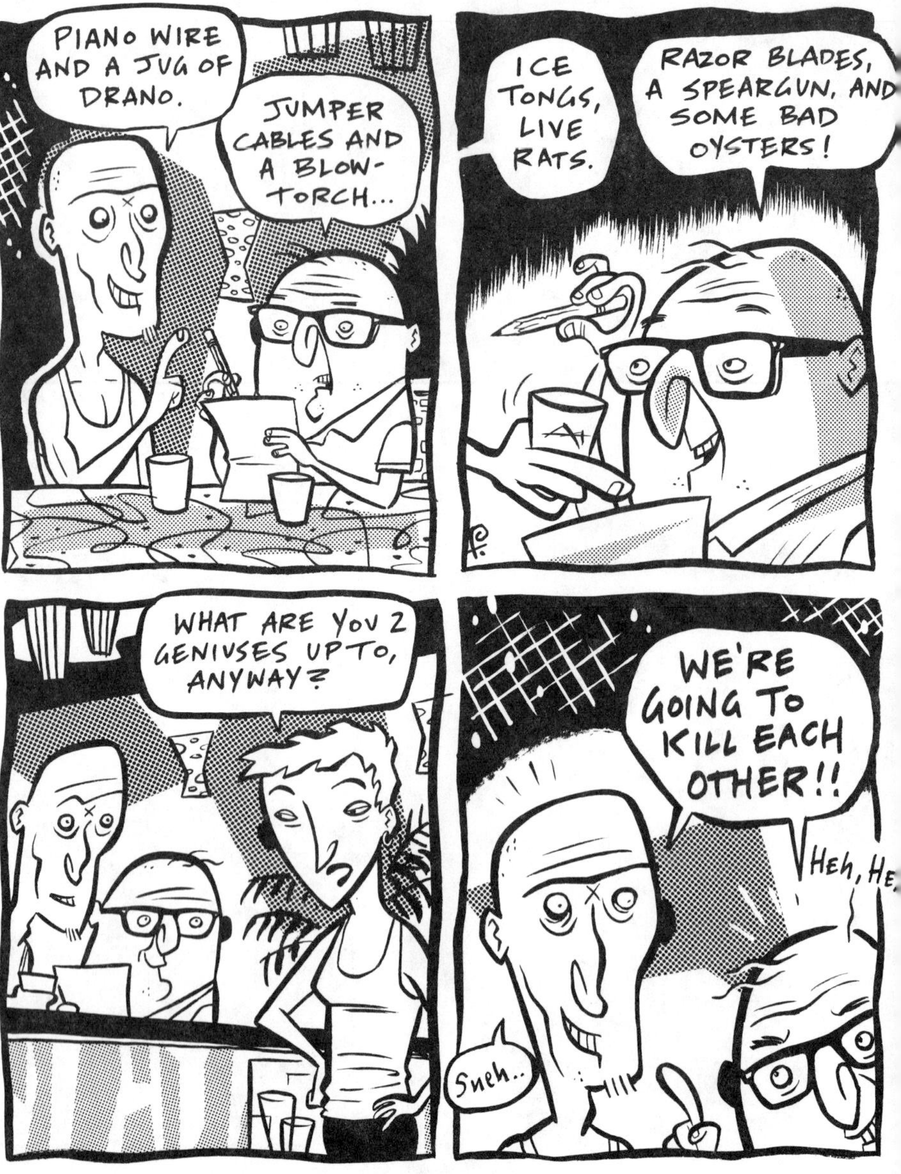
PIANO WIRE AND A JUG OF DRANO.
JUMPER CABLES AND A BLOW-TORCH...
ICE TONGS, LIVE RATS.
RAZOR BLADES, A SPEARGUN, AND SOME BAD OYSTERS!
WHAT ARE YOU 2 GENIUSES UP TO, ANYWAY?
WE'RE GOING TO KILL EACH OTHER!!
Heh, He
Sneh..

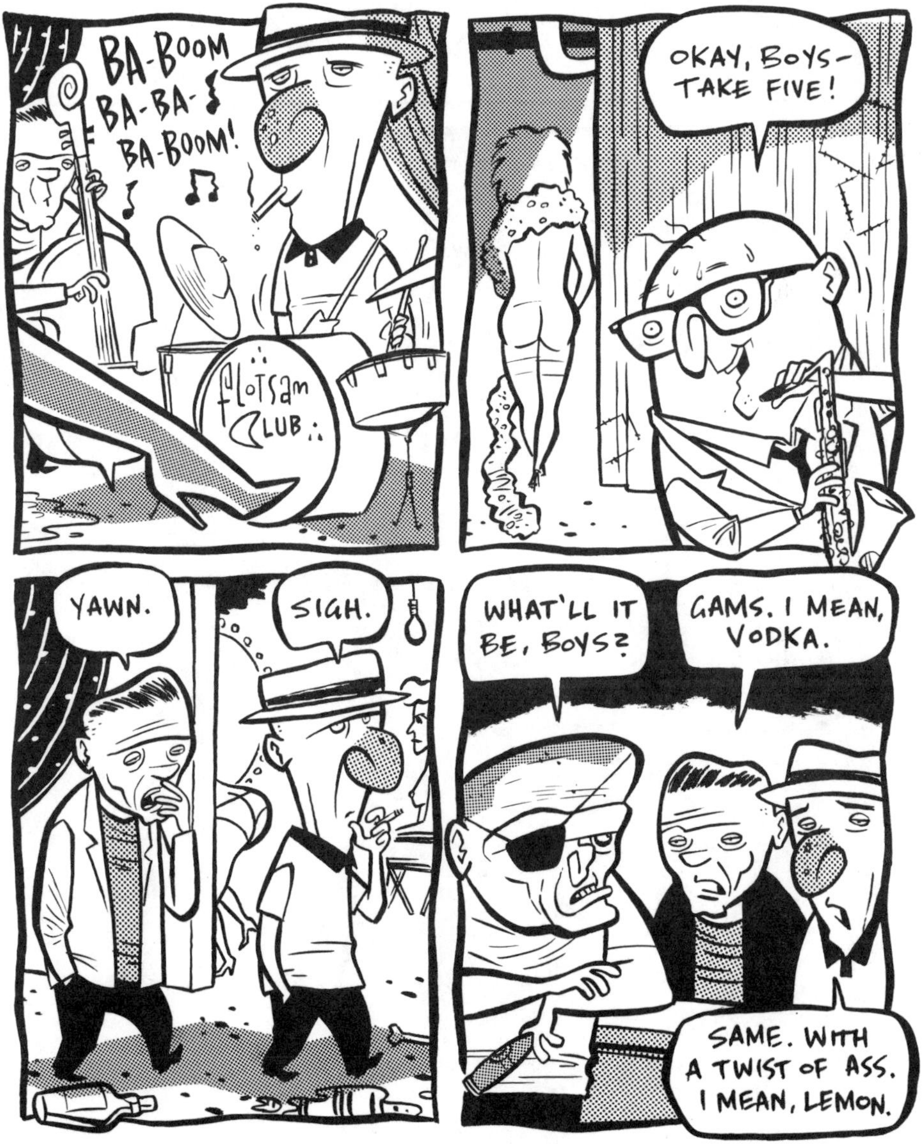
BA-BOOM
BA-BA-
BA-BOOM!
FLOTSAM CLUB
OKAY, BOYS-
TAKE FIVE!
YAWN.
SIGH.
WHAT'LL IT BE, BOYS?
GAMS. I MEAN, VODKA.
SAME. WITH A TWIST OF ASS. I MEAN, LEMON.

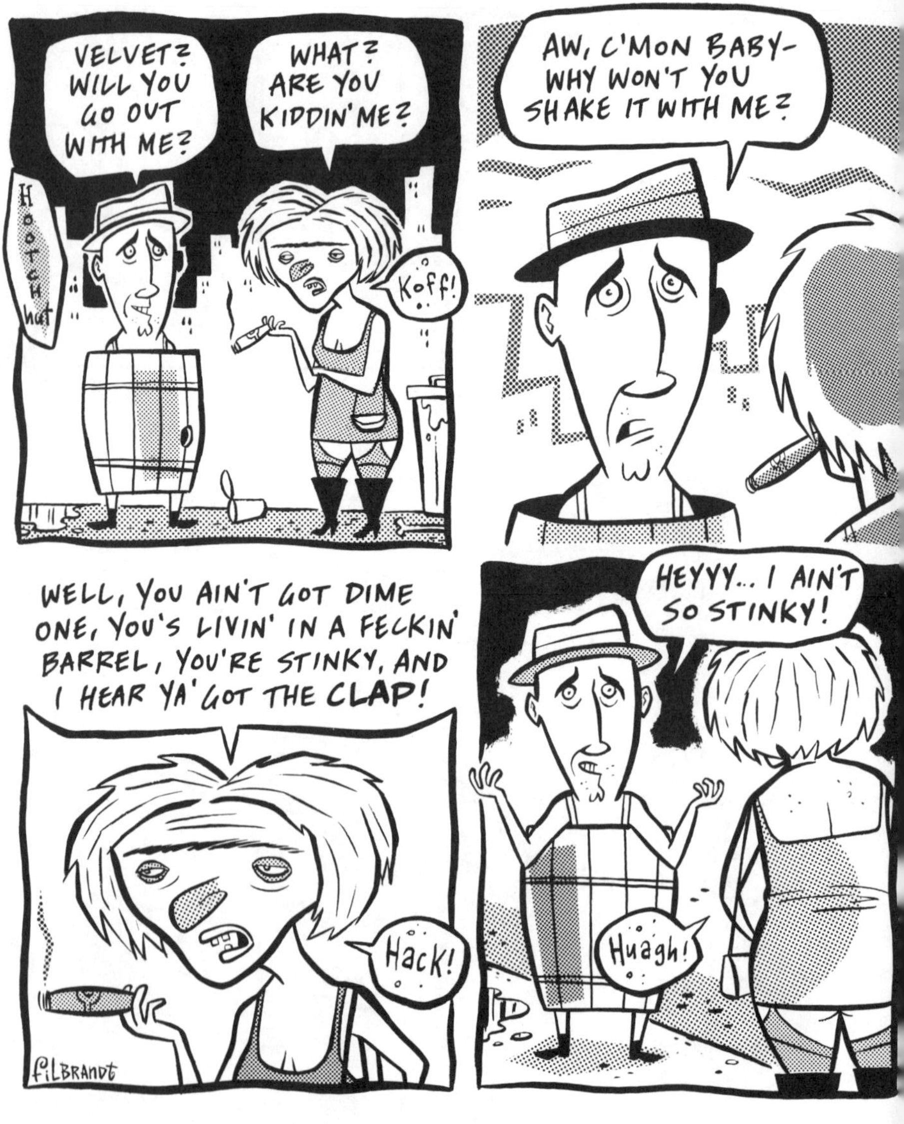
VELVET? WILL YOU GO OUT WITH ME?
WHAT? ARE YOU KIDDIN' ME?
HOOTCH hut
Koff!
AW, C'MON BABY- WHY WON'T YOU SHAKE IT WITH ME?
WELL, YOU AIN'T GOT DIME ONE, YOU'S LIVIN' IN A FECKIN' BARREL, YOU'RE STINKY, AND I HEAR YA' GOT THE CLAP!
Hack!
FILBRANDT
HEYYY... I AIN'T SO STINKY!
Huagh!

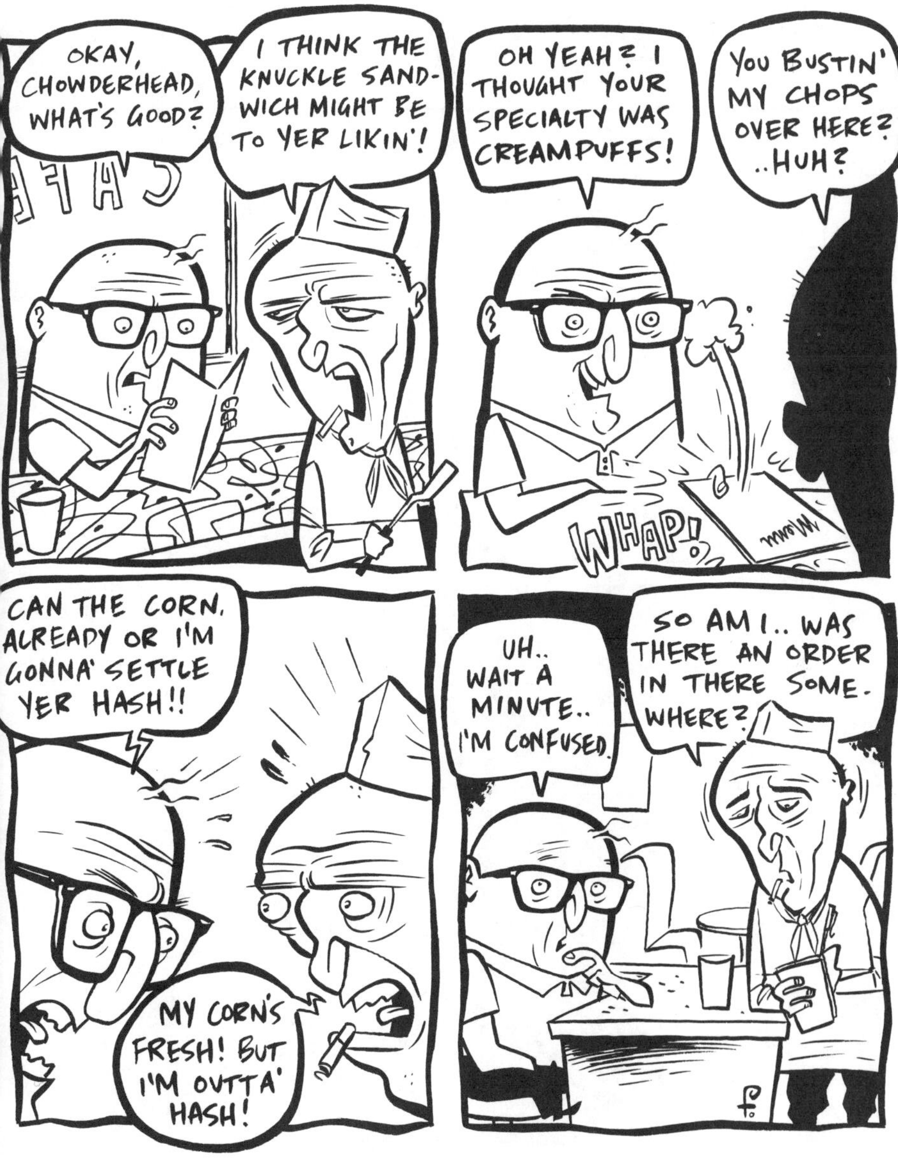
OKAY, CHOWDERHEAD, WHAT'S GOOD?
I THINK THE KNUCKLE SANDWICH MIGHT BE TO YER LIKIN'!
CAFE
OH YEAH? I THOUGHT YOUR SPECIALTY WAS CREAMPUFFS!
YOU BUSTIN' MY CHOPS OVER HERE? ..HUH?
WHAP!
MENU
CAN THE CORN, ALREADY OR I'M GONNA' SETTLE YER HASH!!
MY CORN'S FRESH! BUT I'M OUTTA' HASH!
UH.. WAIT A MINUTE.. I'M CONFUSED.
SO AM I.. WAS THERE AN ORDER IN THERE SOME-WHERE?

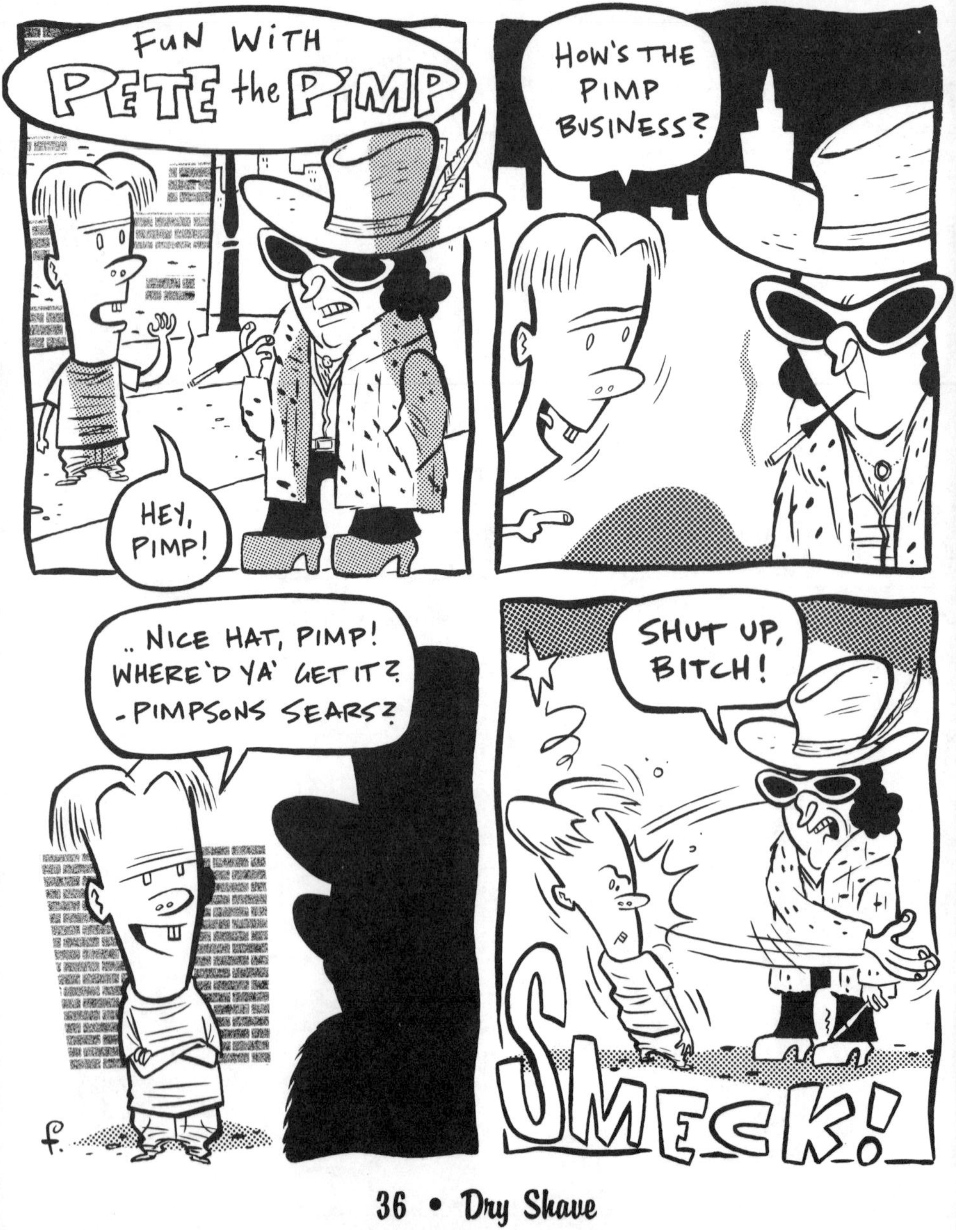
FUN WITH
PETE the PIMP
HEY, PIMP!
HOW'S THE PIMP BUSINESS?
.. NICE HAT, PIMP! WHERE'D YA' GET IT? - PIMPSONS SEARS?
SHUT UP, BITCH!
SMECK!
f.

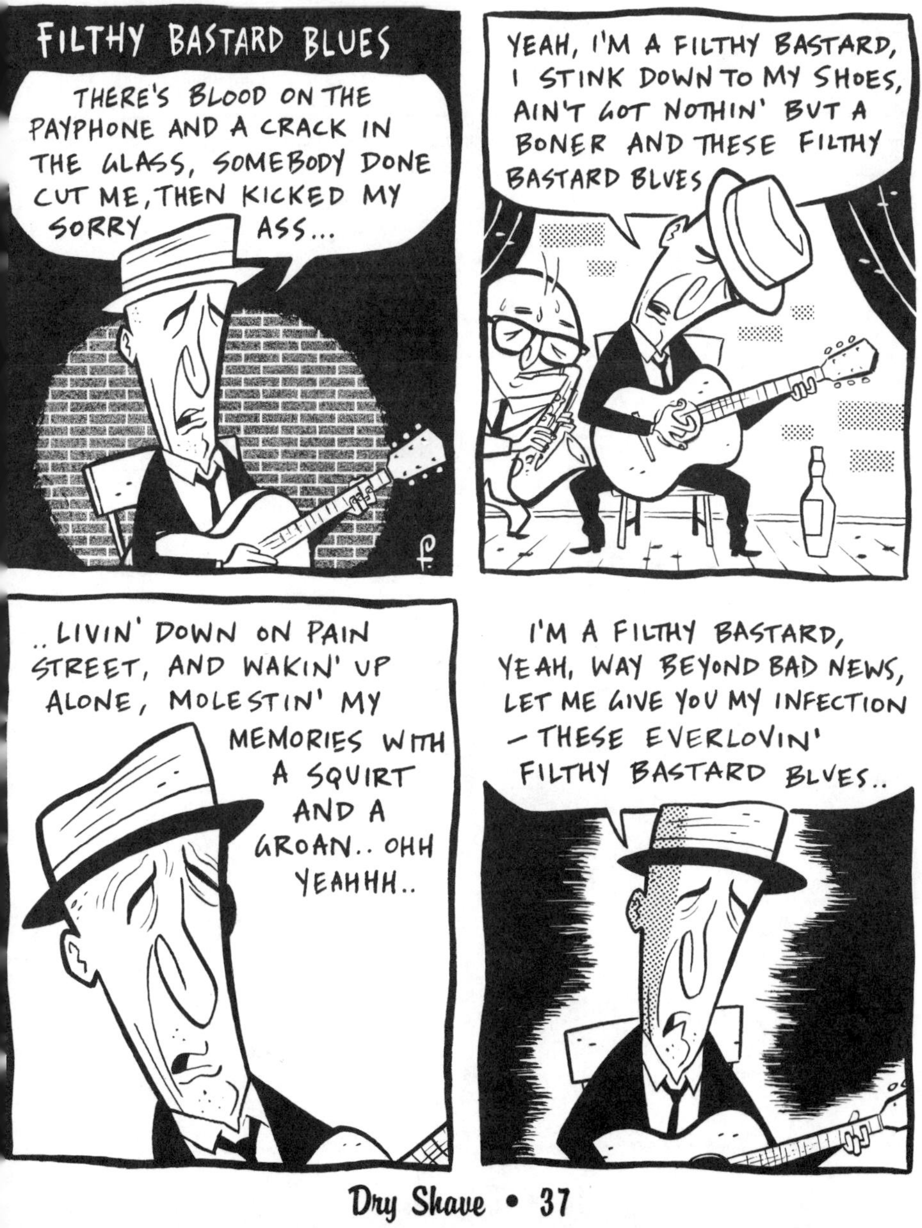
FILTHY BASTARD BLUES
THERE'S BLOOD ON THE PAYPHONE AND A CRACK IN THE GLASS, SOMEBODY DONE CUT ME, THEN KICKED MY SORRY ASS...
YEAH, I'M A FILTHY BASTARD, I STINK DOWN TO MY SHOES, AIN'T GOT NOTHIN' BUT A BONER AND THESE FILTHY BASTARD BLUES
..LIVIN' DOWN ON PAIN STREET, AND WAKIN' UP ALONE, MOLESTIN' MY MEMORIES WITH A SQUIRT AND A GROAN.. OHH YEAHHH..
I'M A FILTHY BASTARD, YEAH, WAY BEYOND BAD NEWS, LET ME GIVE YOU MY INFECTION - THESE EVERLOVIN' FILTHY BASTARD BLUES..

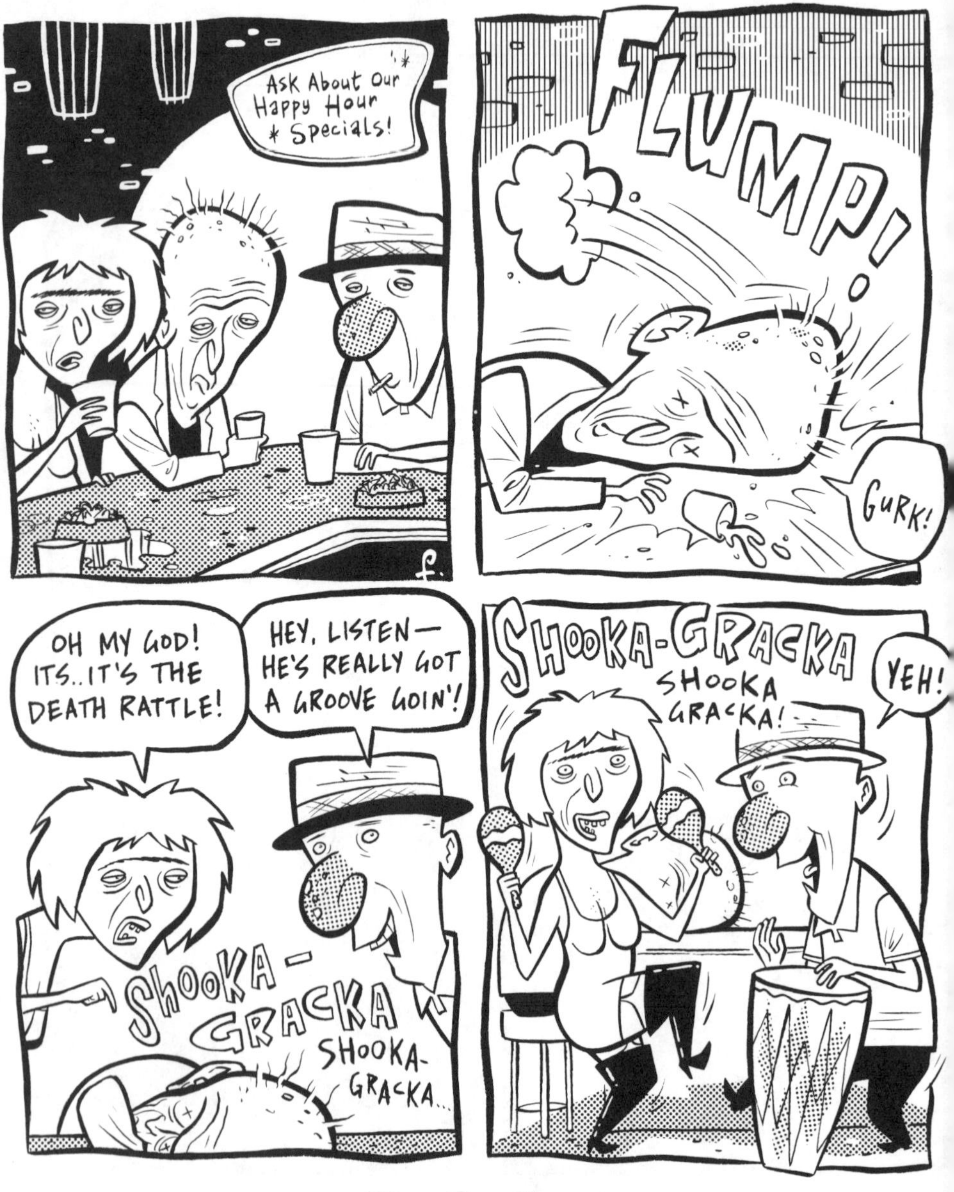
Ask About Our Happy Hour * Specials!
FLUMP!
GURK!
OH MY GOD! ITS..IT'S THE DEATH RATTLE!
HEY, LISTEN— HE'S REALLY GOT A GROOVE GOIN'!
SHOOKA-GRACKA
SHOOKA-GRACKA...
SHOOKA-GRACKA
SHOOKA GRACKA!
YEH!

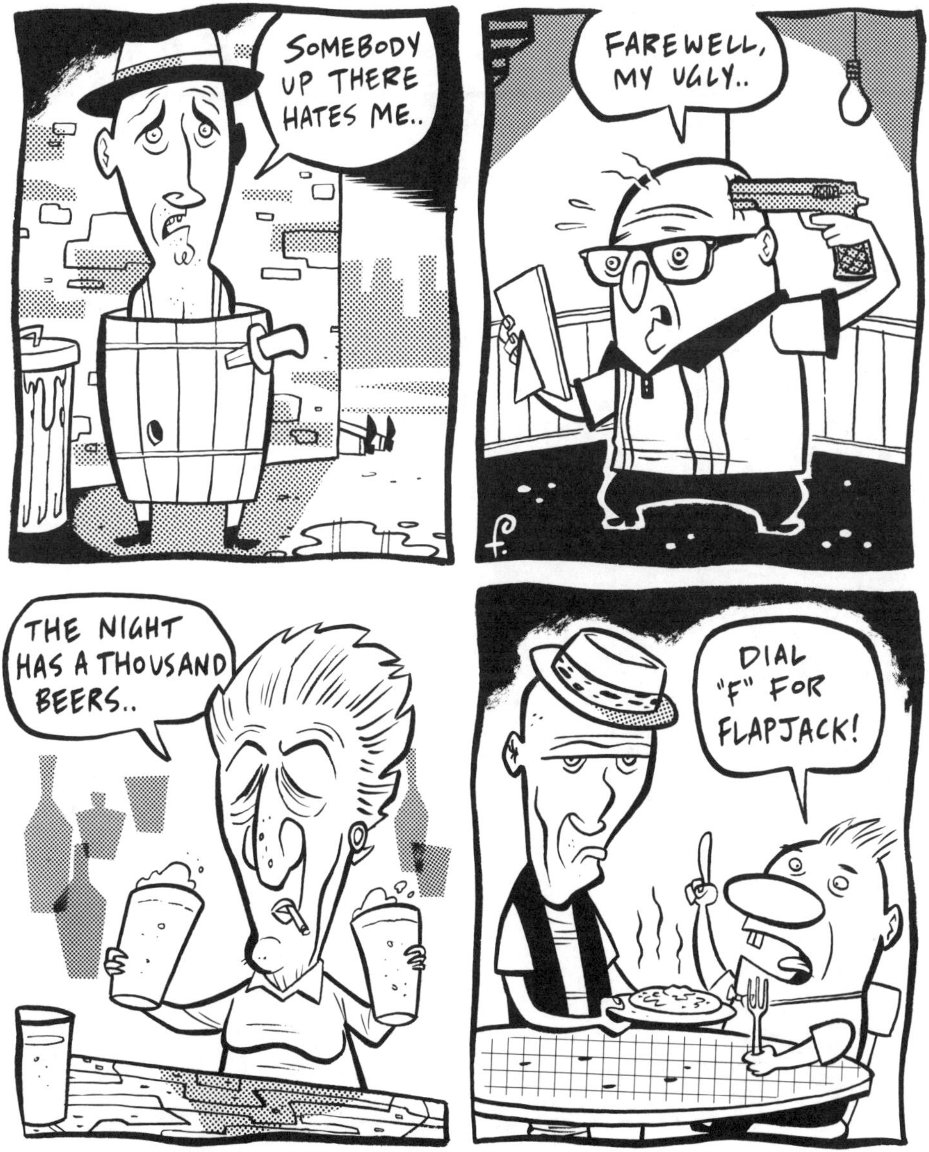
SOMEBODY UP THERE HATES ME..
FAREWELL, MY UGLY..
THE NIGHT HAS A THOUSAND BEERS..
DIAL "F" FOR FLAPJACK!

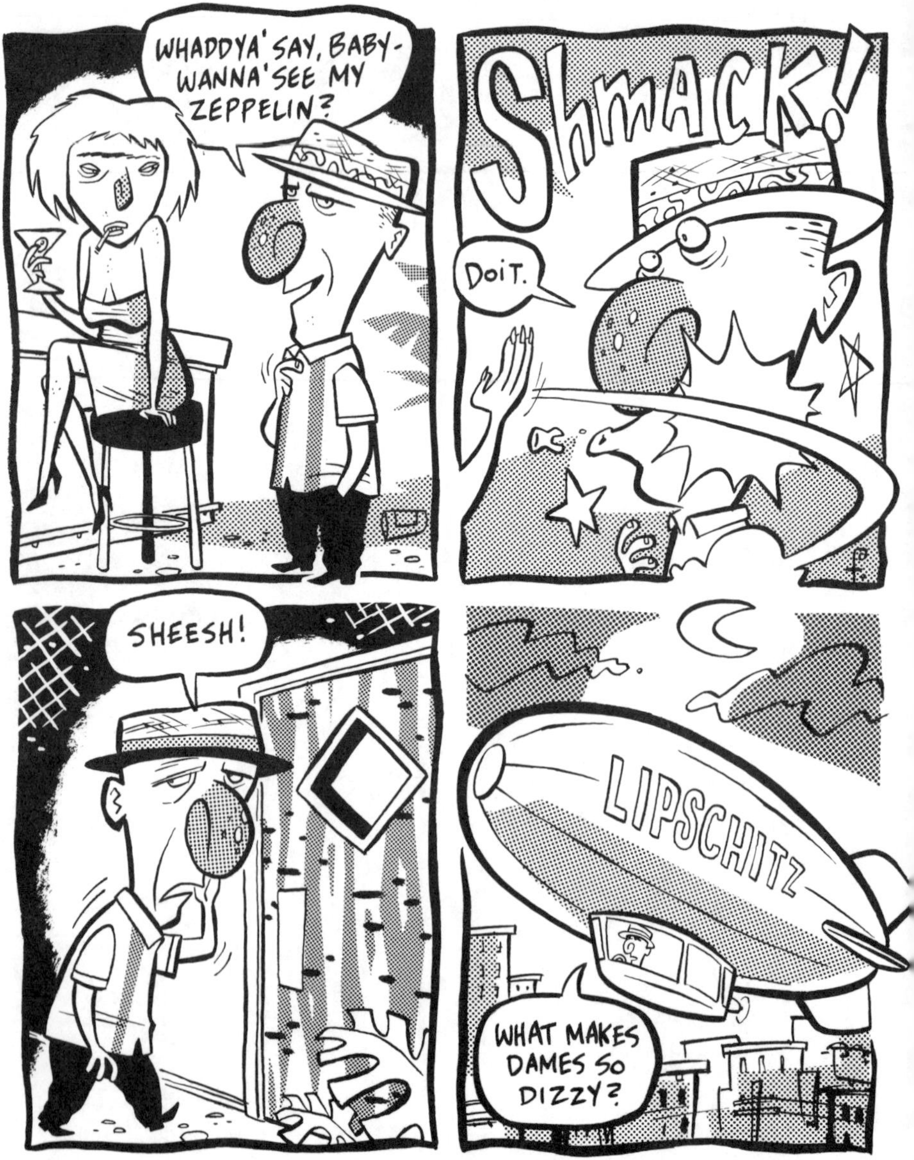
WHADDYA' SAY, BABY-
WANNA' SEE MY
ZEPPELIN?
SHMACK!
DOIT.
SHEESH!
LIPSCHITZ
WHAT MAKES
DAMES SO
DIZZY?

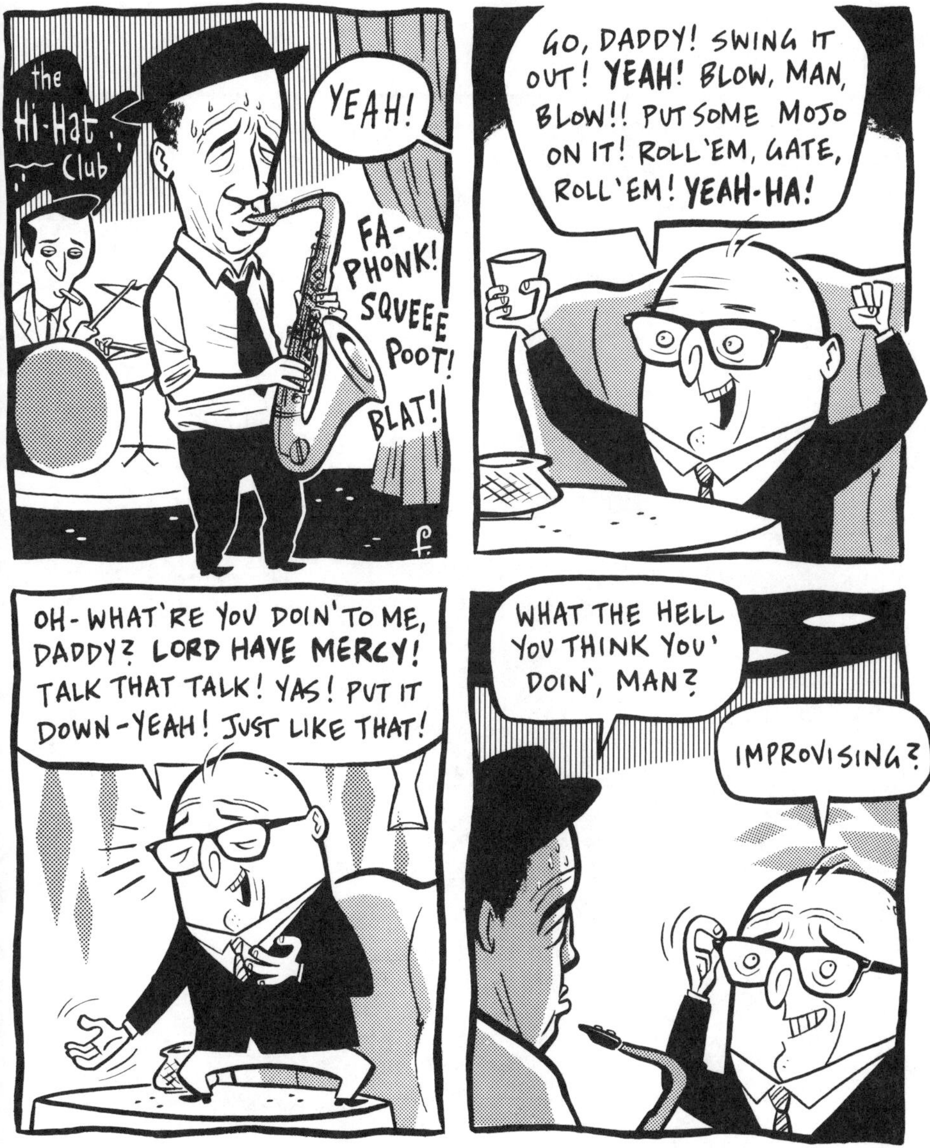
the Hi-Hat Club
YEAH!
FA-PHONK! SQUEEEE POOT! BLAT!
GO, DADDY! SWING IT OUT! YEAH! BLOW, MAN, BLOW!! PUT SOME MOJO ON IT! ROLL'EM, GATE, ROLL'EM! YEAH-HA!
OH-WHAT'RE YOU DOIN' TO ME, DADDY? LORD HAVE MERCY! TALK THAT TALK! YAS! PUT IT DOWN-YEAH! JUST LIKE THAT!
WHAT THE HELL YOU THINK YOU' DOIN', MAN?
IMPROVISING?

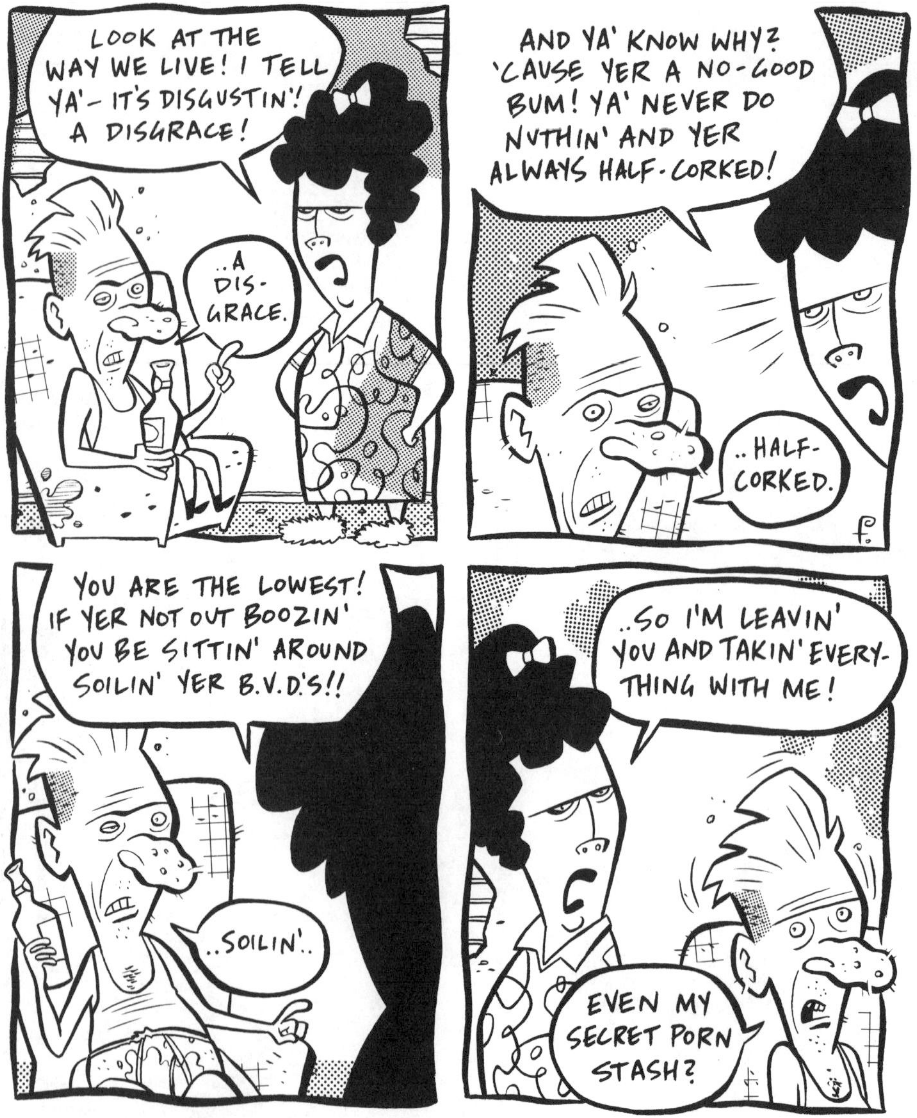
LOOK AT THE WAY WE LIVE! I TELL YA'- IT'S DISGUSTIN'! A DISGRACE!
..A DIS-GRACE.
AND YA' KNOW WHY? 'CAUSE YER A NO-GOOD BUM! YA' NEVER DO NVTHIN' AND YER ALWAYS HALF-CORKED!
.. HALF-CORKED.
YOU ARE THE LOWEST! IF YER NOT OUT BOOZIN' YOU BE SITTIN' AROUND SOILIN' YER B.V.D.'S!!
..SOILIN'..
..SO I'M LEAVIN' YOU AND TAKIN' EVERY-THING WITH ME!
EVEN MY SECRET PORN STASH?

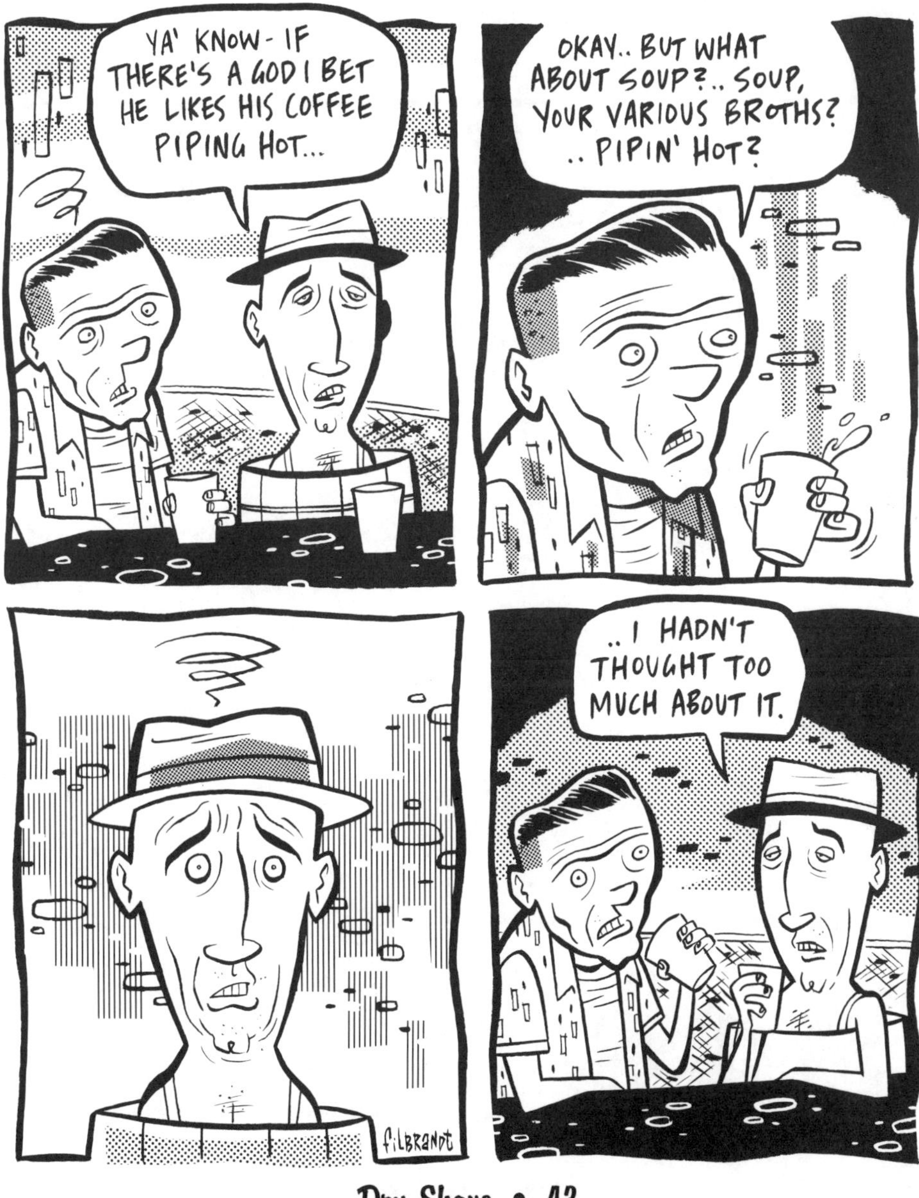
YA' KNOW- IF THERE'S A GOD I BET HE LIKES HIS COFFEE PIPING HOT...
OKAY.. BUT WHAT ABOUT SOUP?.. SOUP, YOUR VARIOUS BROTHS? .. PIPIN' HOT?
.. I HADN'T THOUGHT TOO MUCH ABOUT IT.
filbrandt

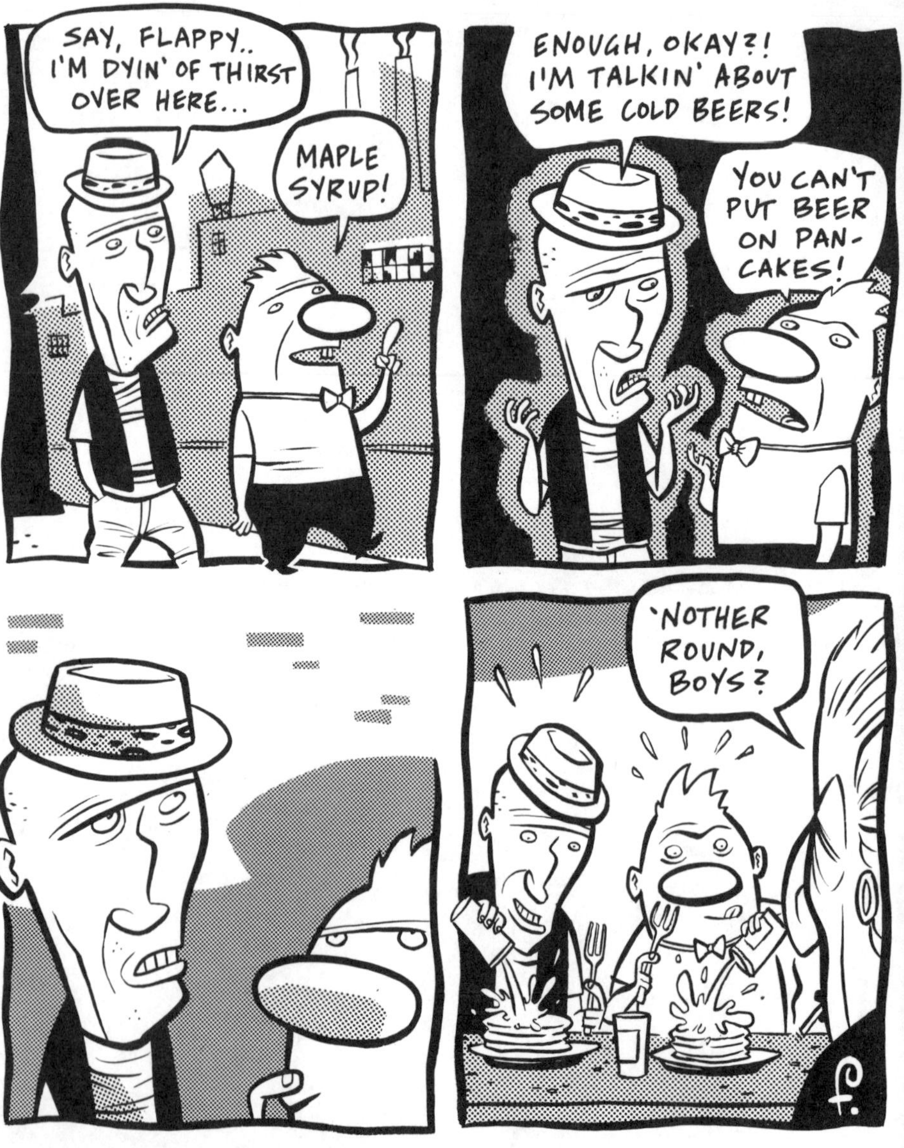
SAY, FLAPPY.. I'M DYIN' OF THIRST OVER HERE...
MAPLE SYRUP!
ENOUGH, OKAY?! I'M TALKIN' ABOUT SOME COLD BEERS!
YOU CAN'T PUT BEER ON PAN-CAKES!
'NOTHER ROUND, BOYS?
f.

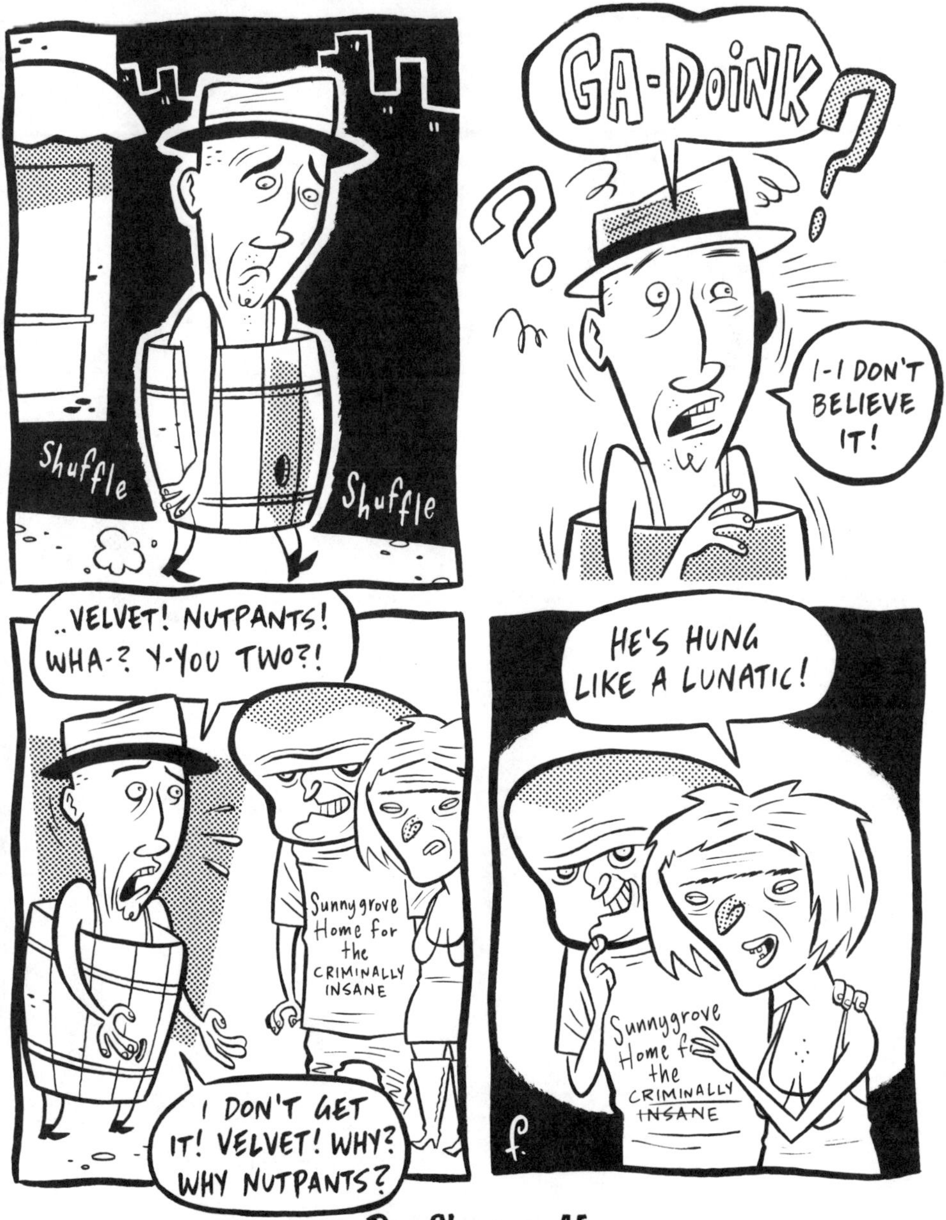

Shuffle
Shuffle
GA-DOINK
I-I DON'T BELIEVE IT!
..VELVET! NUTPANTS! WHA-? Y-YOU TWO?!
Sunnygrove Home for the CRIMINALLY INSANE
I DON'T GET IT! VELVET! WHY? WHY NUTPANTS?
HE'S HUNG LIKE A LUNATIC!
Sunnygrove Home f the CRIMINALLY INSANE
f.

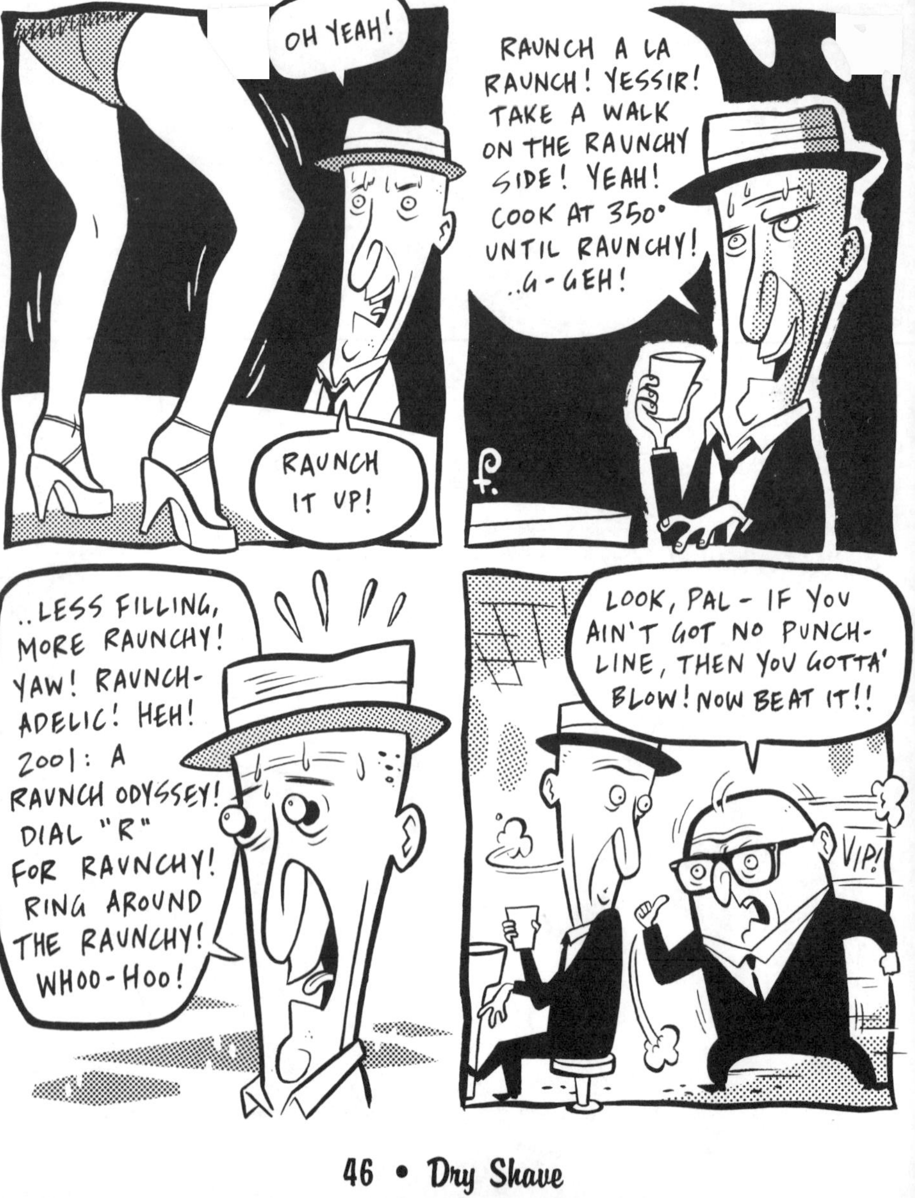
OH YEAH!
RAUNCH IT UP!
RAUNCH A LA RAUNCH! YESSIR! TAKE A WALK ON THE RAUNCHY SIDE! YEAH! COOK AT 350° UNTIL RAUNCHY! ..G-GEH!
f.
..LESS FILLING, MORE RAUNCHY! YAW! RAUNCH-ADELIC! HEH! 2001: A RAUNCH ODYSSEY! DIAL "R" FOR RAUNCHY! RING AROUND THE RAUNCHY! WHOO-HOO!
LOOK, PAL - IF YOU AIN'T GOT NO PUNCH-LINE, THEN YOU GOTTA' BLOW! NOW BEAT IT!!
VIP!

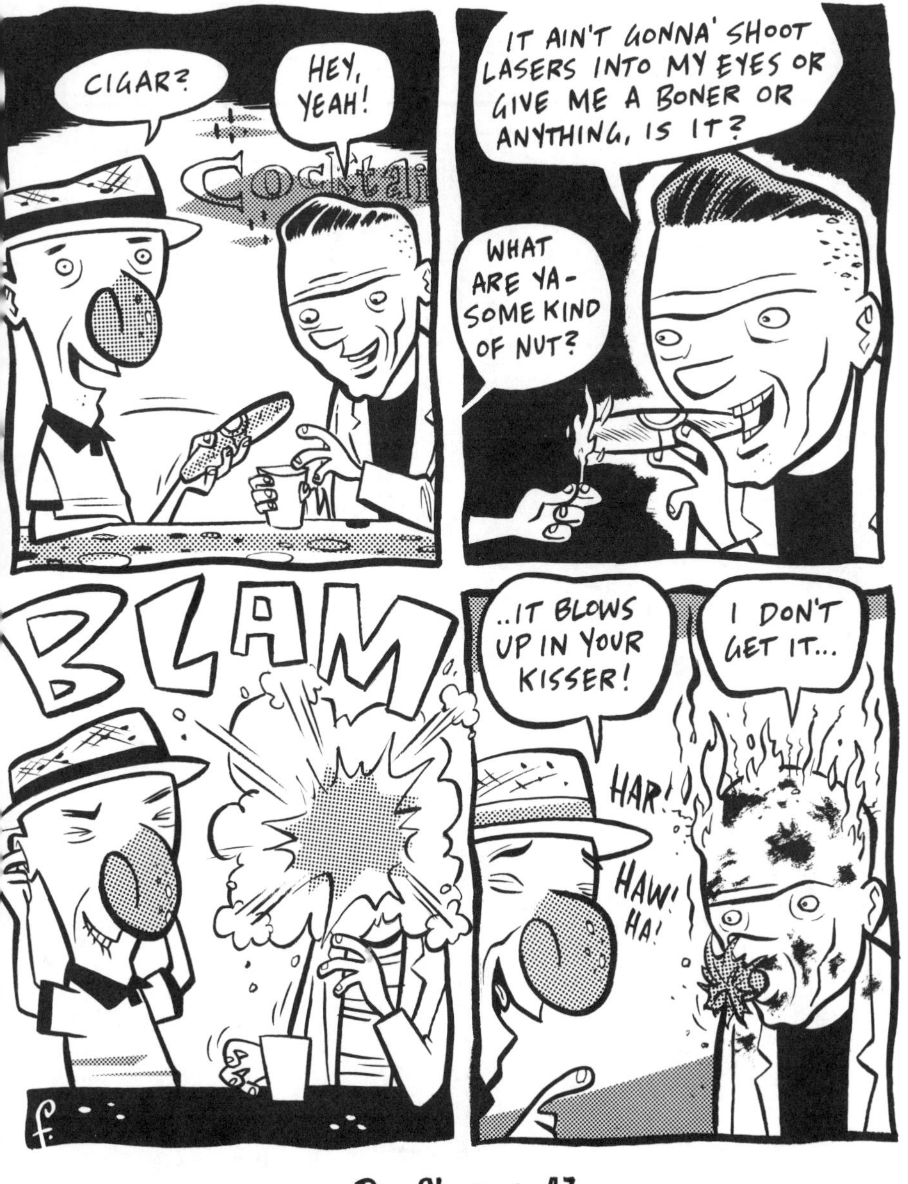
CIGAR?
HEY, YEAH!
Cocktai
IT AIN'T GONNA' SHOOT LASERS INTO MY EYES OR GIVE ME A BONER OR ANYTHING, IS IT?
WHAT ARE YA- SOME KIND OF NUT?
BLAM
..IT BLOWS UP IN YOUR KISSER!
I DON'T GET IT...
HAR!
HAW!
HA!

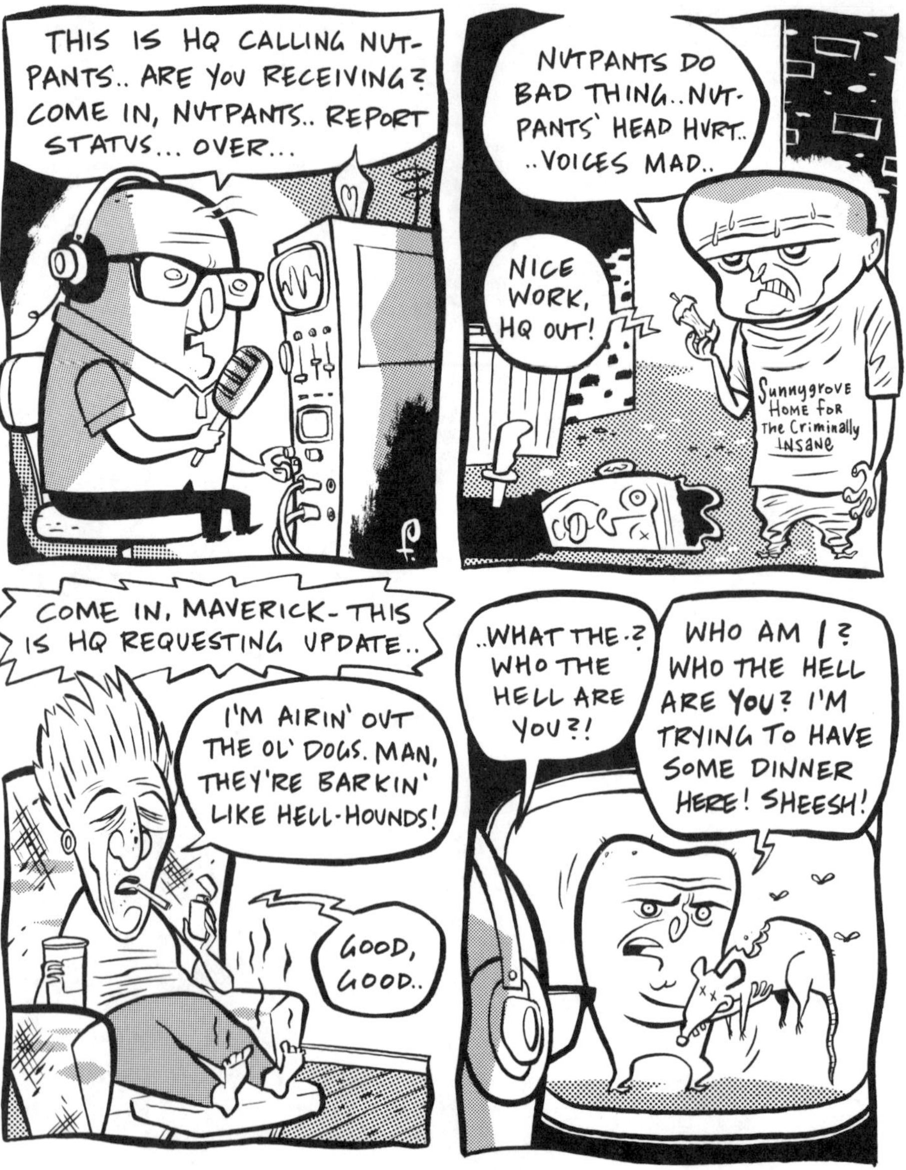
THIS IS HQ CALLING NUT-PANTS.. ARE YOU RECEIVING? COME IN, NUTPANTS.. REPORT STATUS... OVER...
NUTPANTS DO BAD THING..NUT-PANTS' HEAD HURT.. ..VOICES MAD..
NICE WORK, HQ OUT!
Sunnygrove Home for The Criminally Insane
COME IN, MAVERICK- THIS IS HQ REQUESTING UPDATE..
I'M AIRIN' OUT THE OL' DOGS. MAN, THEY'RE BARKIN' LIKE HELL-HOUNDS!
GOOD, GOOD..
..WHAT THE-? WHO THE HELL ARE YOU?!
WHO AM I? WHO THE HELL ARE YOU? I'M TRYING TO HAVE SOME DINNER HERE! SHEESH!

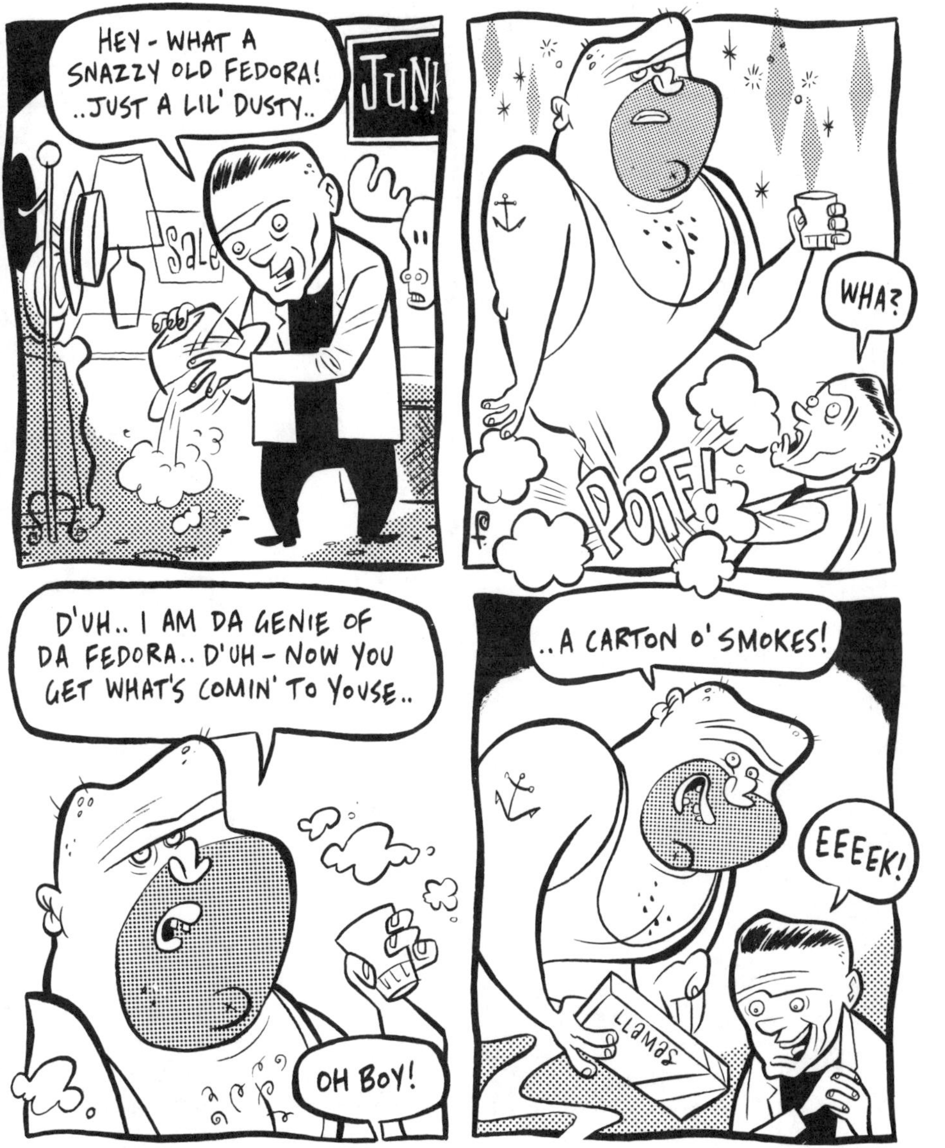
HEY - WHAT A SNAZZY OLD FEDORA! ..JUST A LIL' DUSTY..
JUN
SALE
WHA?
POIF!
D'UH.. I AM DA GENIE OF DA FEDORA.. D'UH - NOW YOU GET WHAT'S COMIN' TO YOUSE..
OH BOY!
..A CARTON O' SMOKES!
EEEEK!

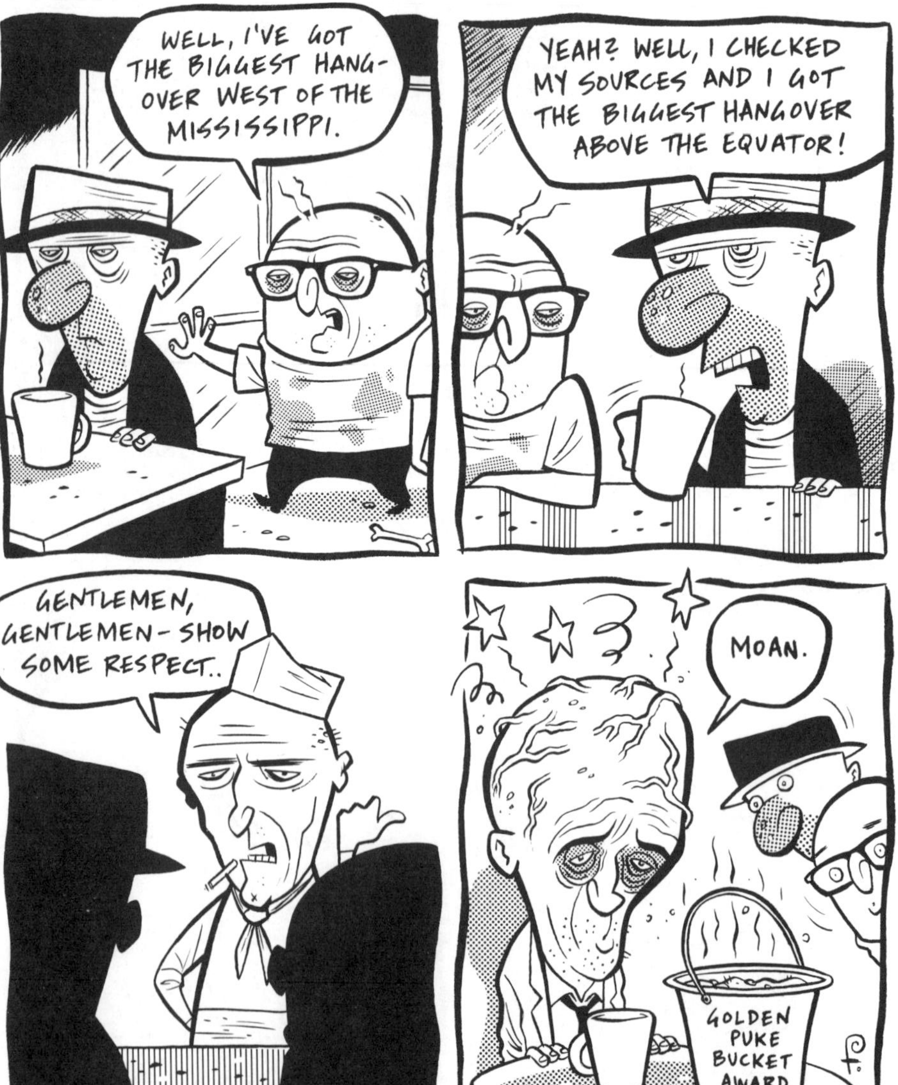
WELL, I'VE GOT THE BIGGEST HANG-OVER WEST OF THE MISSISSIPPI.
YEAH? WELL, I CHECKED MY SOURCES AND I GOT THE BIGGEST HANGOVER ABOVE THE EQUATOR!
GENTLEMEN, GENTLEMEN- SHOW SOME RESPECT..
MOAN.
GOLDEN PUKE BUCKET AWARD

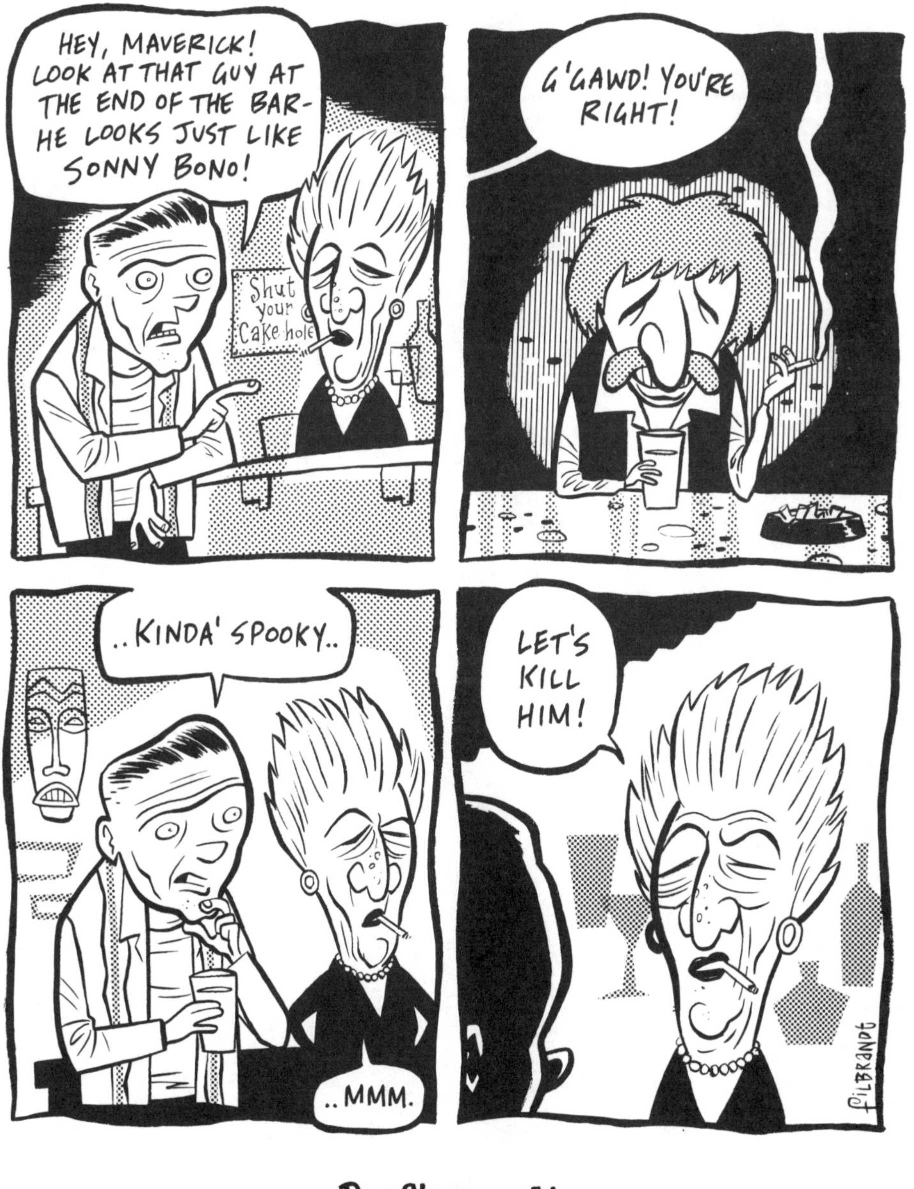
HEY, MAVERICK! LOOK AT THAT GUY AT THE END OF THE BAR- HE LOOKS JUST LIKE SONNY BONO!
Shut your Cake-hole
G'GAWD! YOU'RE RIGHT!
..KINDA' SPOOKY..
..MMM.
LET'S KILL HIM!
FILBRANDT

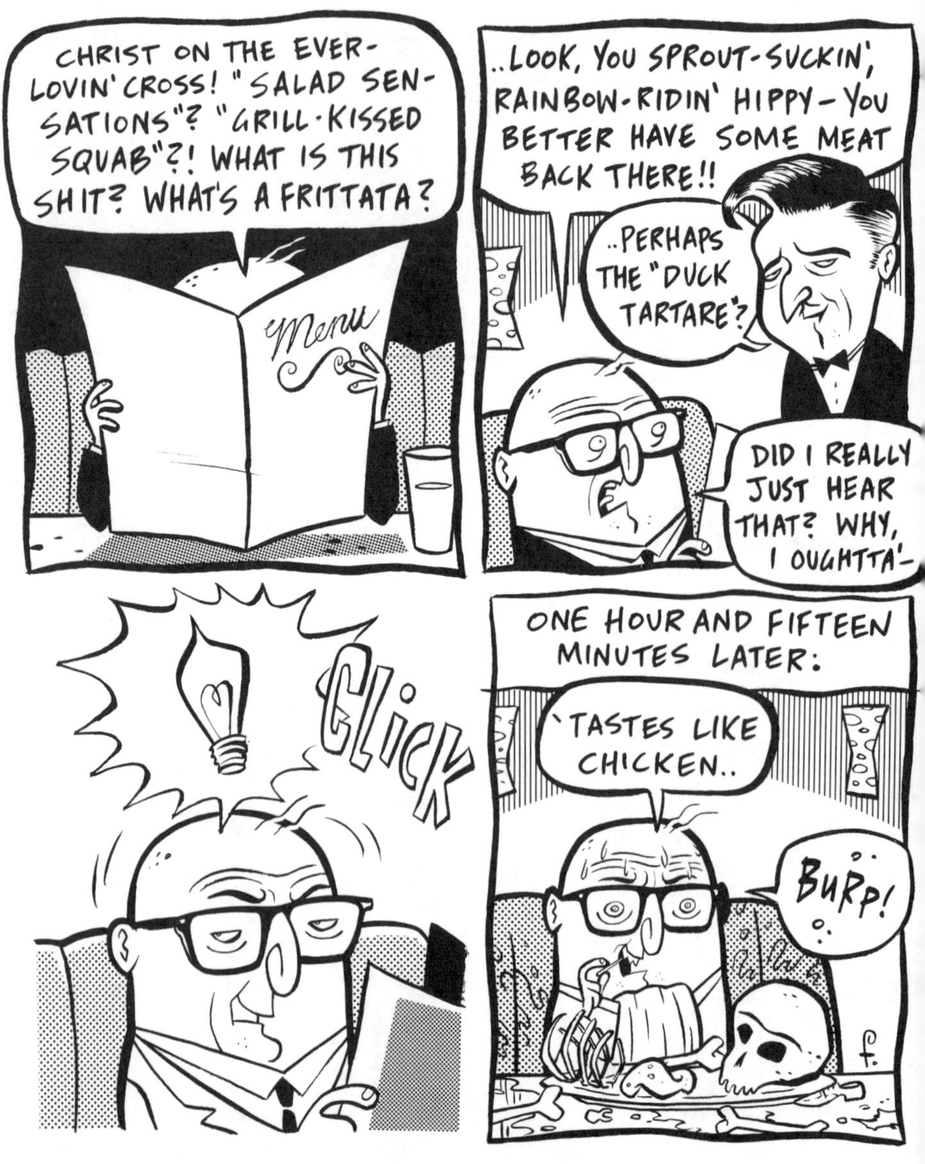
CHRIST ON THE EVER-LOVIN' CROSS! "SALAD SENSATIONS"? "GRILL-KISSED SQUAB"?! WHAT IS THIS SHIT? WHAT'S A FRITTATA?
Menu
..LOOK, YOU SPROUT-SUCKIN', RAINBOW-RIDIN' HIPPY - YOU BETTER HAVE SOME MEAT BACK THERE!!
..PERHAPS THE "DUCK TARTARE"?
DID I REALLY JUST HEAR THAT? WHY, I OUGHTTA'-
CLICK
ONE HOUR AND FIFTEEN MINUTES LATER:
`TASTES LIKE CHICKEN..
BURP!

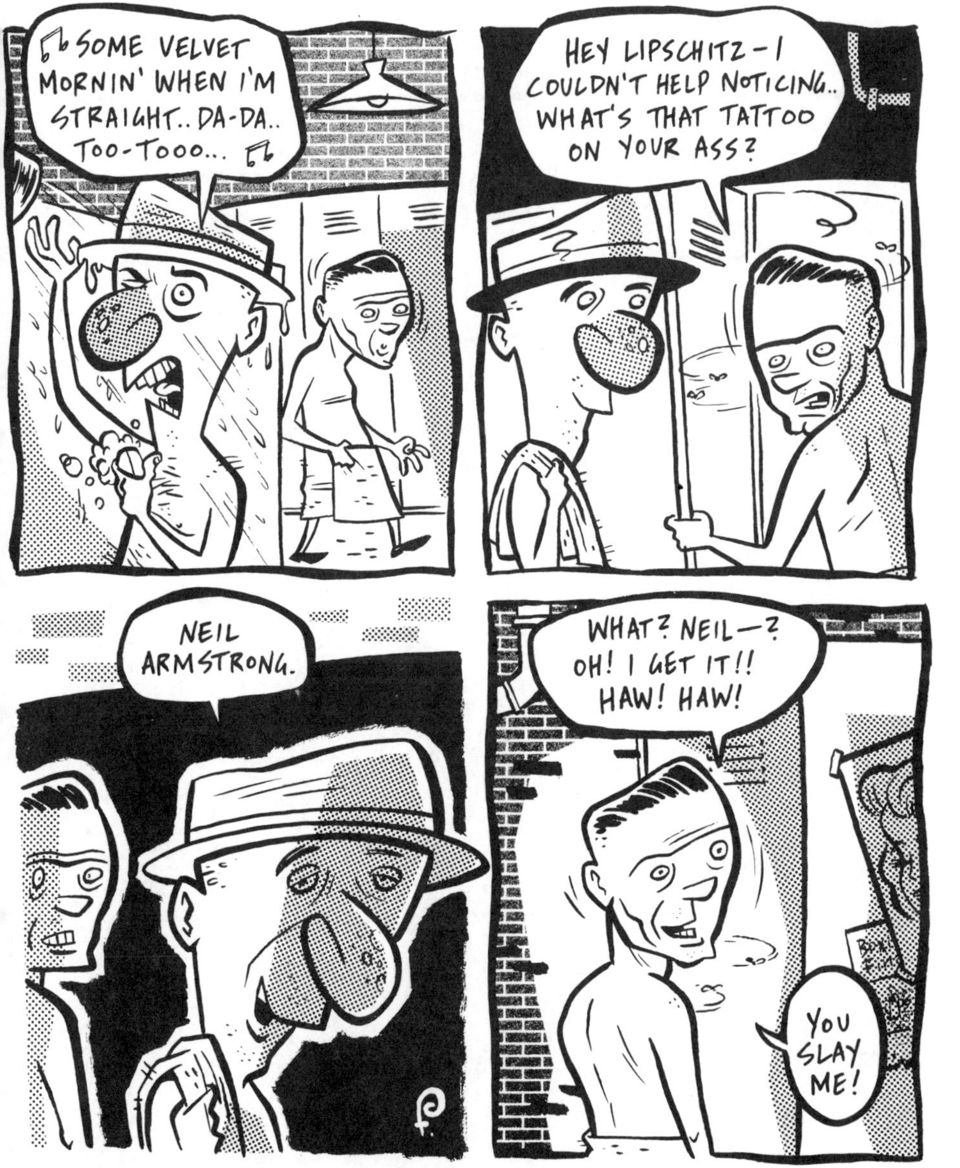
SOME VELVET MORNIN' WHEN I'M STRAIGHT.. DA-DA.. TOO-TOOO...
HEY LIPSCHITZ — I COULDN'T HELP NOTICING.. WHAT'S THAT TATTOO ON YOUR ASS?
NEIL ARMSTRONG.
WHAT? NEIL—? OH! I GET IT!! HAW! HAW!
YOU SLAY ME!

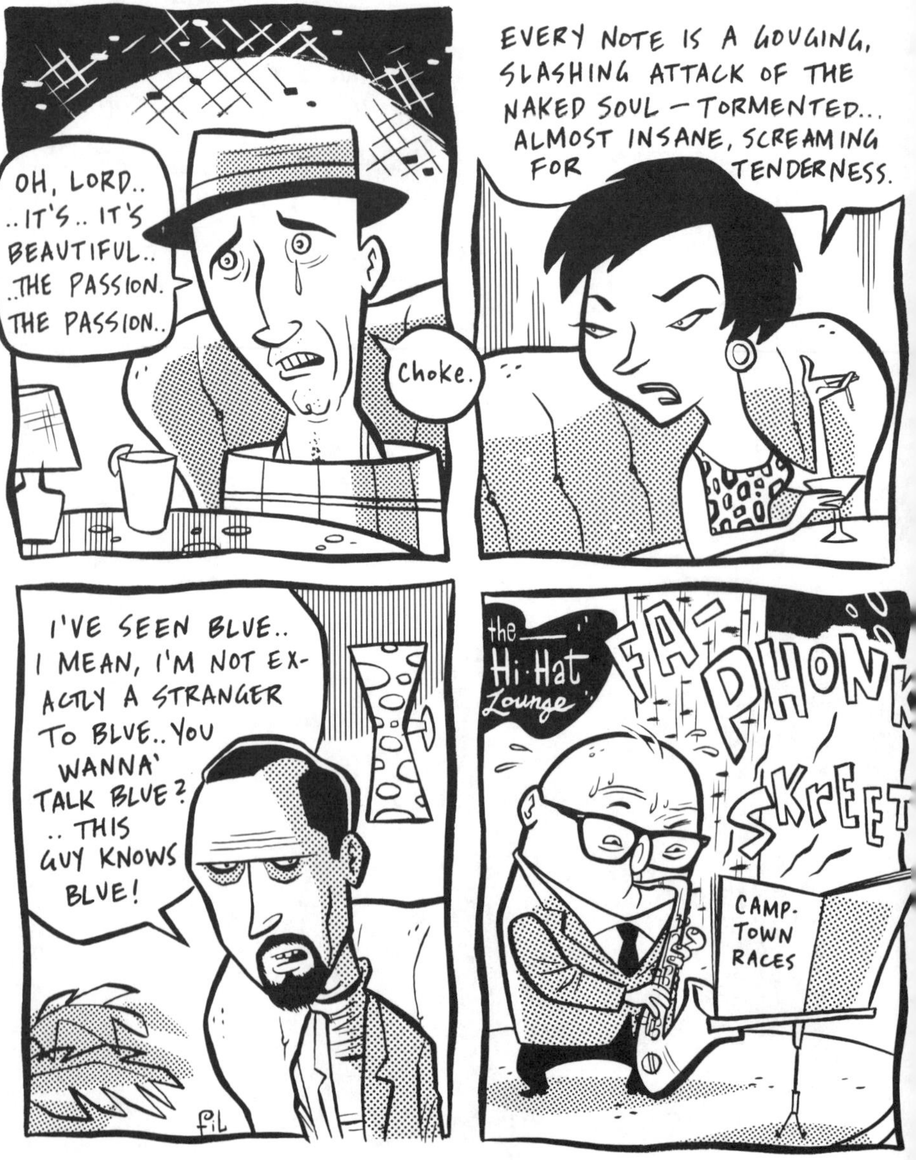

OH, LORD.. ..IT'S.. IT'S BEAUTIFUL.. ..THE PASSION. THE PASSION..
Choke.
EVERY NOTE IS A GOUGING, SLASHING ATTACK OF THE NAKED SOUL — TORMENTED... ALMOST INSANE, SCREAMING FOR TENDERNESS.
I'VE SEEN BLUE.. I MEAN, I'M NOT EXACTLY A STRANGER TO BLUE.. YOU WANNA' TALK BLUE? .. THIS GUY KNOWS BLUE!
fil
the Hi·Hat Lounge
FA-PHONK
SKREET
CAMP-TOWN RACES

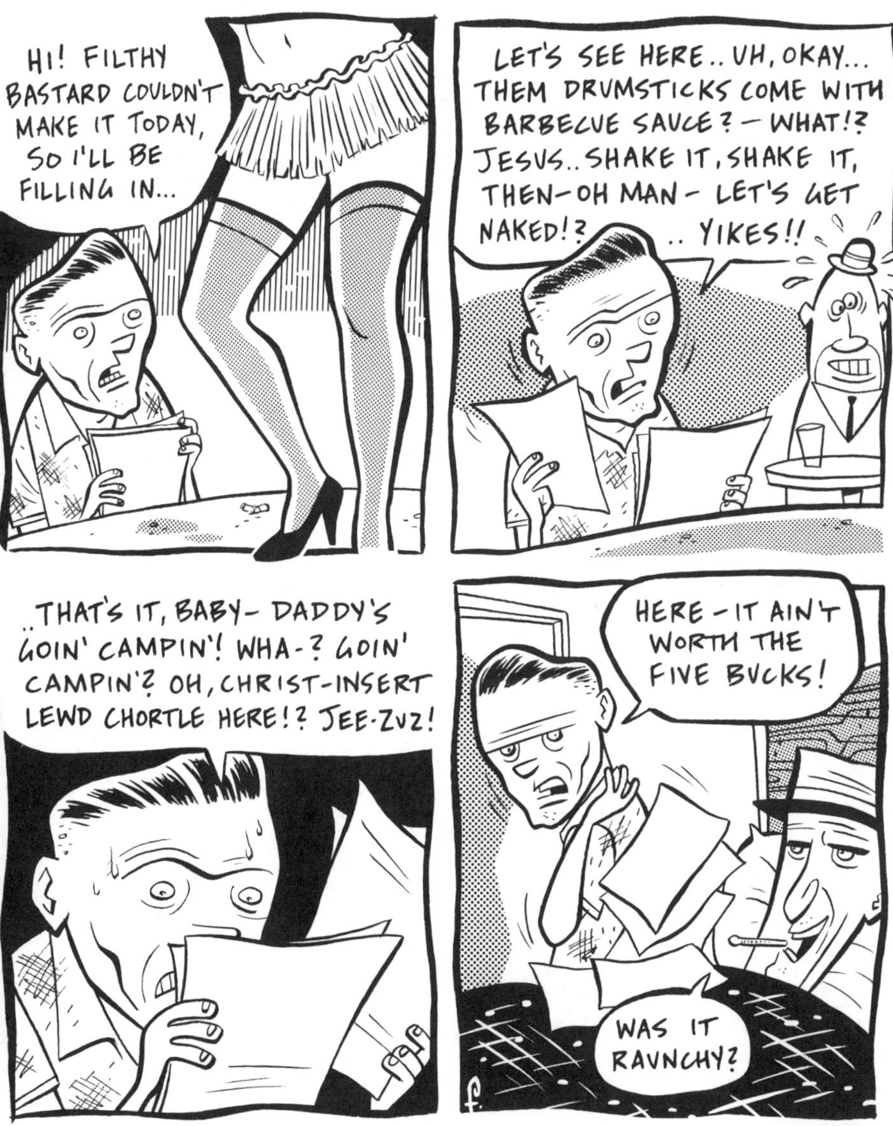
HI! FILTHY BASTARD COULDN'T MAKE IT TODAY, SO I'LL BE FILLING IN...
LET'S SEE HERE.. UH, OKAY... THEM DRUMSTICKS COME WITH BARBECUE SAUCE?—WHAT!? JESUS.. SHAKE IT, SHAKE IT, THEN—OH MAN—LET'S GET NAKED!?
.. YIKES!!
..THAT'S IT, BABY—DADDY'S GOIN' CAMPIN'! WHA-? GOIN' CAMPIN'? OH, CHRIST-INSERT LEWD CHORTLE HERE!? JEE-ZUZ!
HERE—IT AIN'T WORTH THE FIVE BUCKS!
WAS IT RAUNCHY?

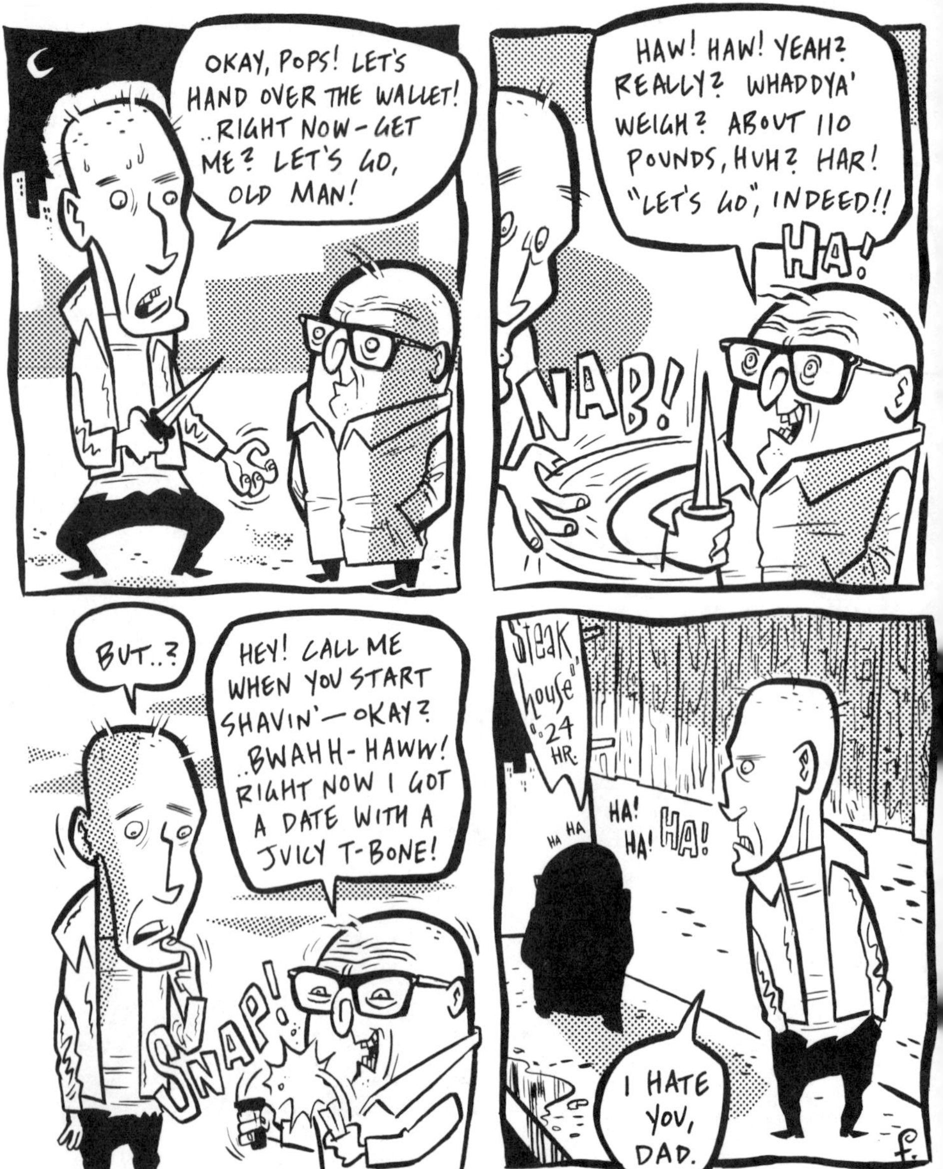
OKAY, POPS! LET'S HAND OVER THE WALLET! ..RIGHT NOW-GET ME? LET'S GO, OLD MAN!
HAW! HAW! YEAH? REALLY? WHADDYA' WEIGH? ABOUT 110 POUNDS, HUH? HAR! "LET'S GO", INDEED!!
HA!
SNAB!
BUT..?
HEY! CALL ME WHEN YOU START SHAVIN'—OKAY? ..BWAHH-HAWW! RIGHT NOW I GOT A DATE WITH A JUICY T-BONE!
SNAP!
Steak house 24 HR.
HA HA
HA HA!
HA! HA!
I HATE YOU, DAD.

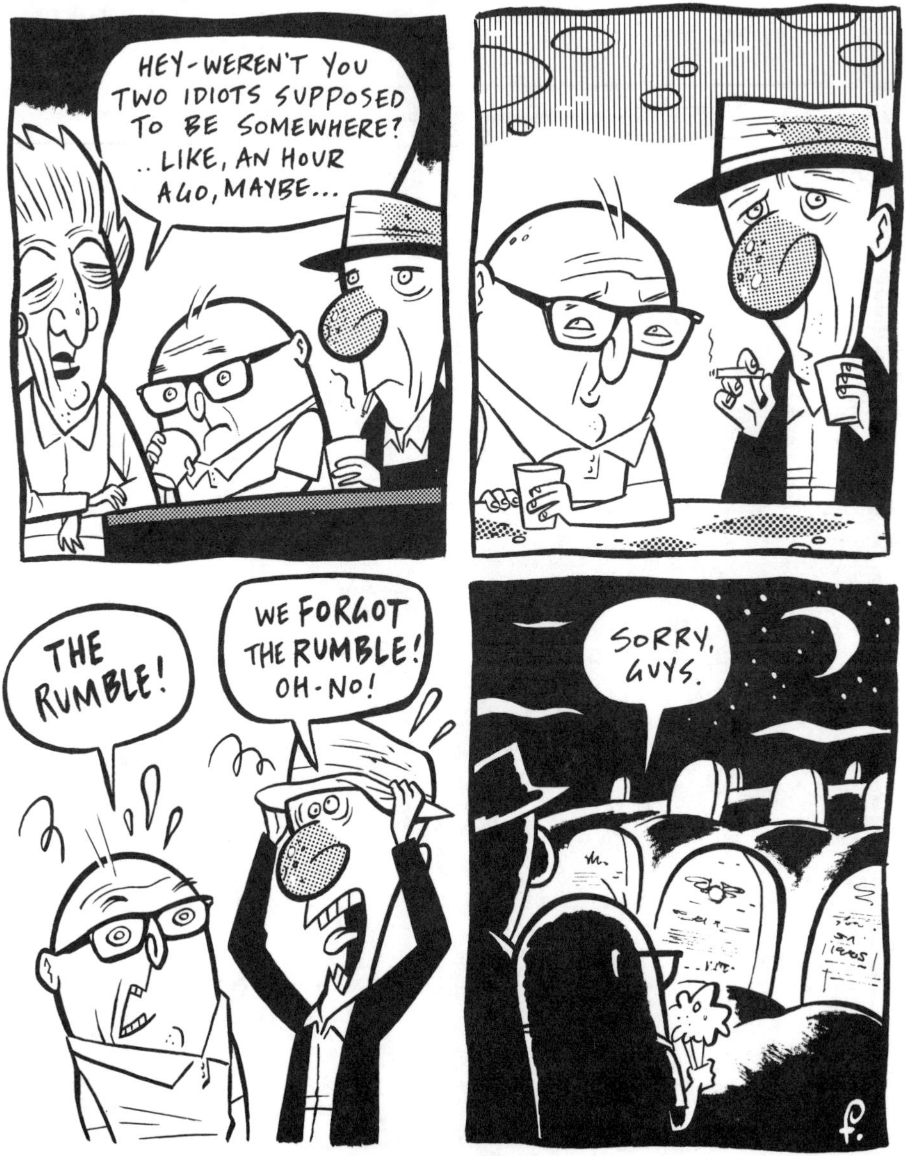
HEY-WEREN'T YOU TWO IDIOTS SUPPOSED TO BE SOMEWHERE? ..LIKE, AN HOUR AGO, MAYBE...
THE RUMBLE!
WE FORGOT THE RUMBLE! OH-NO!
SORRY, GUYS.

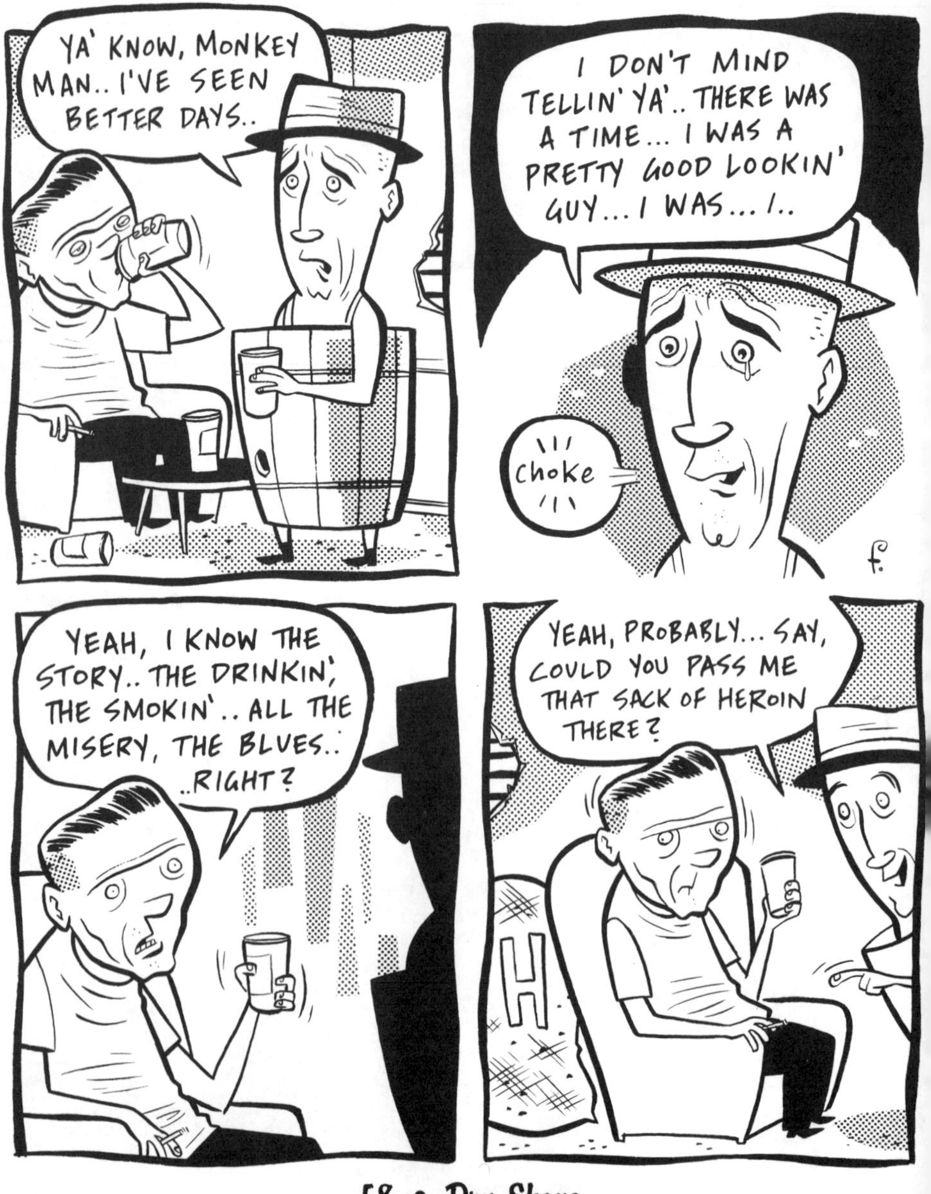
YA' KNOW, MONKEY MAN.. I'VE SEEN BETTER DAYS..
I DON'T MIND TELLIN' YA'.. THERE WAS A TIME... I WAS A PRETTY GOOD LOOKIN' GUY... I WAS... I..
choke
f.
YEAH, I KNOW THE STORY.. THE DRINKIN', THE SMOKIN'.. ALL THE MISERY, THE BLUES.. ..RIGHT?
YEAH, PROBABLY... SAY, COULD YOU PASS ME THAT SACK OF HEROIN THERE?
H

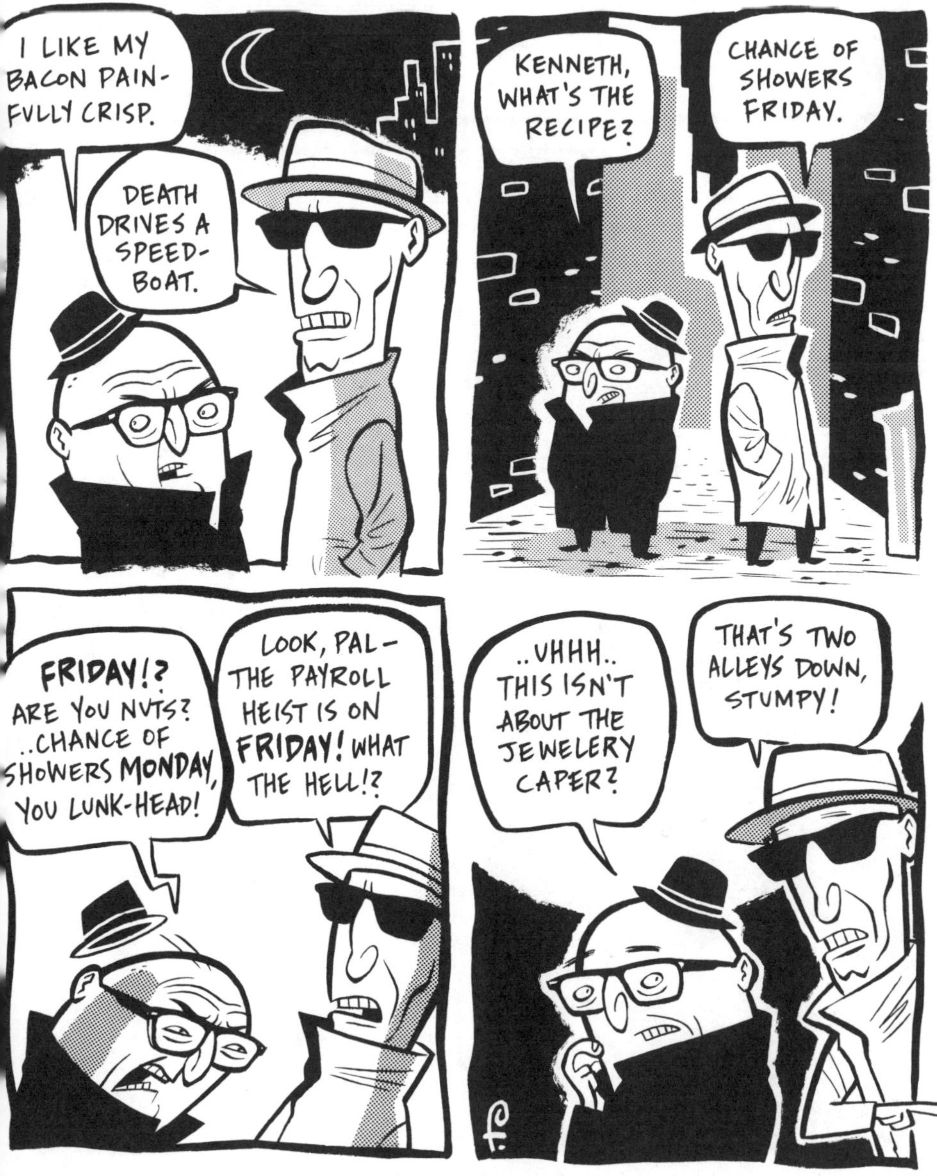
I LIKE MY BACON PAIN-FULLY CRISP.
DEATH DRIVES A SPEED-BOAT.
KENNETH, WHAT'S THE RECIPE?
CHANCE OF SHOWERS FRIDAY.
FRIDAY!? ARE YOU NUTS? ..CHANCE OF SHOWERS MONDAY, YOU LUNK-HEAD!
LOOK, PAL- THE PAYROLL HEIST IS ON FRIDAY! WHAT THE HELL!?
..UHHH.. THIS ISN'T ABOUT THE JEWELERY CAPER?
THAT'S TWO ALLEYS DOWN, STUMPY!

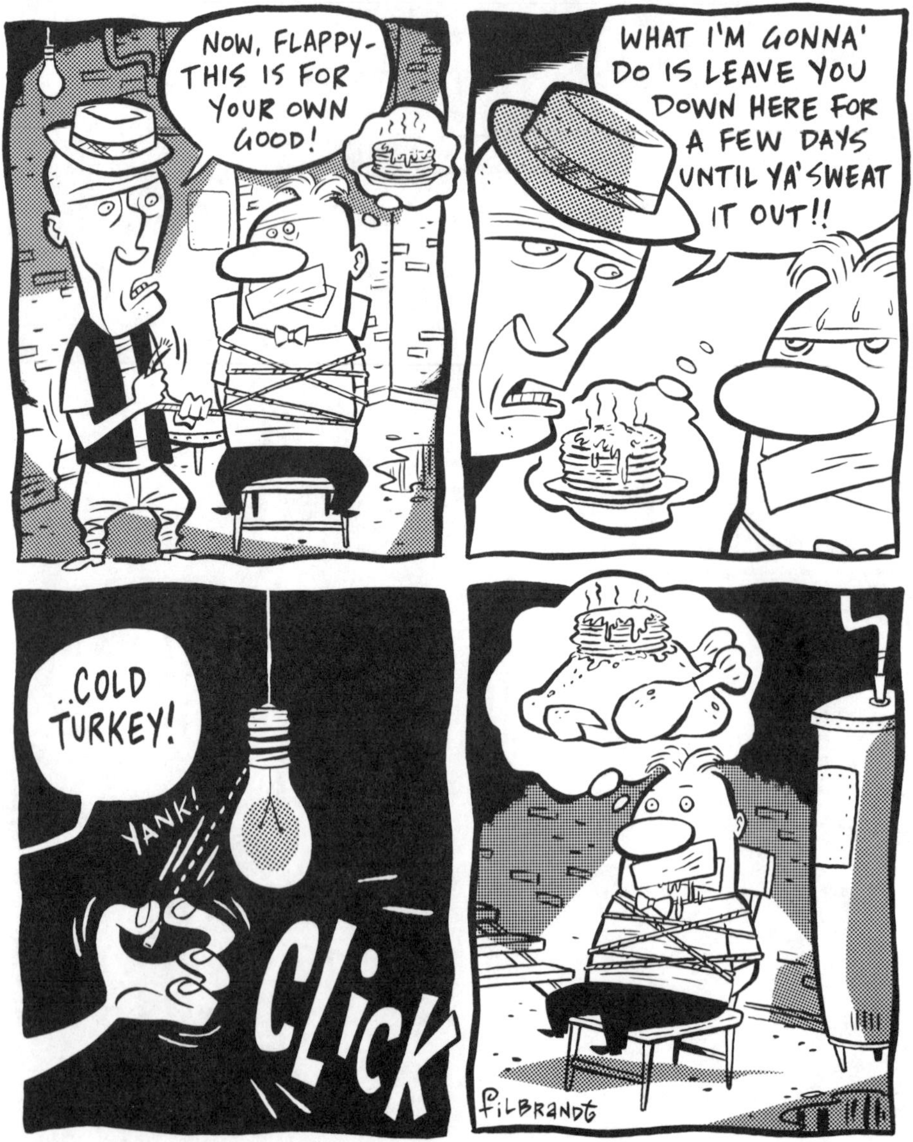
NOW, FLAPPY- THIS IS FOR YOUR OWN GOOD!
WHAT I'M GONNA' DO IS LEAVE YOU DOWN HERE FOR A FEW DAYS UNTIL YA'SWEAT IT OUT!!
..COLD TURKEY!
YANK!
CLICK
FILBRANDT

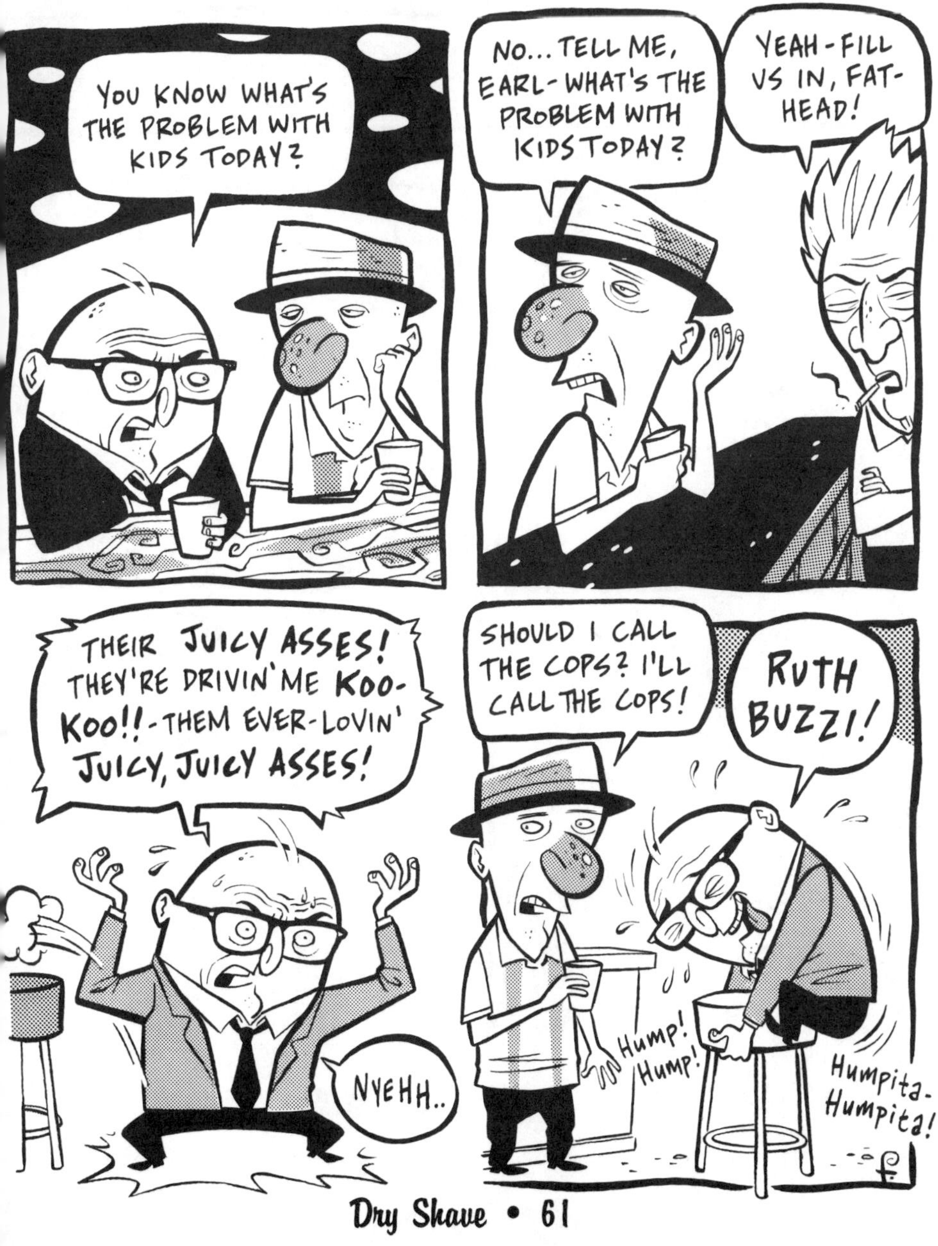

YOU KNOW WHAT'S THE PROBLEM WITH KIDS TODAY?
NO... TELL ME, EARL- WHAT'S THE PROBLEM WITH KIDS TODAY?
YEAH - FILL US IN, FAT-HEAD!
THEIR JUICY ASSES! THEY'RE DRIVIN' ME KOO-KOO!! - THEM EVER-LOVIN' JUICY, JUICY ASSES!
NYEHH..
SHOULD I CALL THE COPS? I'LL CALL THE COPS!
RUTH BUZZI!
Hump! Hump!
Humpita-Humpita!

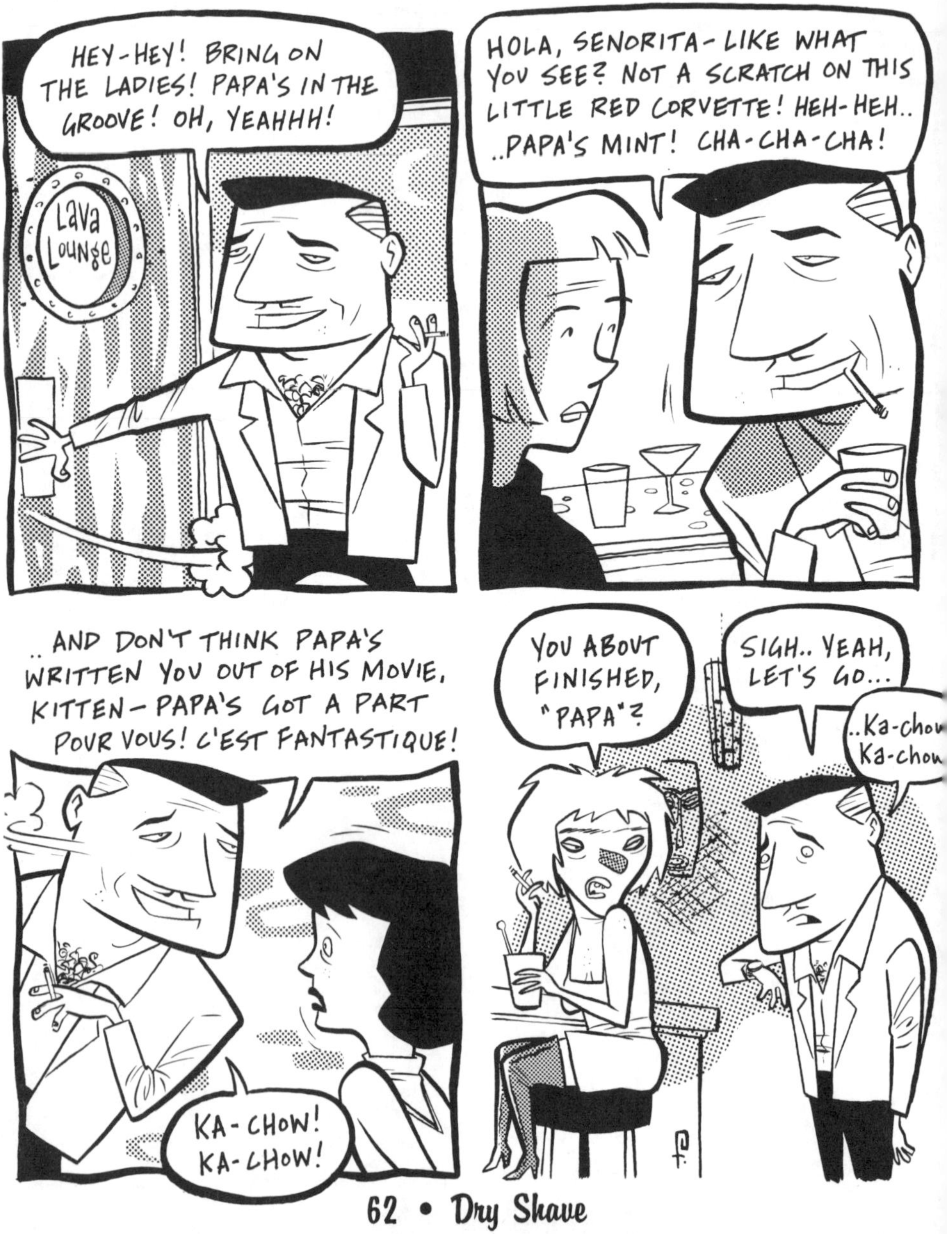
HEY-HEY! BRING ON THE LADIES! PAPA'S IN THE GROOVE! OH, YEAHHH!
LAVA LOUNGE
HOLA, SENORITA- LIKE WHAT YOU SEE? NOT A SCRATCH ON THIS LITTLE RED CORVETTE! HEH-HEH.. ..PAPA'S MINT! CHA-CHA-CHA!
.. AND DON'T THINK PAPA'S WRITTEN YOU OUT OF HIS MOVIE, KITTEN- PAPA'S GOT A PART POUR VOUS! C'EST FANTASTIQUE!
KA-CHOW! KA-CHOW!
YOU ABOUT FINISHED, "PAPA"?
SIGH.. YEAH, LET'S GO...
..Ka-chow Ka-chow

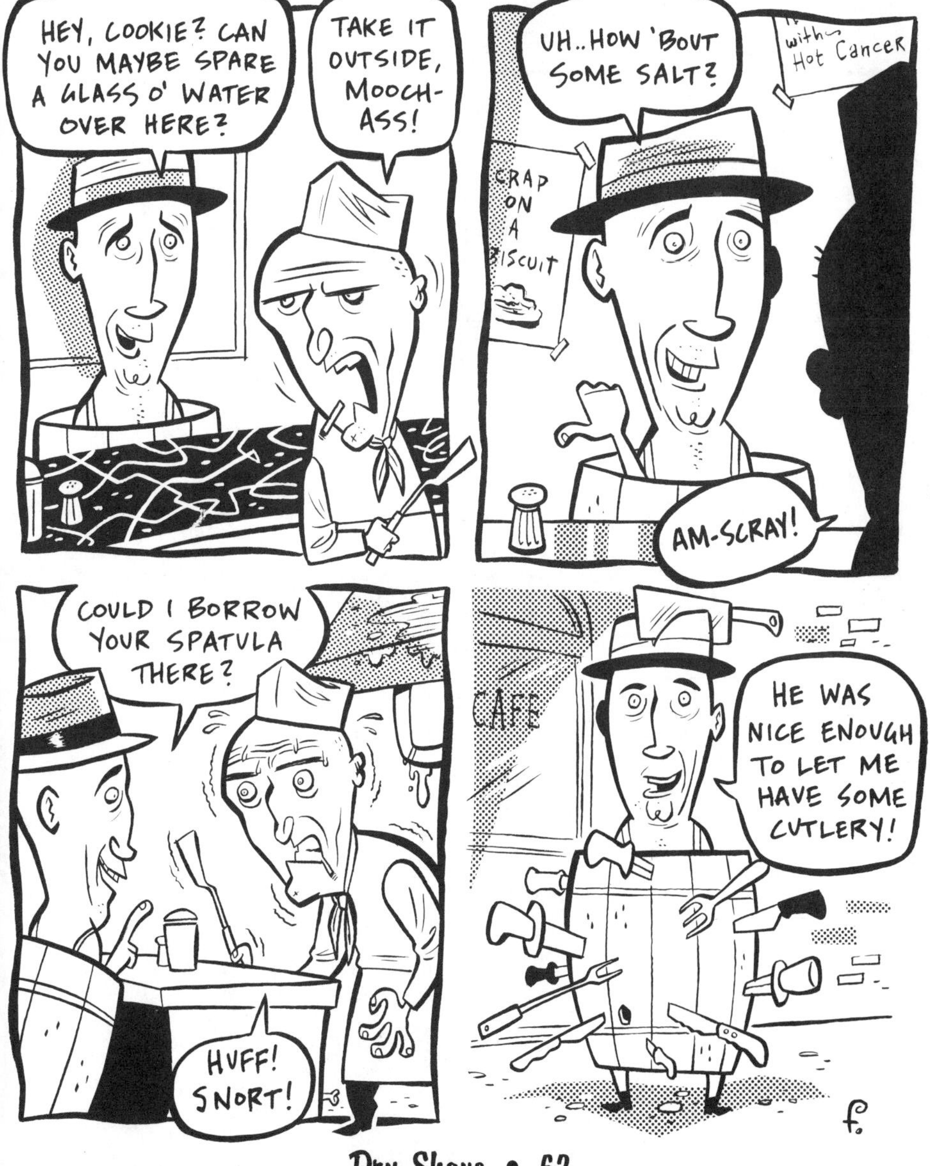
HEY, COOKIE? CAN YOU MAYBE SPARE A GLASS O' WATER OVER HERE?
TAKE IT OUTSIDE, MOOCH-ASS!
UH.. HOW 'BOUT SOME SALT?
with Hot Cancer
CRAP ON A BISCUIT
AM-SCRAY!
COULD I BORROW YOUR SPATULA THERE?
HUFF! SNORT!
CAFE
HE WAS NICE ENOUGH TO LET ME HAVE SOME CUTLERY!
f.

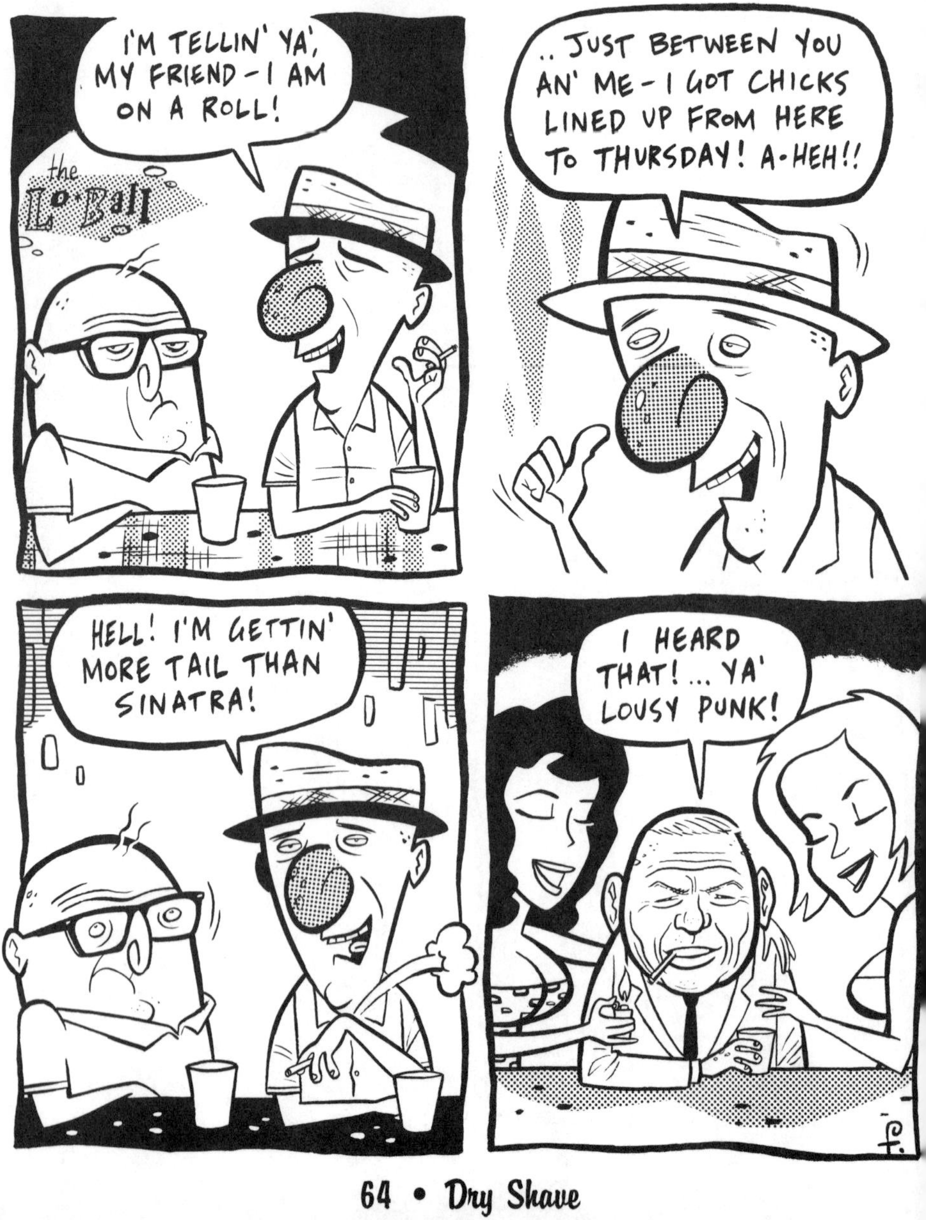
I'M TELLIN' YA', MY FRIEND - I AM ON A ROLL!
the Lo-Ball
.. JUST BETWEEN YOU AN' ME - I GOT CHICKS LINED UP FROM HERE TO THURSDAY! A-HEH!!
HELL! I'M GETTIN' MORE TAIL THAN SINATRA!
I HEARD THAT! ... YA' LOUSY PUNK!

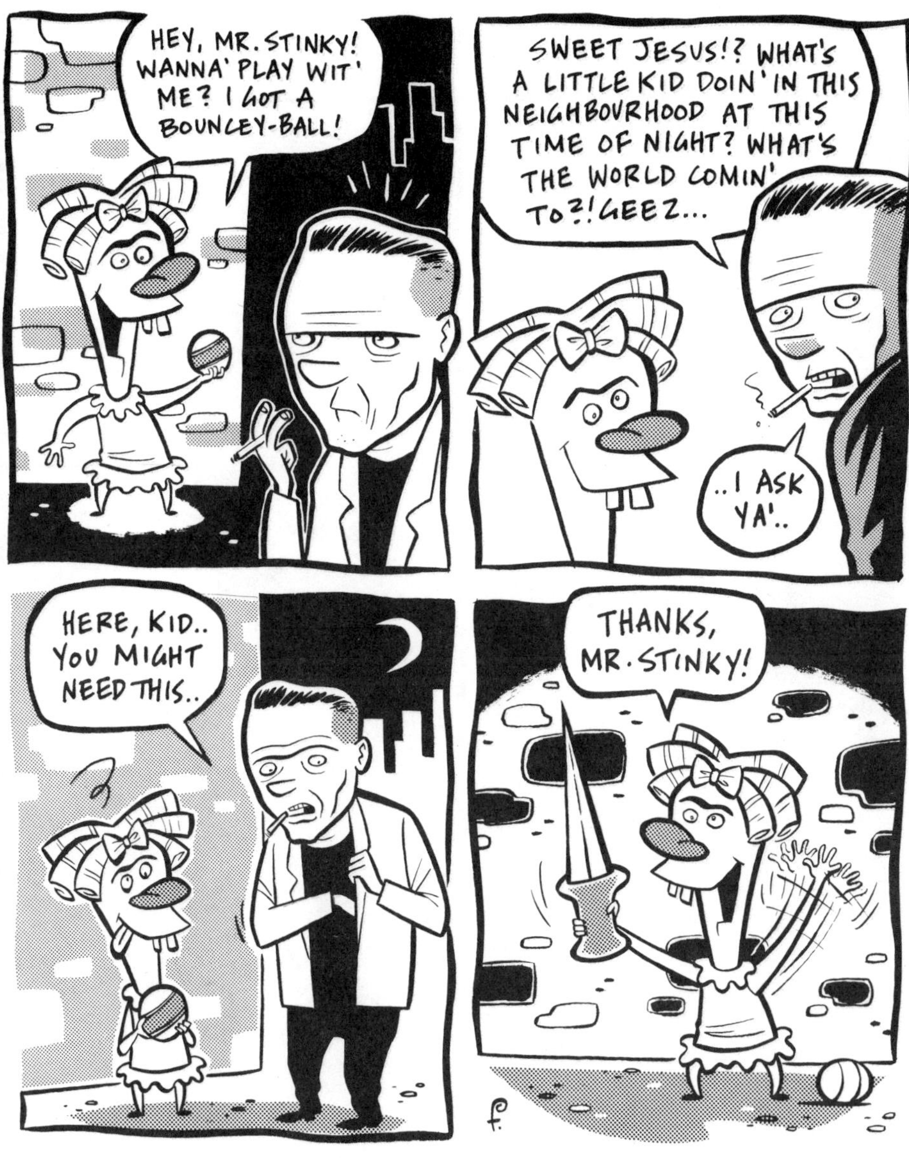
HEY, MR. STINKY! WANNA' PLAY WIT' ME? I GOT A BOUNCEY-BALL!
SWEET JESUS!? WHAT'S A LITTLE KID DOIN' IN THIS NEIGHBOURHOOD AT THIS TIME OF NIGHT? WHAT'S THE WORLD COMIN' TO?!GEEZ...
..I ASK YA'..
HERE, KID.. YOU MIGHT NEED THIS..
THANKS, MR. STINKY!
f.

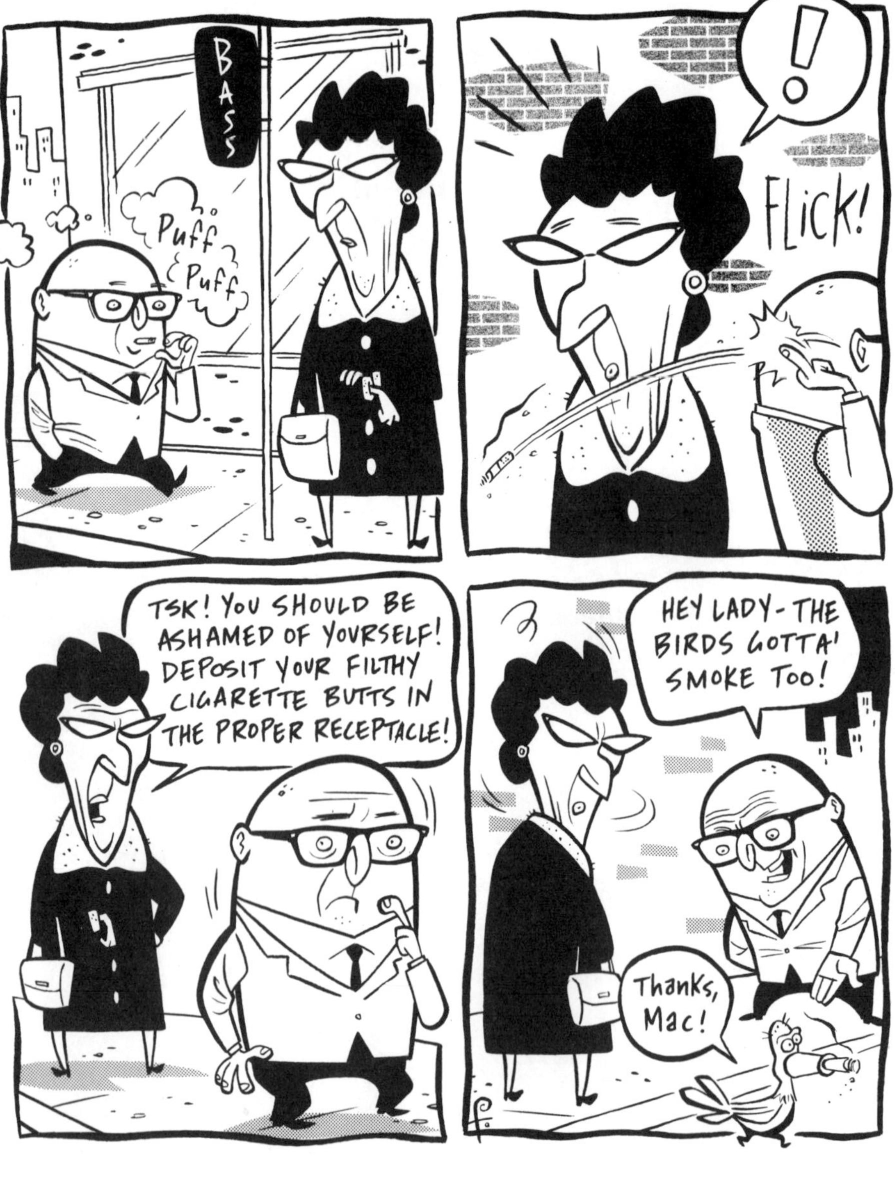
BASS
Puff Puff
!
FLICK!
TSK! YOU SHOULD BE ASHAMED OF YOURSELF! DEPOSIT YOUR FILTHY CIGARETTE BUTTS IN THE PROPER RECEPTACLE!
HEY LADY - THE BIRDS GOTTA' SMOKE TOO!
Thanks, Mac!

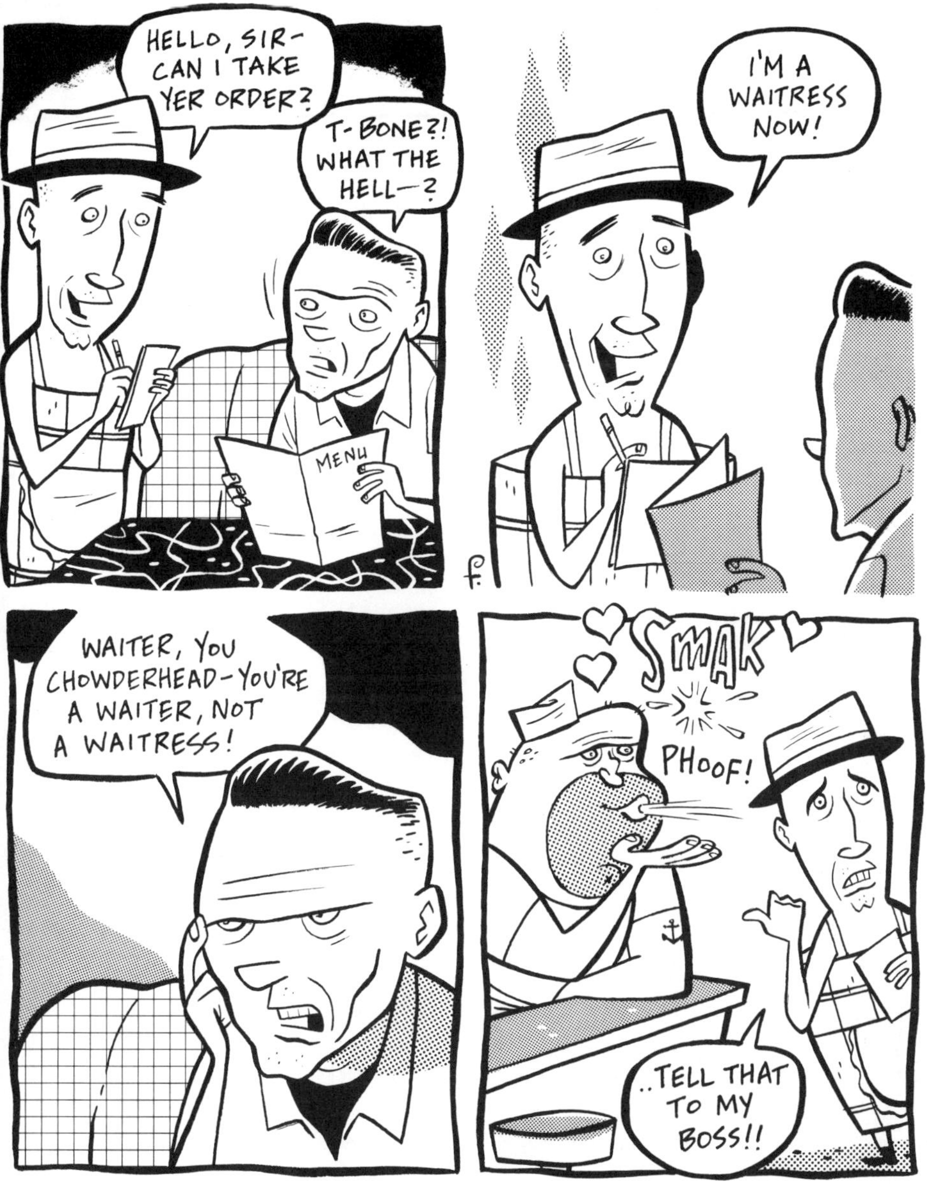
HELLO, SIR-
CAN I TAKE
YER ORDER?
T-BONE?!
WHAT THE
HELL—?
MENU
I'M A
WAITRESS
NOW!
WAITER, YOU
CHOWDERHEAD-YOU'RE
A WAITER, NOT
A WAITRESS!
SMAK
PHOOF!
..TELL THAT
TO MY
BOSS!!

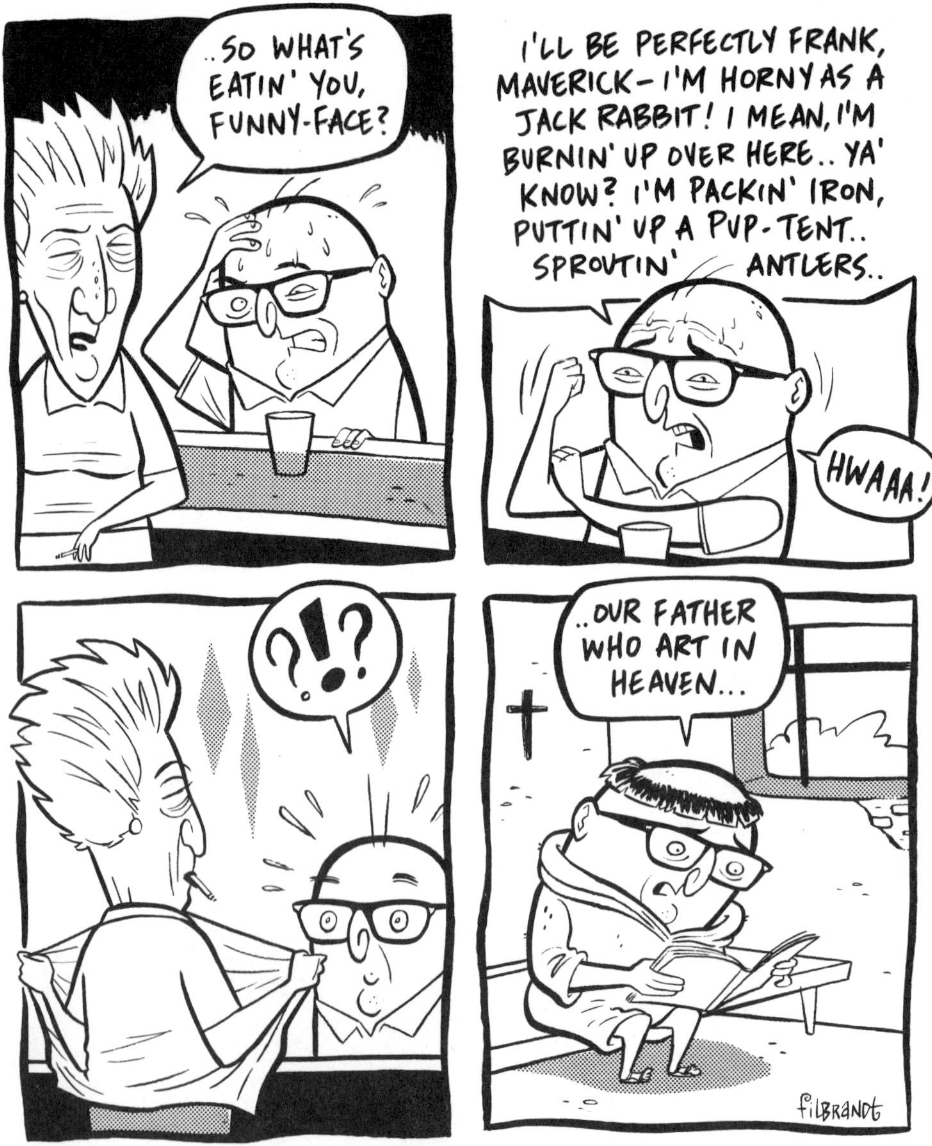
..SO WHAT'S EATIN' YOU, FUNNY-FACE?
I'LL BE PERFECTLY FRANK, MAVERICK– I'M HORNY AS A JACK RABBIT! I MEAN, I'M BURNIN' UP OVER HERE.. YA' KNOW? I'M PACKIN' IRON, PUTTIN' UP A PUP-TENT.. SPROUTIN' ANTLERS..
HWAAA!
?!?
..OUR FATHER WHO ART IN HEAVEN...
FILBRANDT

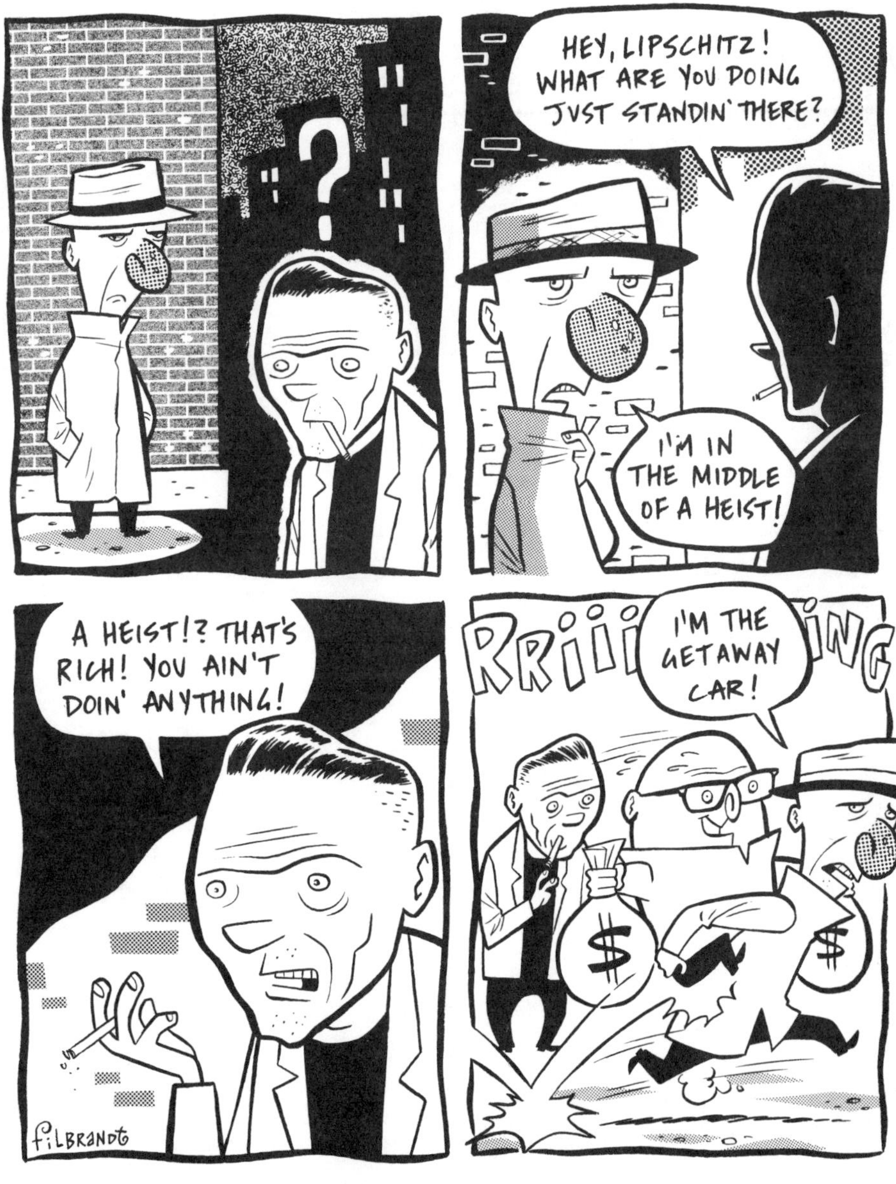
HEY, LIPSCHITZ! WHAT ARE YOU DOING JUST STANDIN' THERE?
I'M IN THE MIDDLE OF A HEIST!
A HEIST!? THAT'S RICH! YOU AIN'T DOIN' ANYTHING!
FILBRANDT
RRIIIING
I'M THE GETAWAY CAR!

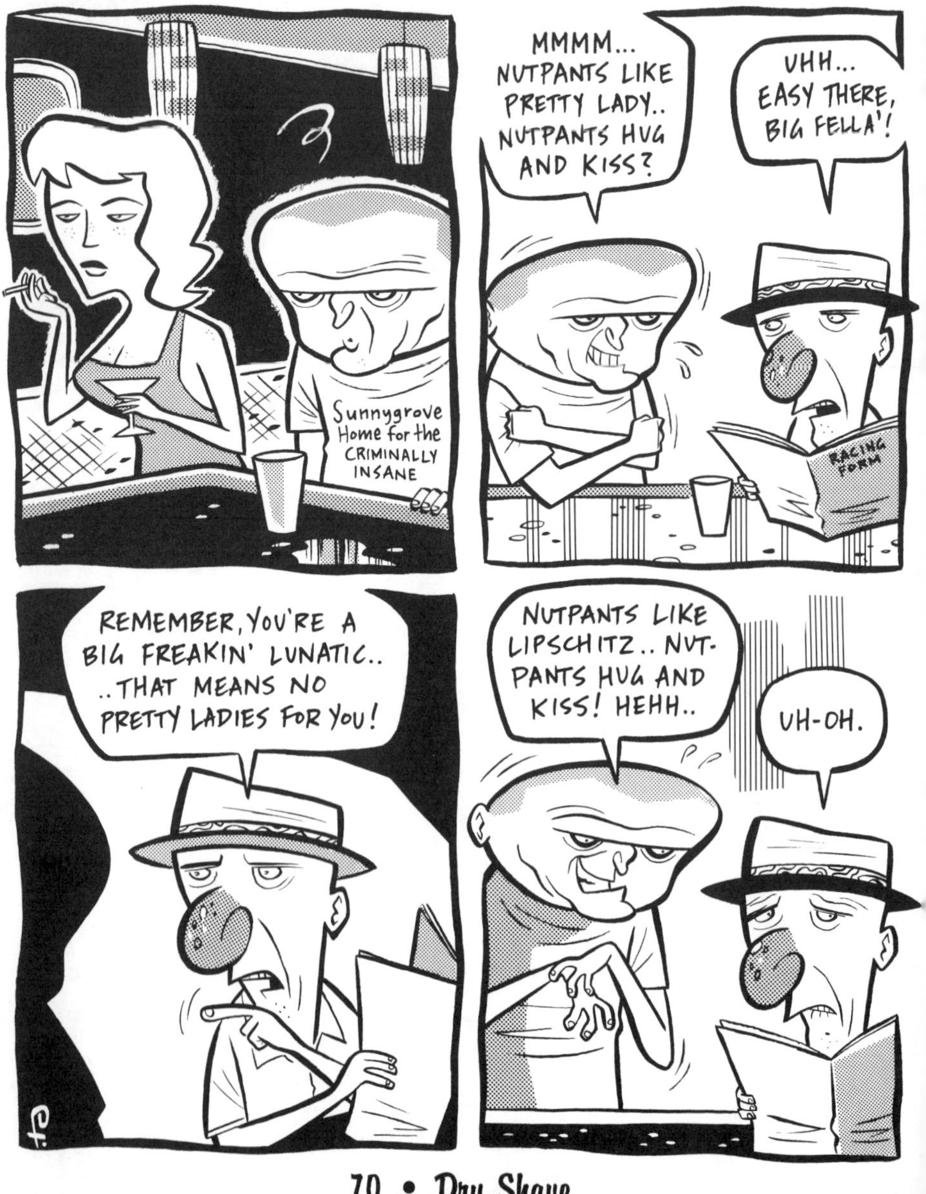

Sunnygrove Home for the CRIMINALLY INSANE
MMMM... NUTPANTS LIKE PRETTY LADY.. NUTPANTS HUG AND KISS?
UHH... EASY THERE, BIG FELLA'!
REMEMBER, YOU'RE A BIG FREAKIN' LUNATIC.. ..THAT MEANS NO PRETTY LADIES FOR YOU!
NUTPANTS LIKE LIPSCHITZ.. NUT-PANTS HUG AND KISS! HEHH..
UH-OH.

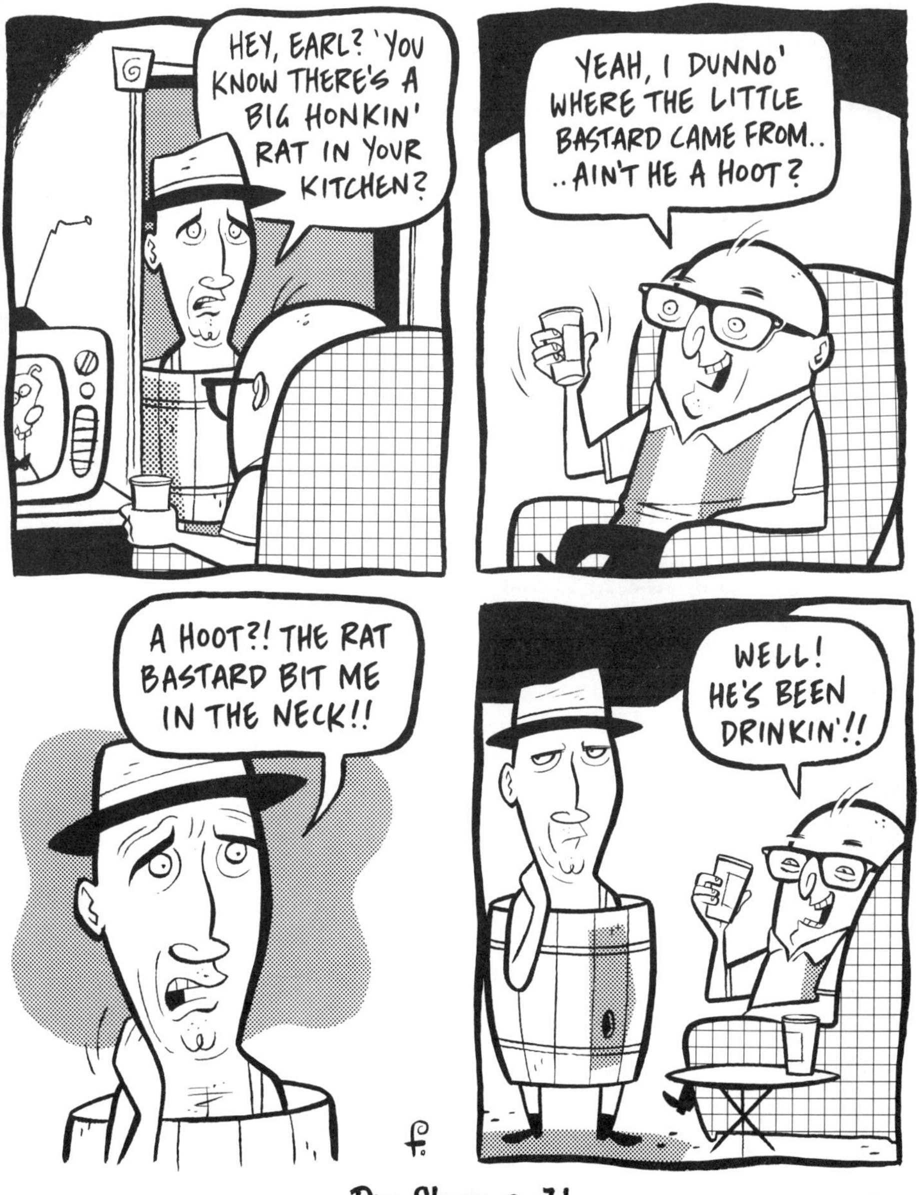
HEY, EARL? 'YOU KNOW THERE'S A BIG HONKIN' RAT IN YOUR KITCHEN?
YEAH, I DUNNO' WHERE THE LITTLE BASTARD CAME FROM.. ..AIN'T HE A HOOT?
A HOOT?! THE RAT BASTARD BIT ME IN THE NECK!!
WELL! HE'S BEEN DRINKIN'!!
f.

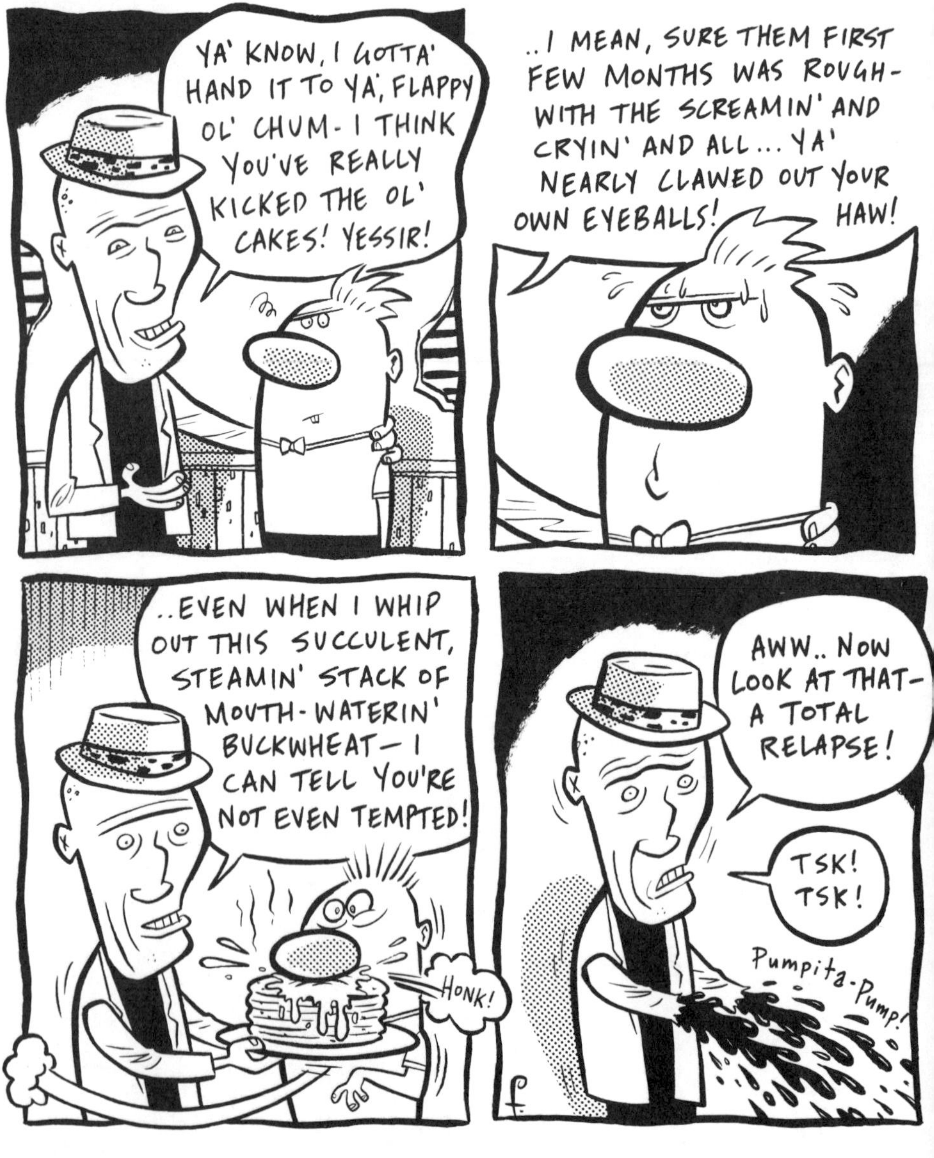
YA' KNOW, I GOTTA' HAND IT TO YA', FLAPPY OL' CHUM- I THINK YOU'VE REALLY KICKED THE OL' CAKES! YESSIR!
..I MEAN, SURE THEM FIRST FEW MONTHS WAS ROUGH- WITH THE SCREAMIN' AND CRYIN' AND ALL... YA' NEARLY CLAWED OUT YOUR OWN EYEBALLS! HAW!
..EVEN WHEN I WHIP OUT THIS SUCCULENT, STEAMIN' STACK OF MOUTH-WATERIN' BUCKWHEAT— I CAN TELL YOU'RE NOT EVEN TEMPTED!
HONK!
AWW.. NOW LOOK AT THAT- A TOTAL RELAPSE!
TSK! TSK!
Pumpita-Pump!

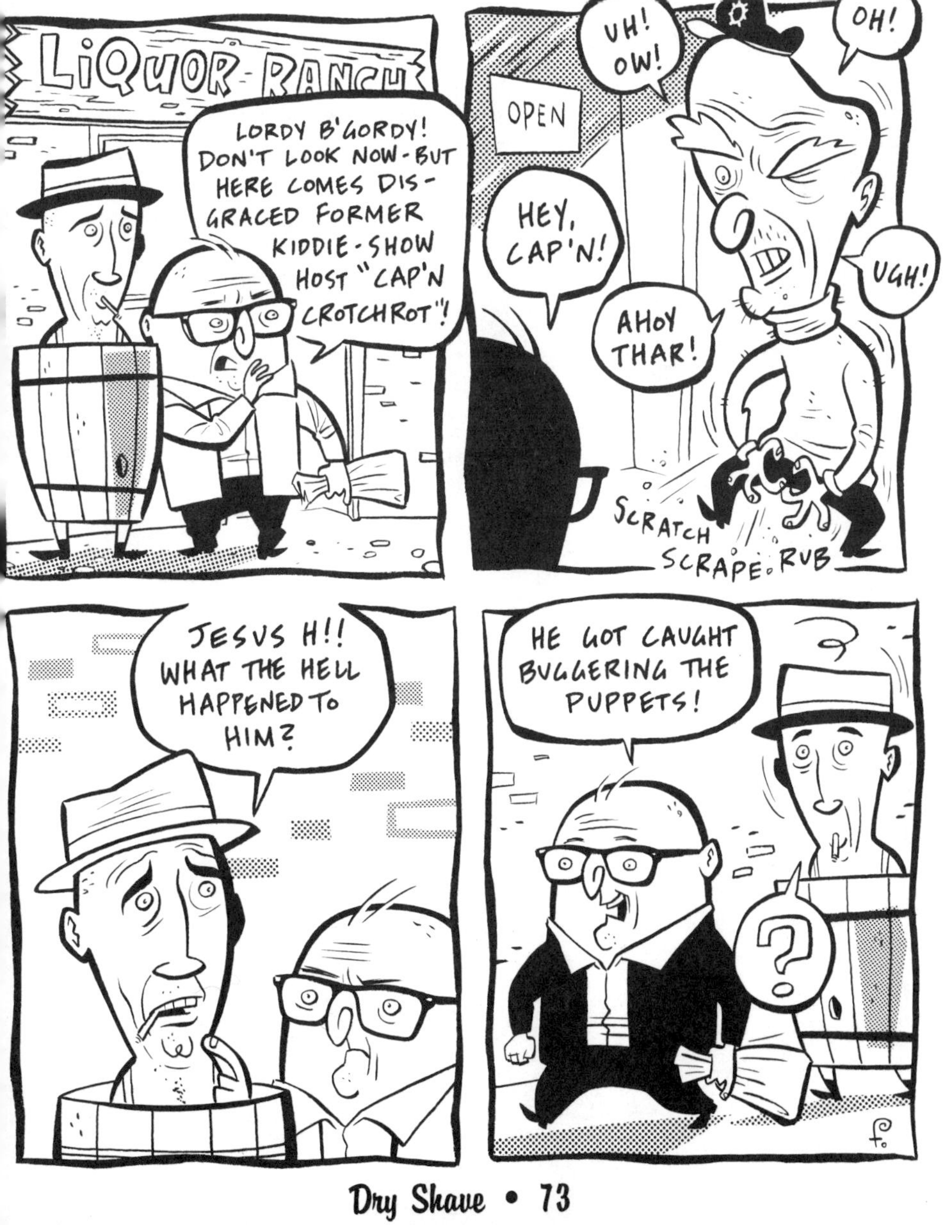
LIQUOR RANCH
LORDY B'GORDY! DON'T LOOK NOW - BUT HERE COMES DIS-GRACED FORMER KIDDIE-SHOW HOST "CAP'N CROTCHROT"!
OPEN
UH! OW!
OH!
HEY, CAP'N!
AHOY THAR!
UGH!
SCRATCH SCRAPE RUB
JESUS H!! WHAT THE HELL HAPPENED TO HIM?
HE GOT CAUGHT BUGGERING THE PUPPETS!
?
f.

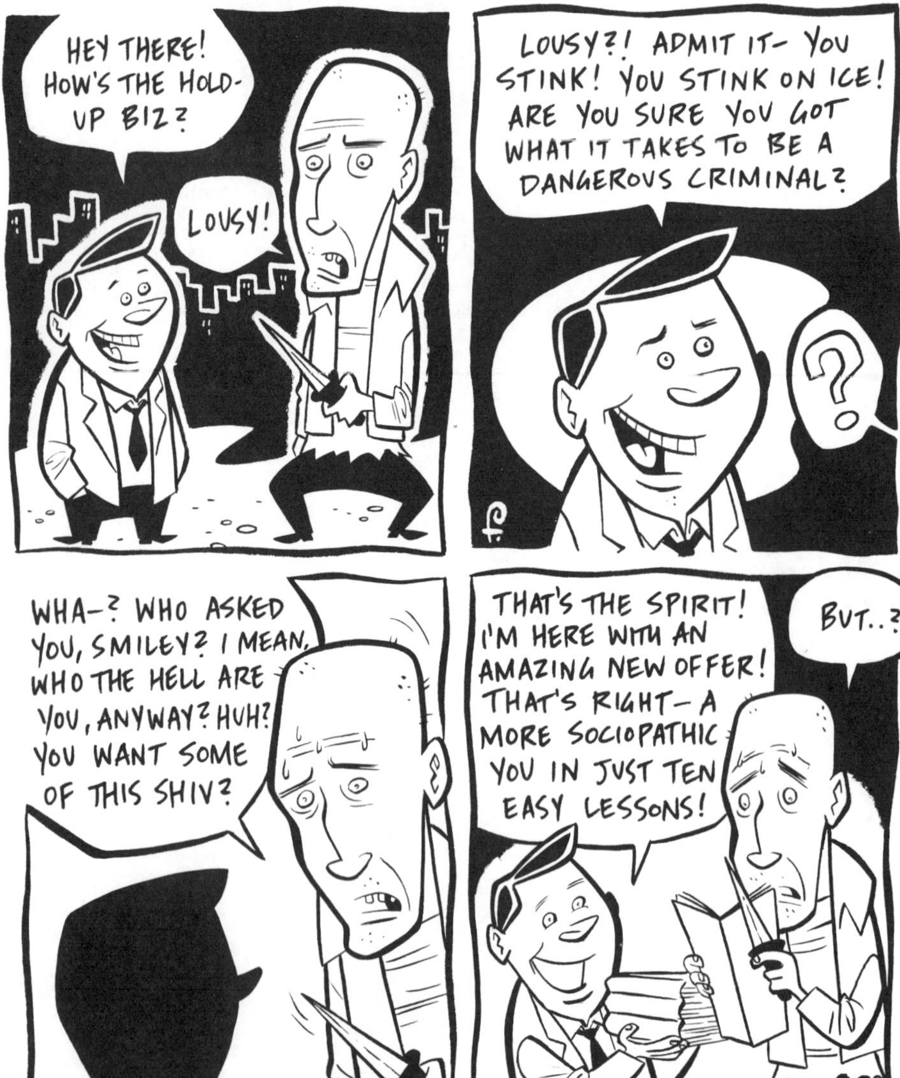
HEY THERE! HOW'S THE HOLD-UP BIZ?
LOUSY!
LOUSY?! ADMIT IT- YOU STINK! YOU STINK ON ICE! ARE YOU SURE YOU GOT WHAT IT TAKES TO BE A DANGEROUS CRIMINAL?
?
WHA-? WHO ASKED YOU, SMILEY? I MEAN, WHO THE HELL ARE YOU, ANYWAY? HUH? YOU WANT SOME OF THIS SHIV?
THAT'S THE SPIRIT! I'M HERE WITH AN AMAZING NEW OFFER! THAT'S RIGHT- A MORE SOCIOPATHIC YOU IN JUST TEN EASY LESSONS!
BUT..?

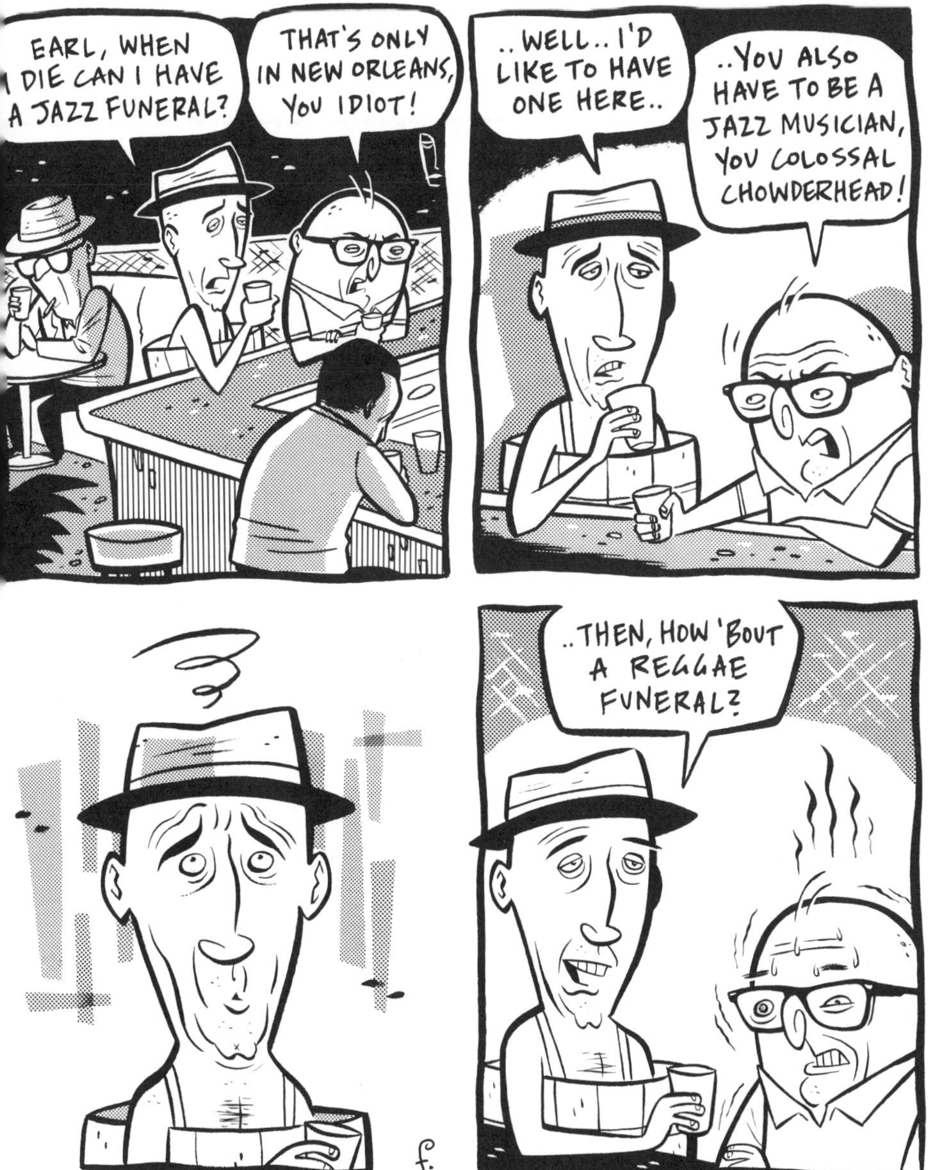
EARL, WHEN I DIE CAN I HAVE A JAZZ FUNERAL?
THAT'S ONLY IN NEW ORLEANS, YOU IDIOT!
..WELL.. I'D LIKE TO HAVE ONE HERE..
..YOU ALSO HAVE TO BE A JAZZ MUSICIAN, YOU COLOSSAL CHOWDERHEAD!
..THEN, HOW 'BOUT A REGGAE FUNERAL?
f.

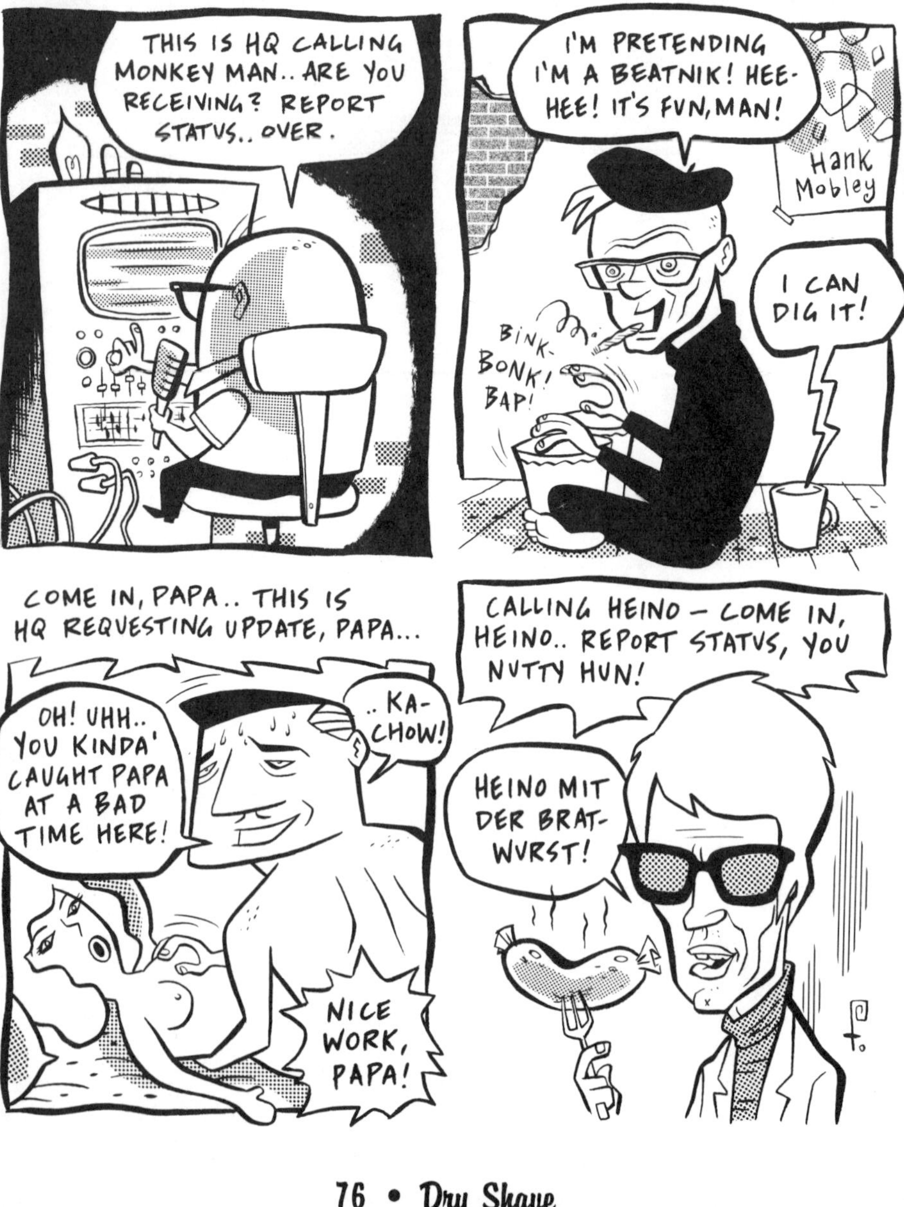
THIS IS HQ CALLING MONKEY MAN.. ARE YOU RECEIVING? REPORT STATUS.. OVER.
I'M PRETENDING I'M A BEATNIK! HEE-HEE! IT'S FUN, MAN!
Hank Mobley
I CAN DIG IT!
BINK-BONK! BAP!
COME IN, PAPA.. THIS IS HQ REQUESTING UPDATE, PAPA...
OH! UHH.. YOU KINDA' CAUGHT PAPA AT A BAD TIME HERE!
..KA-CHOW!
NICE WORK, PAPA!
CALLING HEINO – COME IN, HEINO.. REPORT STATUS, YOU NUTTY HUN!
HEINO MIT DER BRAT-WURST!

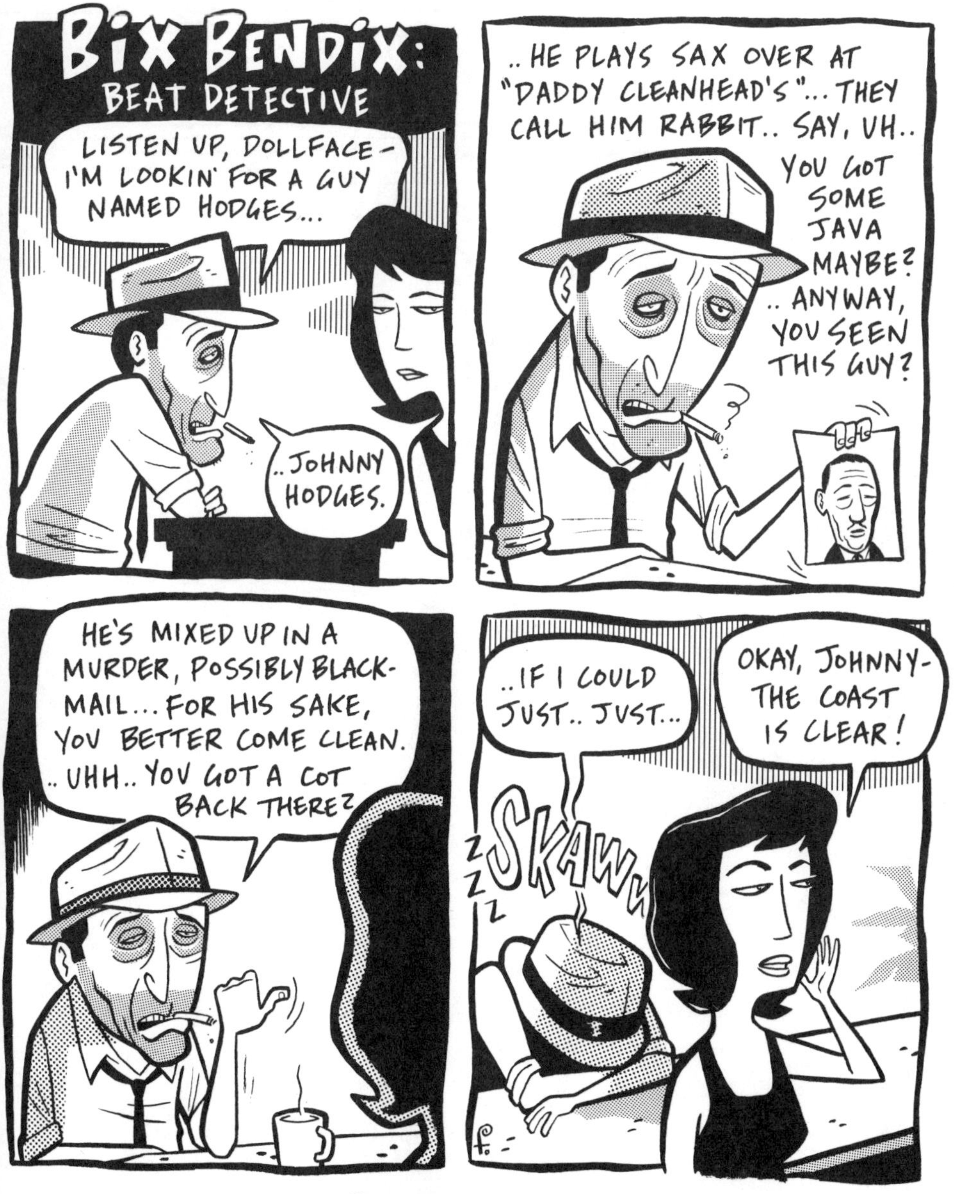
BIX BENDIX:
BEAT DETECTIVE
LISTEN UP, DOLLFACE - I'M LOOKIN' FOR A GUY NAMED HODGES...
..JOHNNY HODGES.
..HE PLAYS SAX OVER AT "DADDY CLEANHEAD'S"... THEY CALL HIM RABBIT.. SAY, UH..
YOU GOT SOME JAVA MAYBE?
.. ANYWAY, YOU SEEN THIS GUY?
HE'S MIXED UP IN A MURDER, POSSIBLY BLACK-MAIL... FOR HIS SAKE, YOU BETTER COME CLEAN. .. UHH.. YOU GOT A COT BACK THERE?
..IF I COULD JUST.. JUST...
OKAY, JOHNNY - THE COAST IS CLEAR!
ZZZ
SKAWW

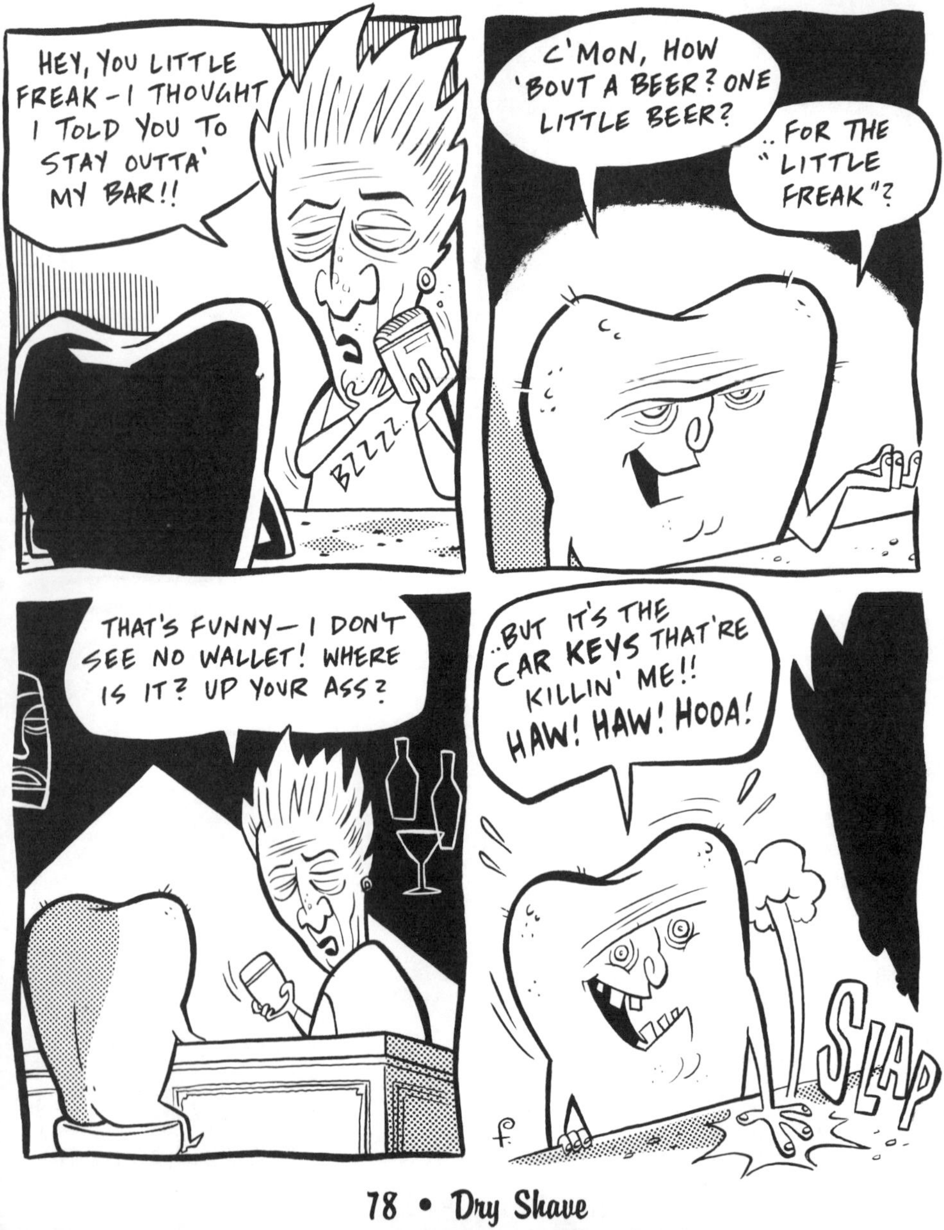
HEY, YOU LITTLE FREAK - I THOUGHT I TOLD YOU TO STAY OUTTA' MY BAR!!
BZZZZ
C'MON, HOW 'BOUT A BEER? ONE LITTLE BEER?
..FOR THE "LITTLE FREAK"?
THAT'S FUNNY— I DON'T SEE NO WALLET! WHERE IS IT? UP YOUR ASS?
..BUT IT'S THE CAR KEYS THAT'RE KILLIN' ME!! HAW! HAW! HOOA!
SLAP

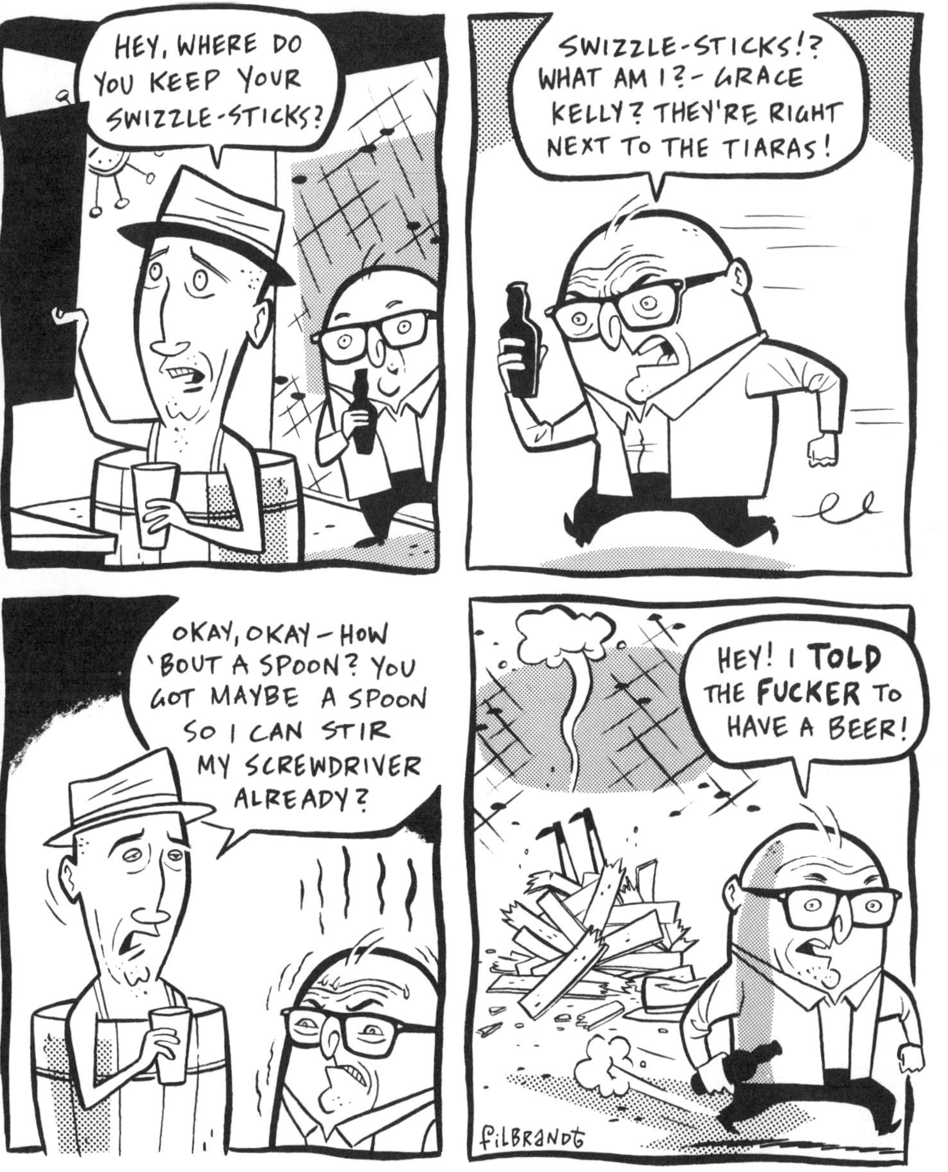
HEY, WHERE DO YOU KEEP YOUR SWIZZLE-STICKS?
SWIZZLE-STICKS!? WHAT AM I?- GRACE KELLY? THEY'RE RIGHT NEXT TO THE TIARAS!
OKAY, OKAY - HOW 'BOUT A SPOON? YOU GOT MAYBE A SPOON SO I CAN STIR MY SCREWDRIVER ALREADY?
HEY! I **TOLD** THE **FUCKER** TO HAVE A BEER!
FILBRANDT

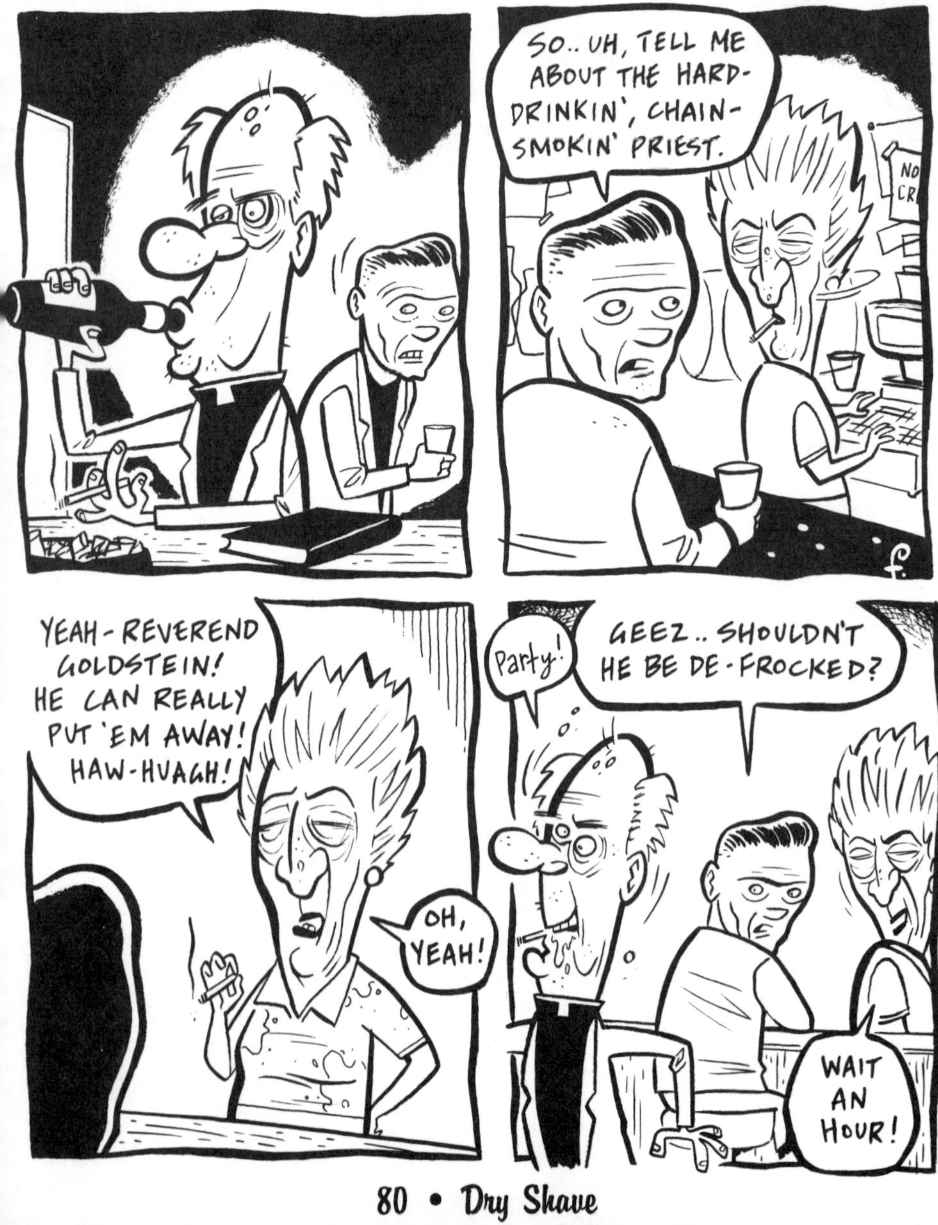
SO.. UH, TELL ME ABOUT THE HARD-DRINKIN', CHAIN-SMOKIN' PRIEST.
YEAH - REVEREND GOLDSTEIN! HE CAN REALLY PUT 'EM AWAY! HAW-HUAGH!
OH, YEAH!
Party!
GEEZ.. SHOULDN'T HE BE DE-FROCKED?
WAIT AN HOUR!

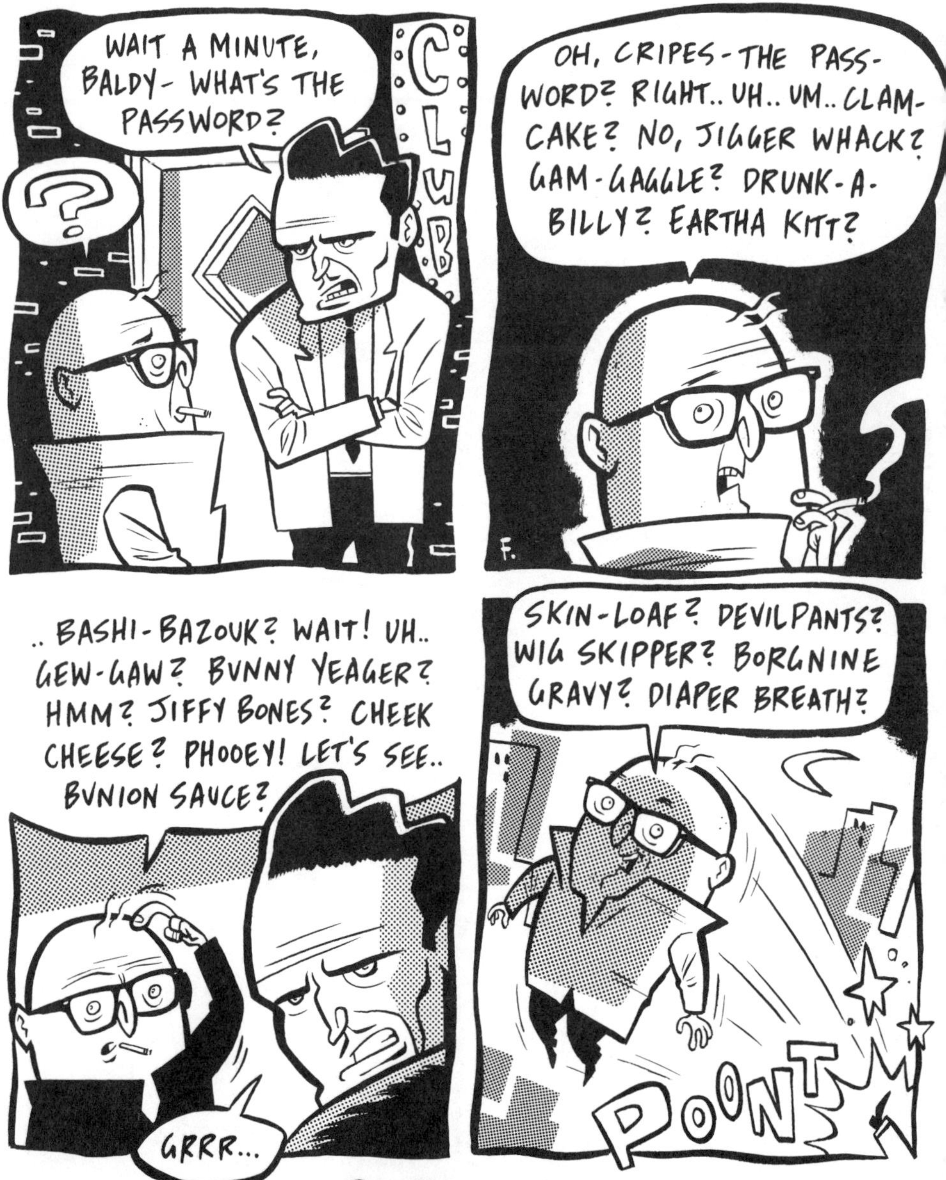
WAIT A MINUTE, BALDY- WHAT'S THE PASSWORD?
?
CLUB
OH, CRIPES - THE PASSWORD? RIGHT.. UH.. UM.. CLAMCAKE? NO, JIGGER WHACK? GAM-GAGGLE? DRUNK-A-BILLY? EARTHA KITT?
F.
.. BASHI-BAZOUK? WAIT! UH.. GEW-GAW? BUNNY YEAGER? HMM? JIFFY BONES? CHEEK CHEESE? PHOOEY! LET'S SEE.. BUNION SAUCE?
GRRR...
SKIN-LOAF? DEVILPANTS? WIG SKIPPER? BORGNINE GRAVY? DIAPER BREATH?
POONT

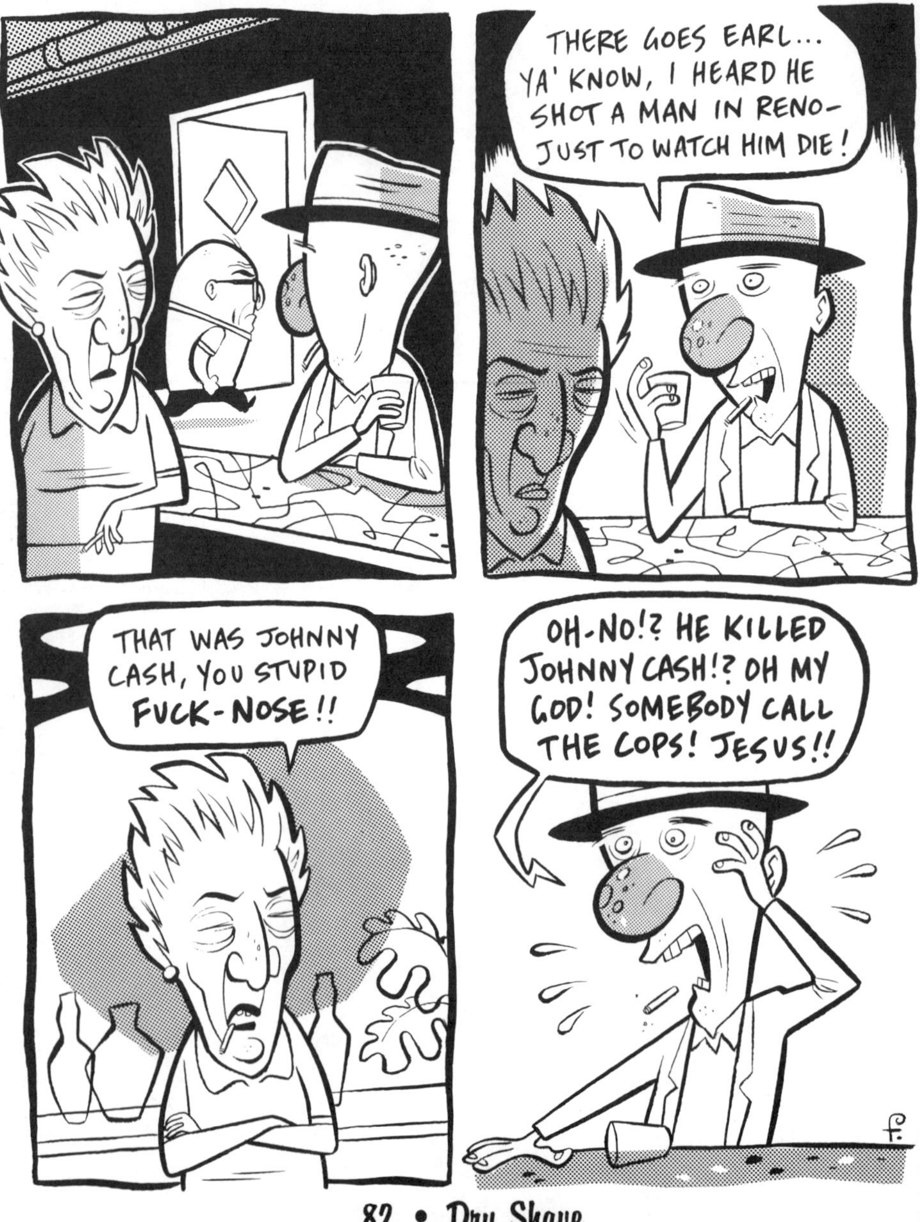
THERE GOES EARL... YA' KNOW, I HEARD HE SHOT A MAN IN RENO- JUST TO WATCH HIM DIE!
THAT WAS JOHNNY CASH, YOU STUPID FUCK-NOSE!!
OH-NO!? HE KILLED JOHNNY CASH!? OH MY GOD! SOMEBODY CALL THE COPS! JESUS!!
f.

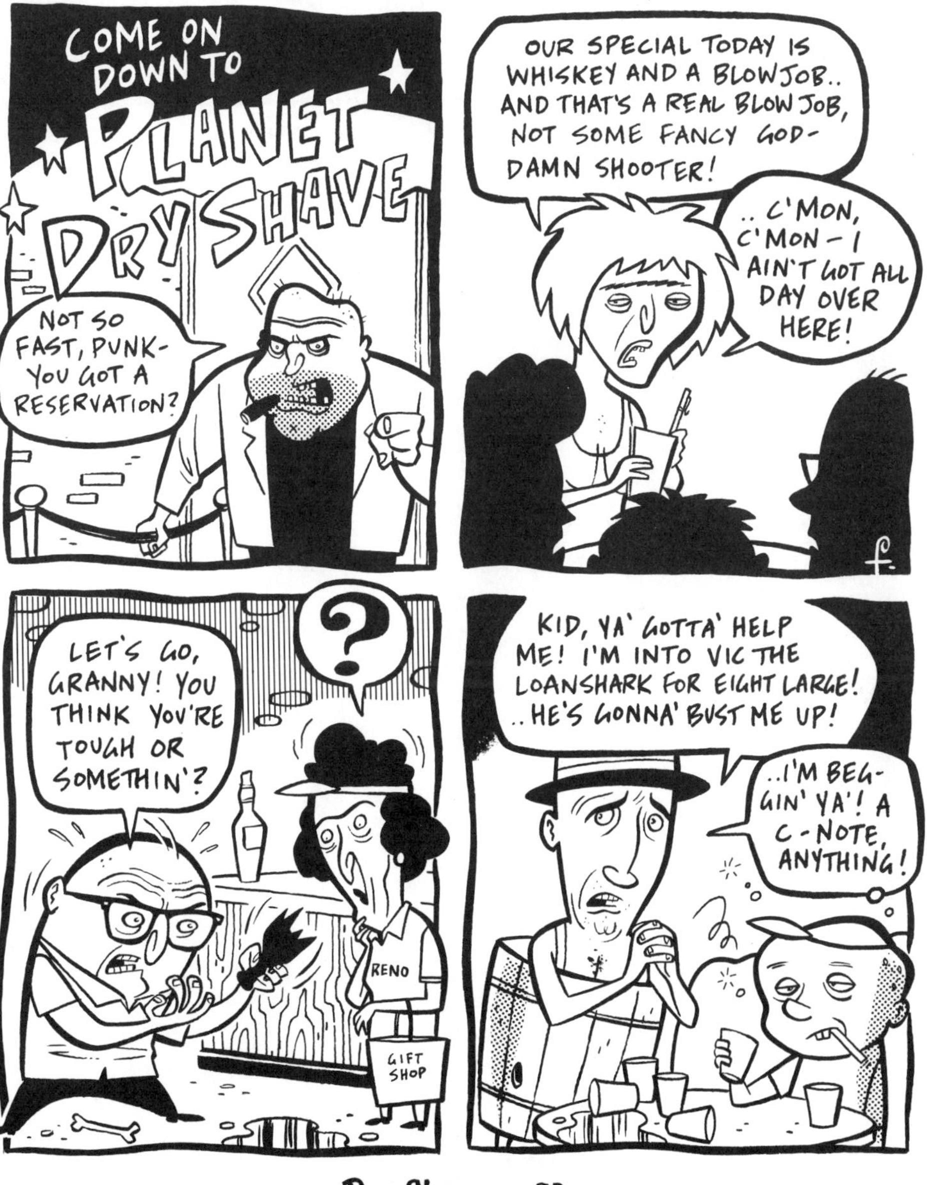
COME ON DOWN TO
PLANET DRY SHAVE
NOT SO FAST, PUNK- YOU GOT A RESERVATION?
OUR SPECIAL TODAY IS WHISKEY AND A BLOWJOB.. AND THAT'S A REAL BLOW JOB, NOT SOME FANCY GOD-DAMN SHOOTER!
.. C'MON, C'MON - I AIN'T GOT ALL DAY OVER HERE!
LET'S GO, GRANNY! YOU THINK YOU'RE TOUGH OR SOMETHIN'?
?
RENO
GIFT SHOP
KID, YA' GOTTA' HELP ME! I'M INTO VIC THE LOANSHARK FOR EIGHT LARGE! .. HE'S GONNA' BUST ME UP!
..I'M BEG-GIN' YA'! A C-NOTE, ANYTHING!

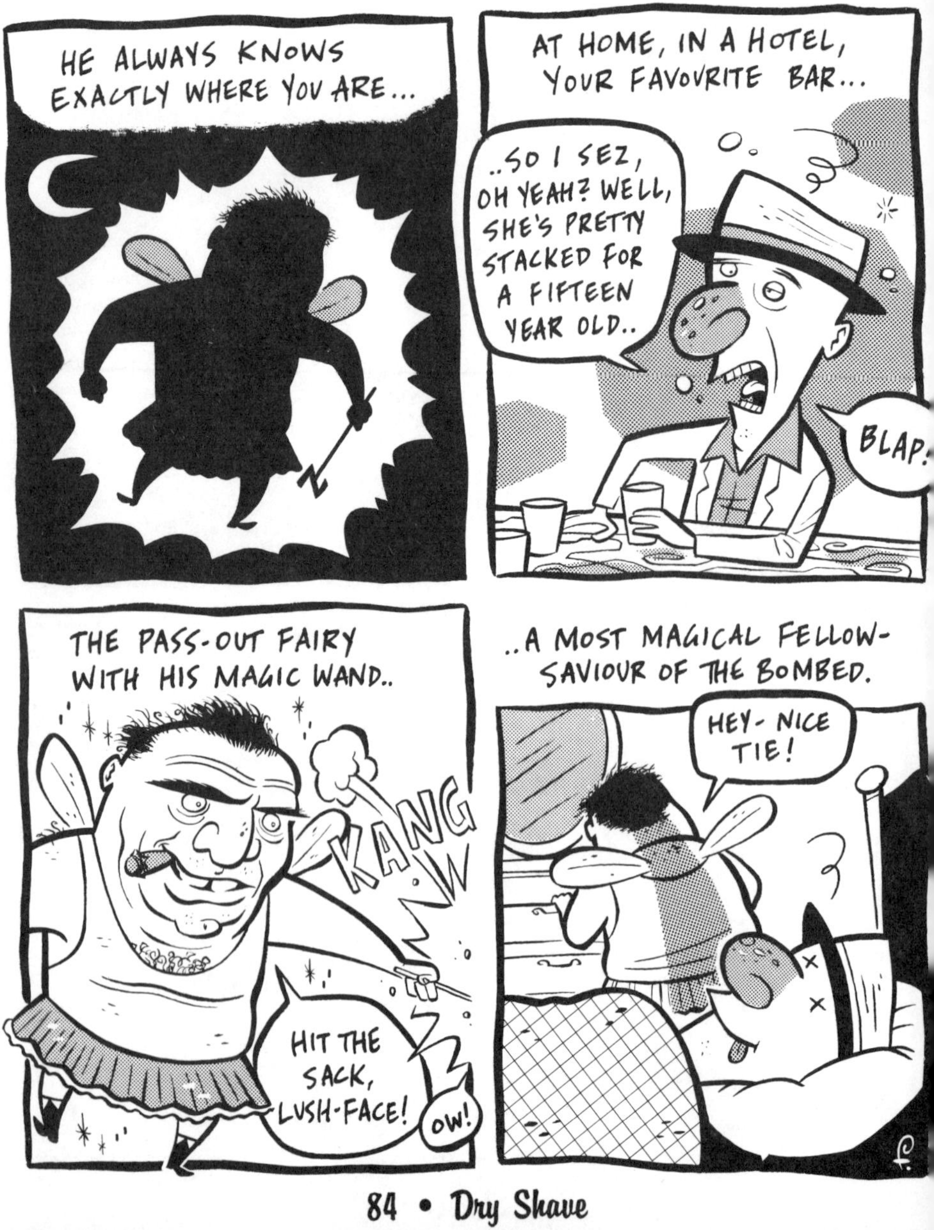
HE ALWAYS KNOWS EXACTLY WHERE YOU ARE...
AT HOME, IN A HOTEL, YOUR FAVOURITE BAR...
..SO I SEZ, OH YEAH? WELL, SHE'S PRETTY STACKED FOR A FIFTEEN YEAR OLD..
BLAP!
THE PASS-OUT FAIRY WITH HIS MAGIC WAND..
KANG
HIT THE SACK, LUSH-FACE!
OW!
..A MOST MAGICAL FELLOW- SAVIOUR OF THE BOMBED.
HEY- NICE TIE!

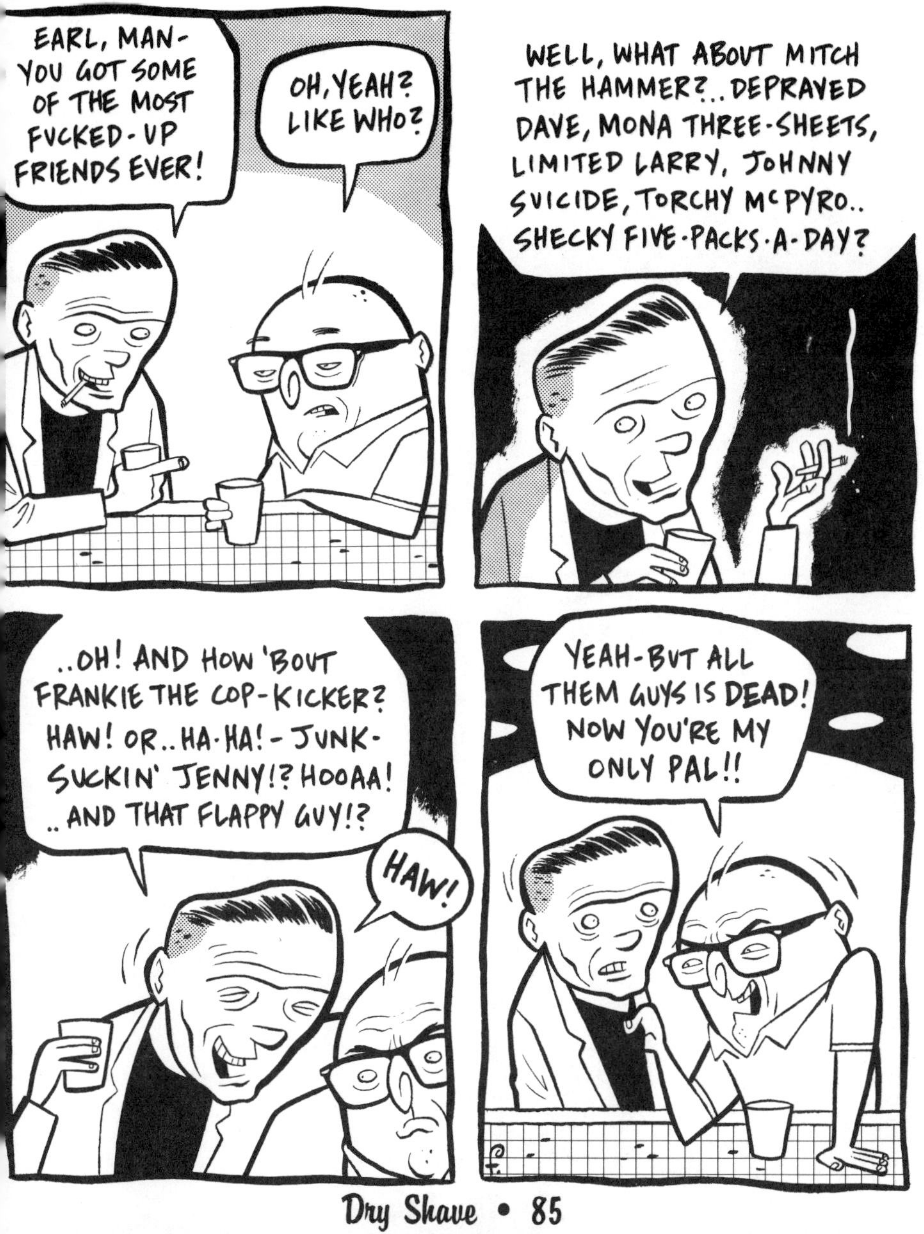
EARL, MAN- YOU GOT SOME OF THE MOST FUCKED-UP FRIENDS EVER!
OH, YEAH? LIKE WHO?
WELL, WHAT ABOUT MITCH THE HAMMER?.. DEPRAVED DAVE, MONA THREE-SHEETS, LIMITED LARRY, JOHNNY SUICIDE, TORCHY McPYRO.. SHECKY FIVE-PACKS-A-DAY?
..OH! AND HOW 'BOUT FRANKIE THE COP-KICKER? HAW! OR.. HA-HA! - JUNK-SUCKIN' JENNY!? HOOAA! .. AND THAT FLAPPY GUY!?
HAW!
YEAH-BUT ALL THEM GUYS IS DEAD! NOW YOU'RE MY ONLY PAL!!

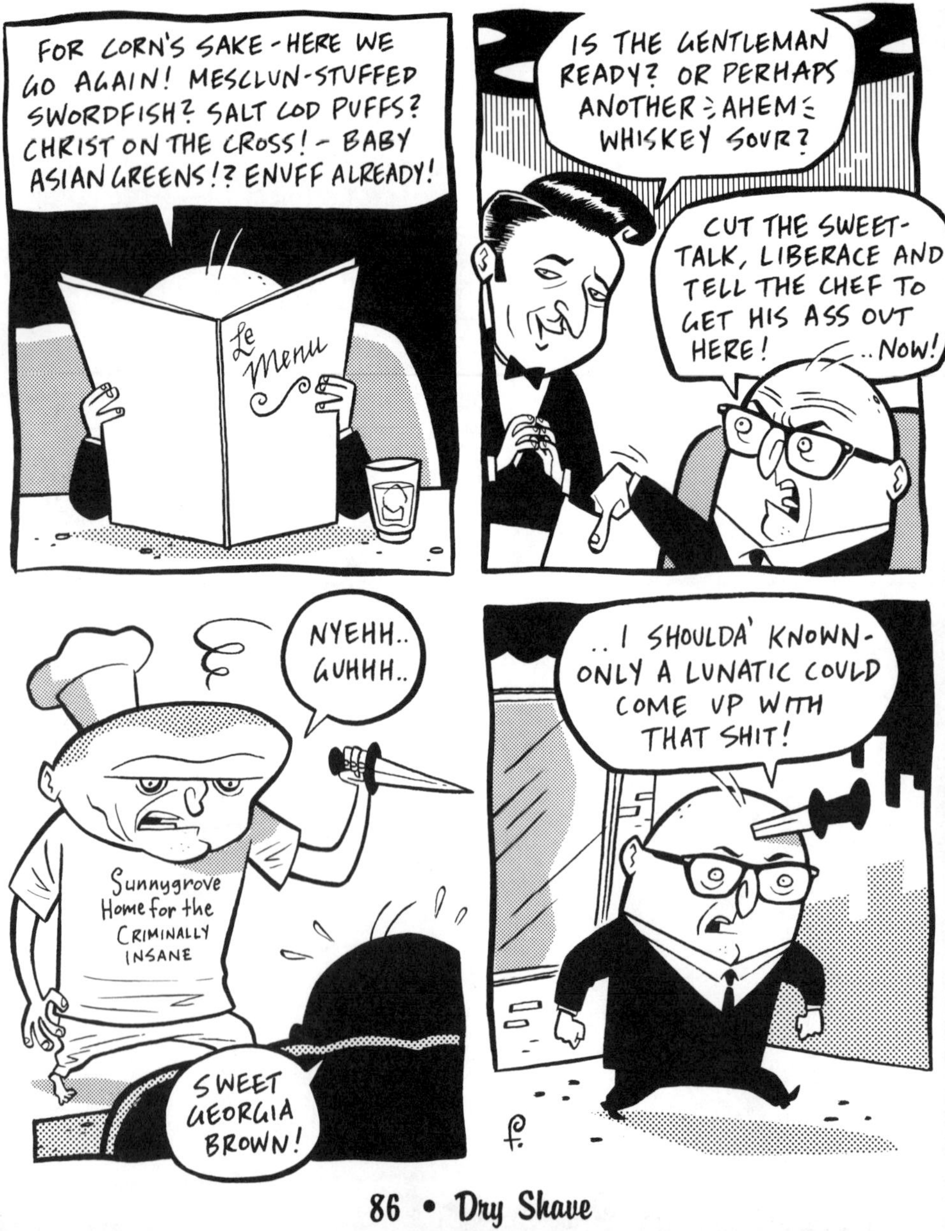
FOR CORN'S SAKE - HERE WE GO AGAIN! MESCLUN-STUFFED SWORDFISH? SALT COD PUFFS? CHRIST ON THE CROSS! - BABY ASIAN GREENS!? ENUFF ALREADY!
Le Menu
IS THE GENTLEMAN READY? OR PERHAPS ANOTHER ≈AHEM≈ WHISKEY SOUR?
CUT THE SWEET-TALK, LIBERACE AND TELL THE CHEF TO GET HIS ASS OUT HERE! ..NOW!
NYEHH.. GUHHH..
Sunnygrove Home for the CRIMINALLY INSANE
SWEET GEORGIA BROWN!
..I SHOULDA' KNOWN- ONLY A LUNATIC COULD COME UP WITH THAT SHIT!
f.

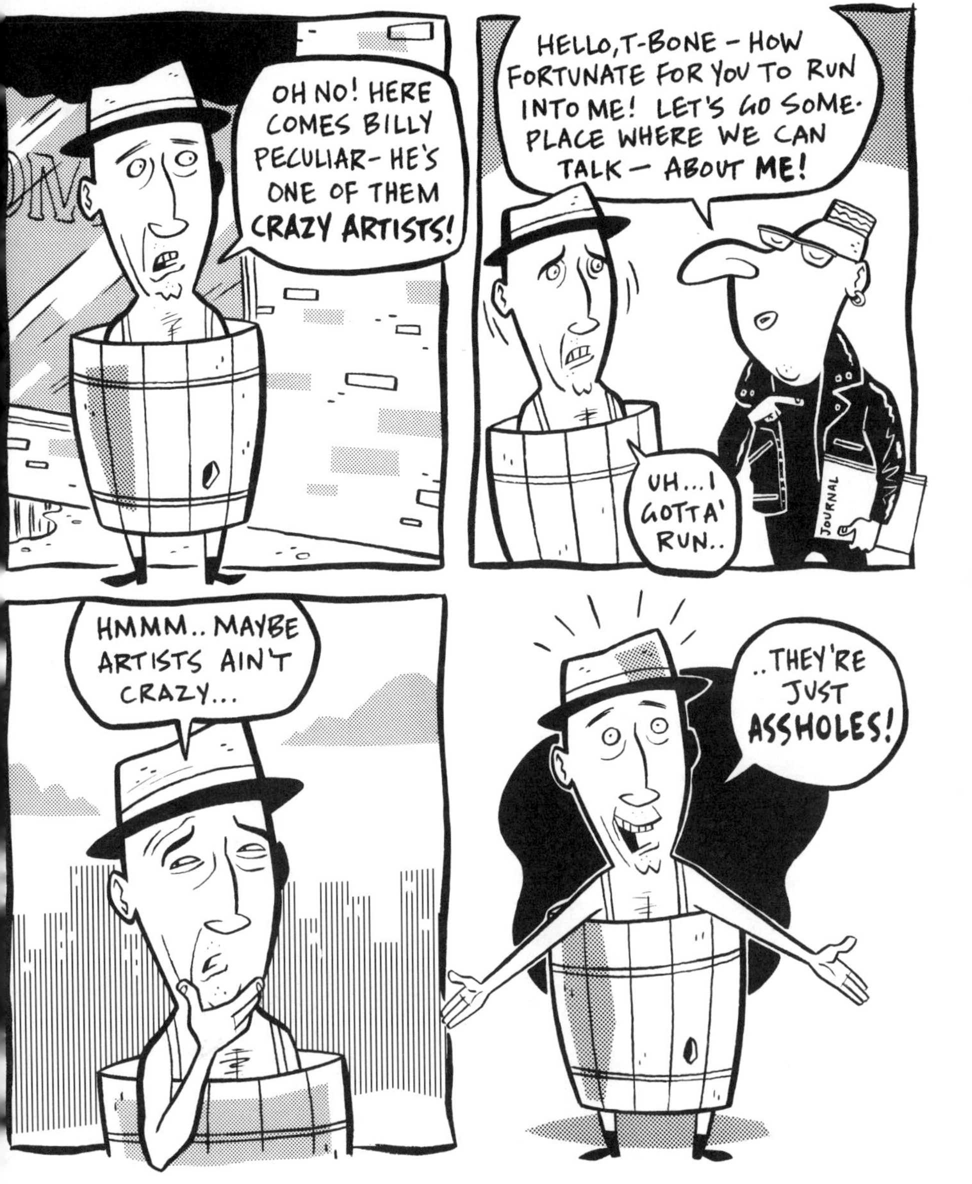
OH NO! HERE COMES BILLY PECULIAR- HE'S ONE OF THEM CRAZY ARTISTS!
HELLO, T-BONE - HOW FORTUNATE FOR YOU TO RUN INTO ME! LET'S GO SOME-PLACE WHERE WE CAN TALK - ABOUT ME!
UH...I GOTTA' RUN..
JOURNAL
HMMM.. MAYBE ARTISTS AIN'T CRAZY...
..THEY'RE JUST ASSHOLES!

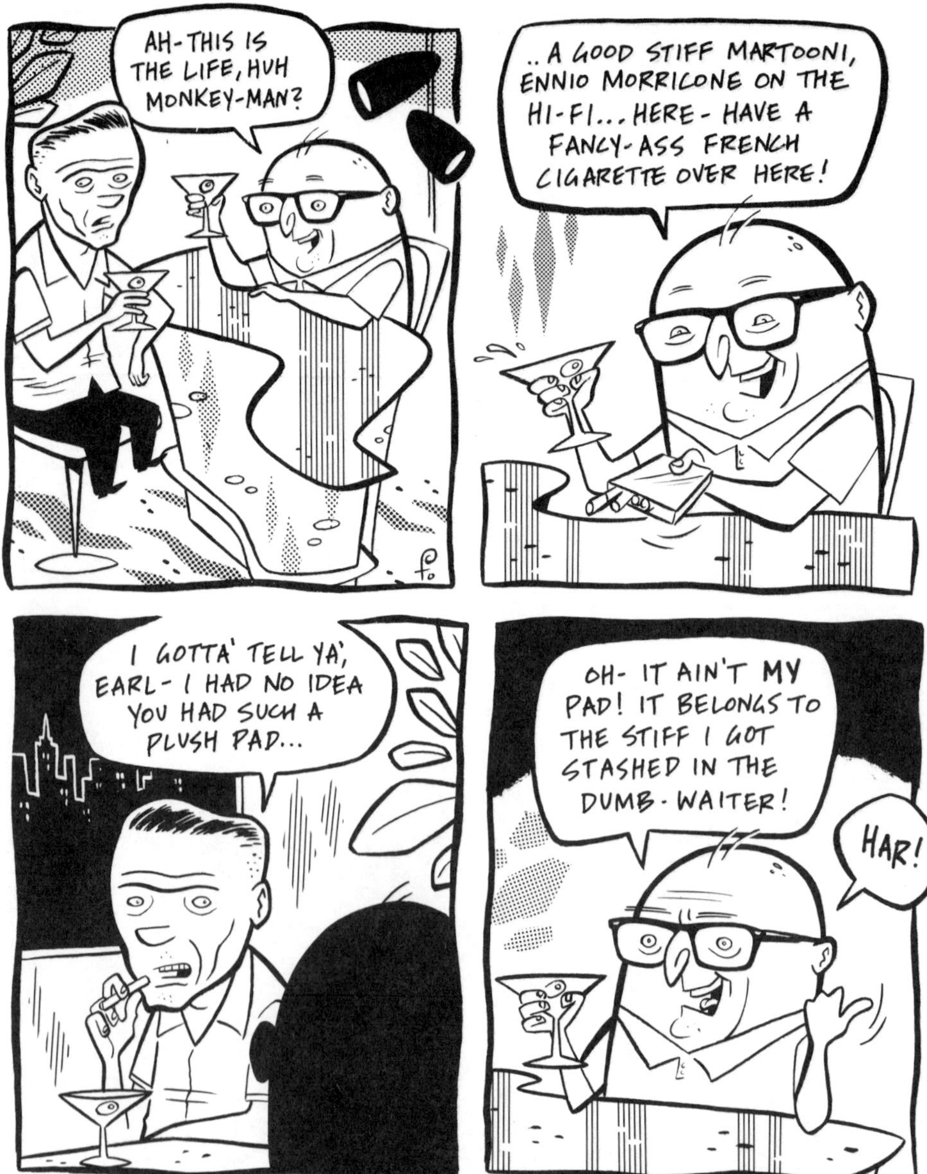
AH-THIS IS THE LIFE, HUH MONKEY-MAN?
..A GOOD STIFF MARTOONI, ENNIO MORRICONE ON THE HI-FI... HERE- HAVE A FANCY-ASS FRENCH CIGARETTE OVER HERE!
I GOTTA' TELL YA', EARL- I HAD NO IDEA YOU HAD SUCH A PLUSH PAD...
OH- IT AIN'T MY PAD! IT BELONGS TO THE STIFF I GOT STASHED IN THE DUMB-WAITER!
HAR!

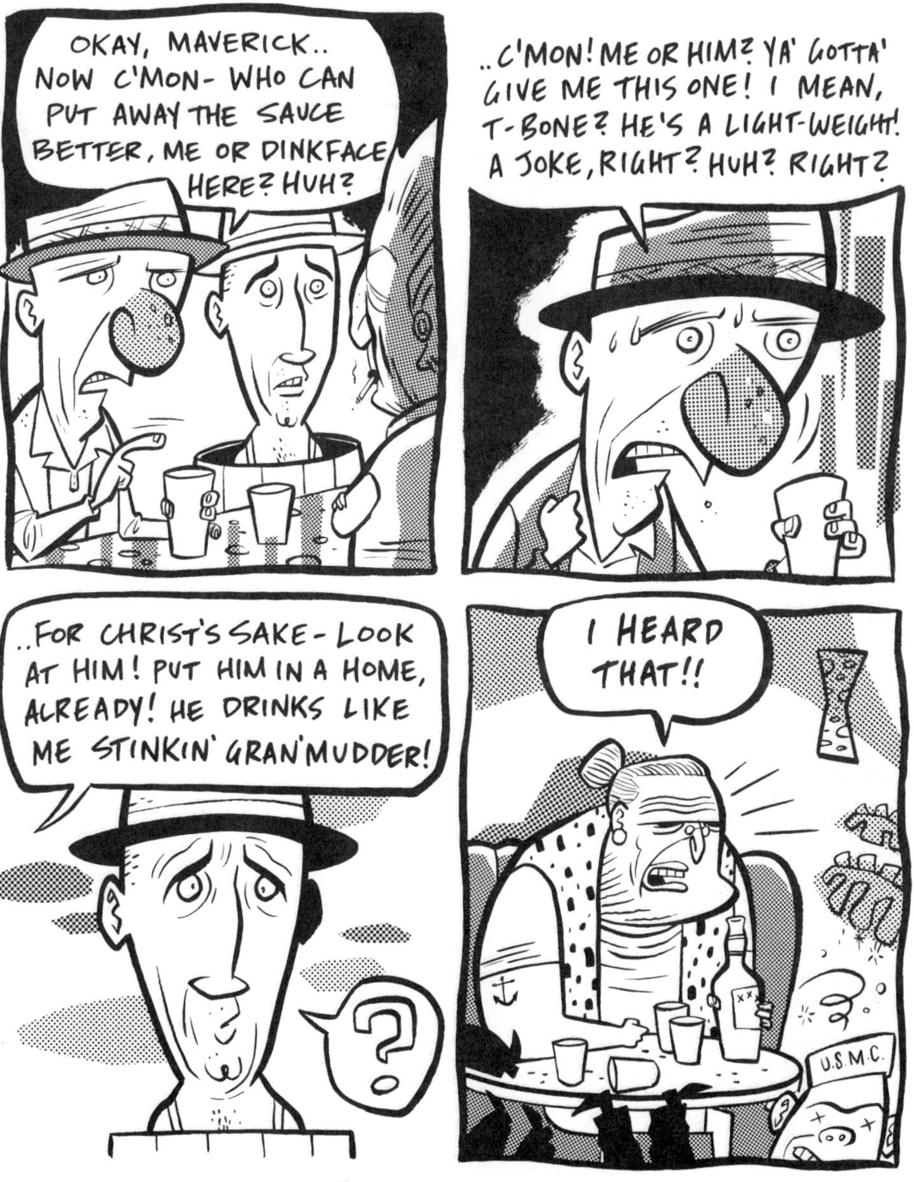
OKAY, MAVERICK.. NOW C'MON- WHO CAN PUT AWAY THE SAUCE BETTER, ME OR DINKFACE HERE? HUH?
..C'MON! ME OR HIM? YA' GOTTA' GIVE ME THIS ONE! I MEAN, T-BONE? HE'S A LIGHT-WEIGHT! A JOKE, RIGHT? HUH? RIGHT?
..FOR CHRIST'S SAKE - LOOK AT HIM! PUT HIM IN A HOME, ALREADY! HE DRINKS LIKE ME STINKIN' GRAN'MUDDER!
?
I HEARD THAT!!
U.S.M.C.

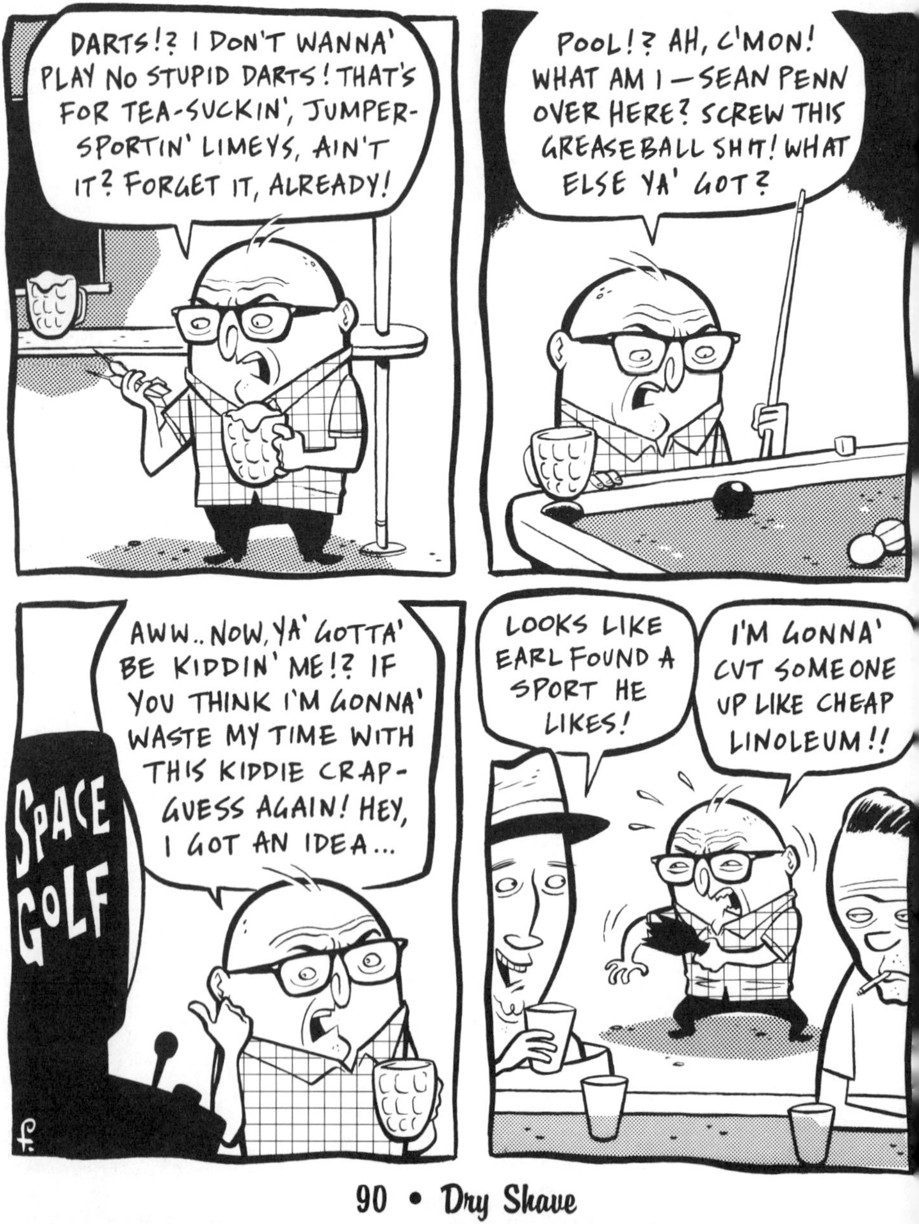
DARTS!? I DON'T WANNA' PLAY NO STUPID DARTS! THAT'S FOR TEA-SUCKIN', JUMPER-SPORTIN' LIMEYS, AIN'T IT? FORGET IT, ALREADY!
POOL!? AH, C'MON! WHAT AM I—SEAN PENN OVER HERE? SCREW THIS GREASEBALL SHIT! WHAT ELSE YA' GOT?
AWW.. NOW, YA' GOTTA' BE KIDDIN' ME!? IF YOU THINK I'M GONNA' WASTE MY TIME WITH THIS KIDDIE CRAP-GUESS AGAIN! HEY, I GOT AN IDEA...
SPACE GOLF
LOOKS LIKE EARL FOUND A SPORT HE LIKES!
I'M GONNA' CUT SOMEONE UP LIKE CHEAP LINOLEUM!!

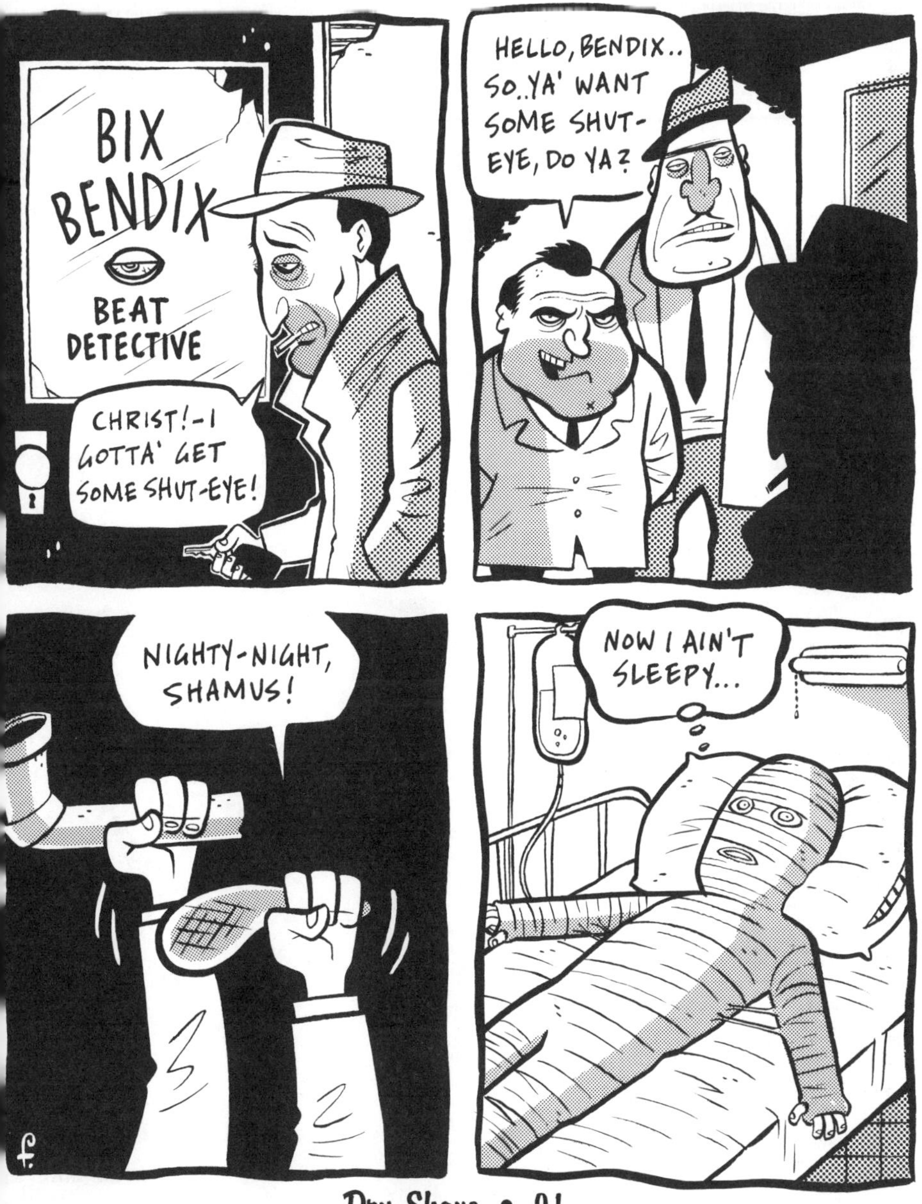
BIX BENDIX
BEAT DETECTIVE
CHRIST!-I GOTTA' GET SOME SHUT-EYE!
HELLO, BENDIX.. SO..YA' WANT SOME SHUT-EYE, DO YA?
NIGHTY-NIGHT, SHAMUS!
NOW I AIN'T SLEEPY...

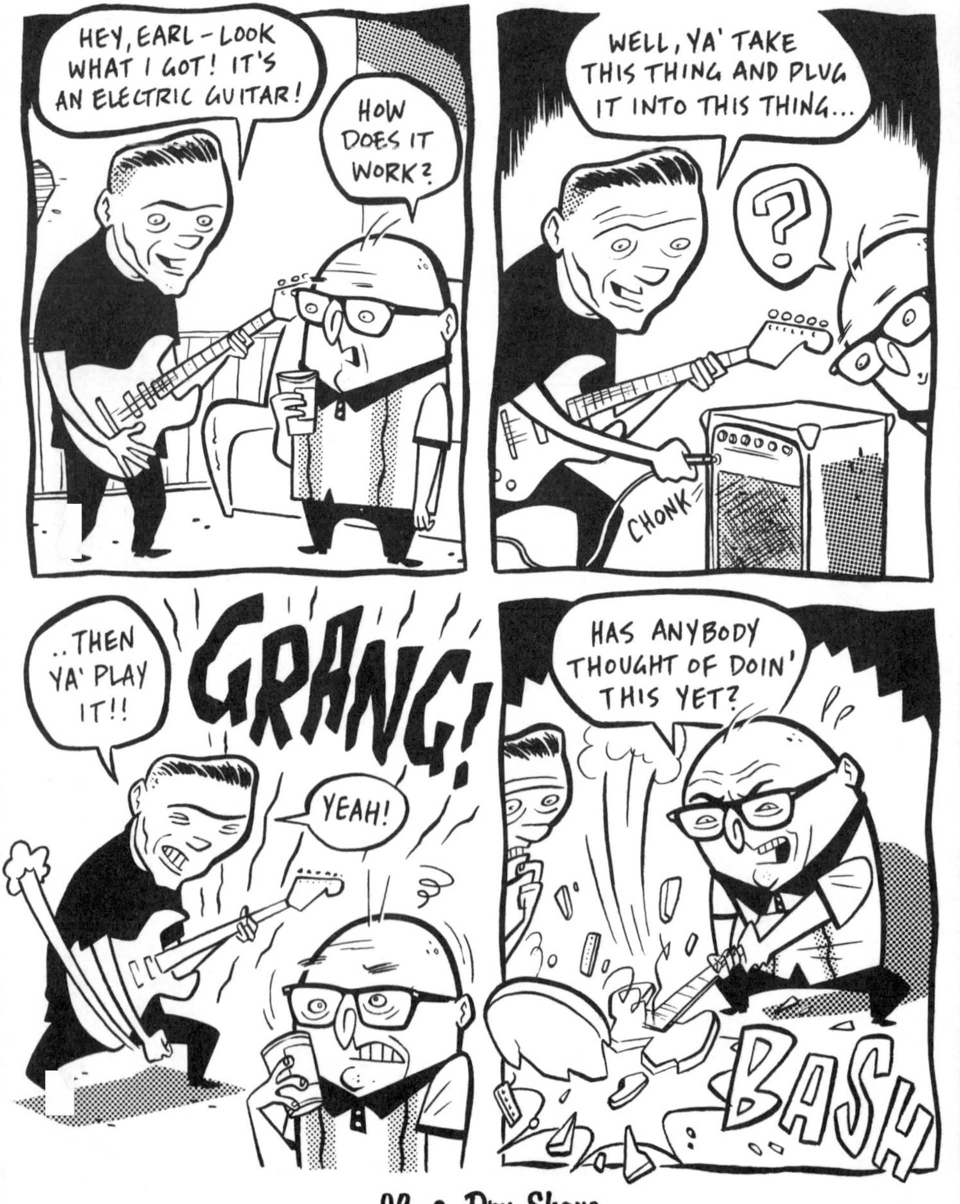
HEY, EARL - LOOK WHAT I GOT! IT'S AN ELECTRIC GUITAR!
HOW DOES IT WORK?
WELL, YA' TAKE THIS THING AND PLUG IT INTO THIS THING...
?
CHONK
..THEN YA' PLAY IT!!
GRANG!
YEAH!
HAS ANYBODY THOUGHT OF DOIN' THIS YET?
BASH

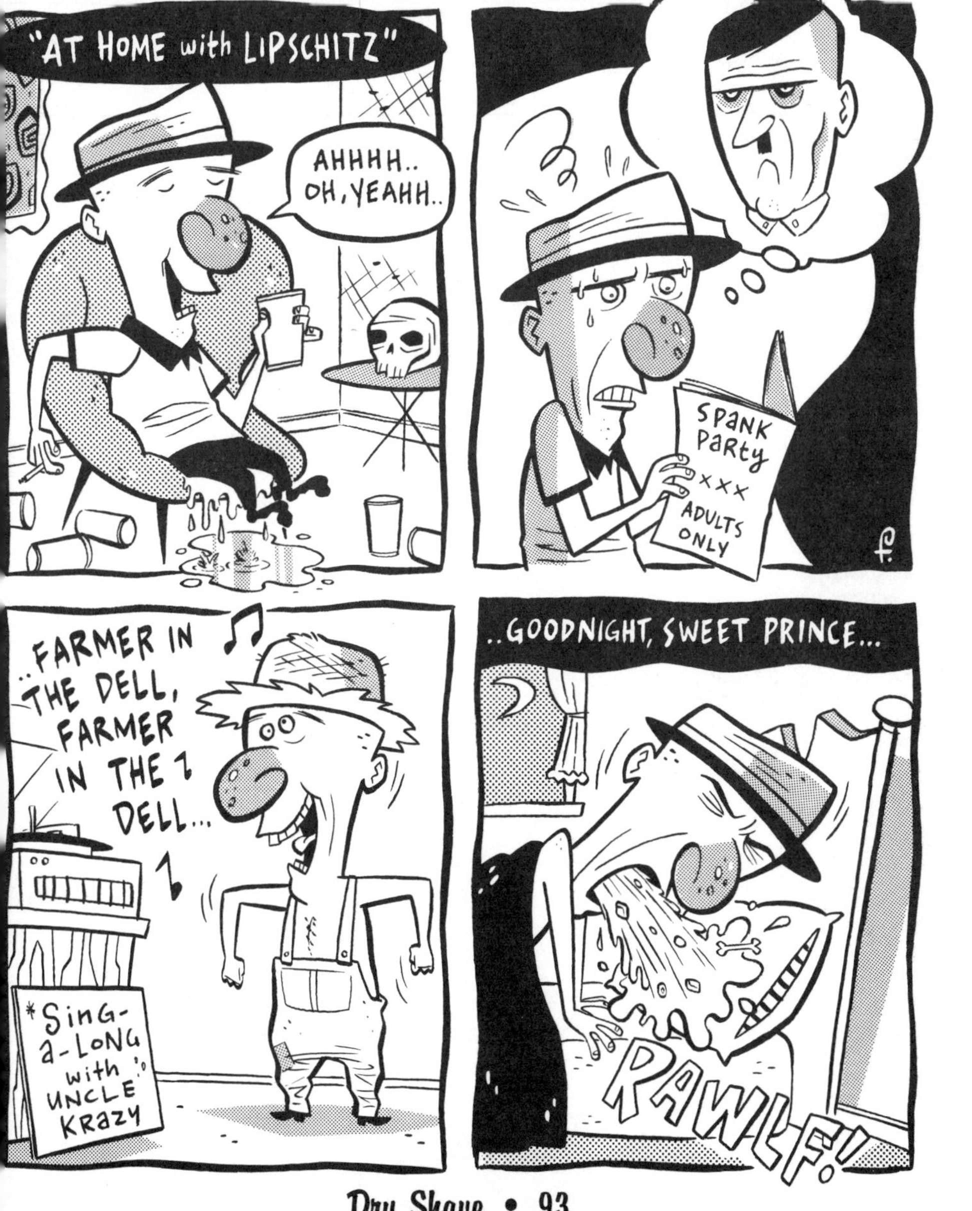
"AT HOME with LIPSCHITZ"
AHHHH.. OH, YEAHH..
SPANK PARTY XXX ADULTS ONLY
..FARMER IN THE DELL, FARMER IN THE DELL...
*SING-A-LONG with UNCLE KRAZY
..GOODNIGHT, SWEET PRINCE...
RAWLF!

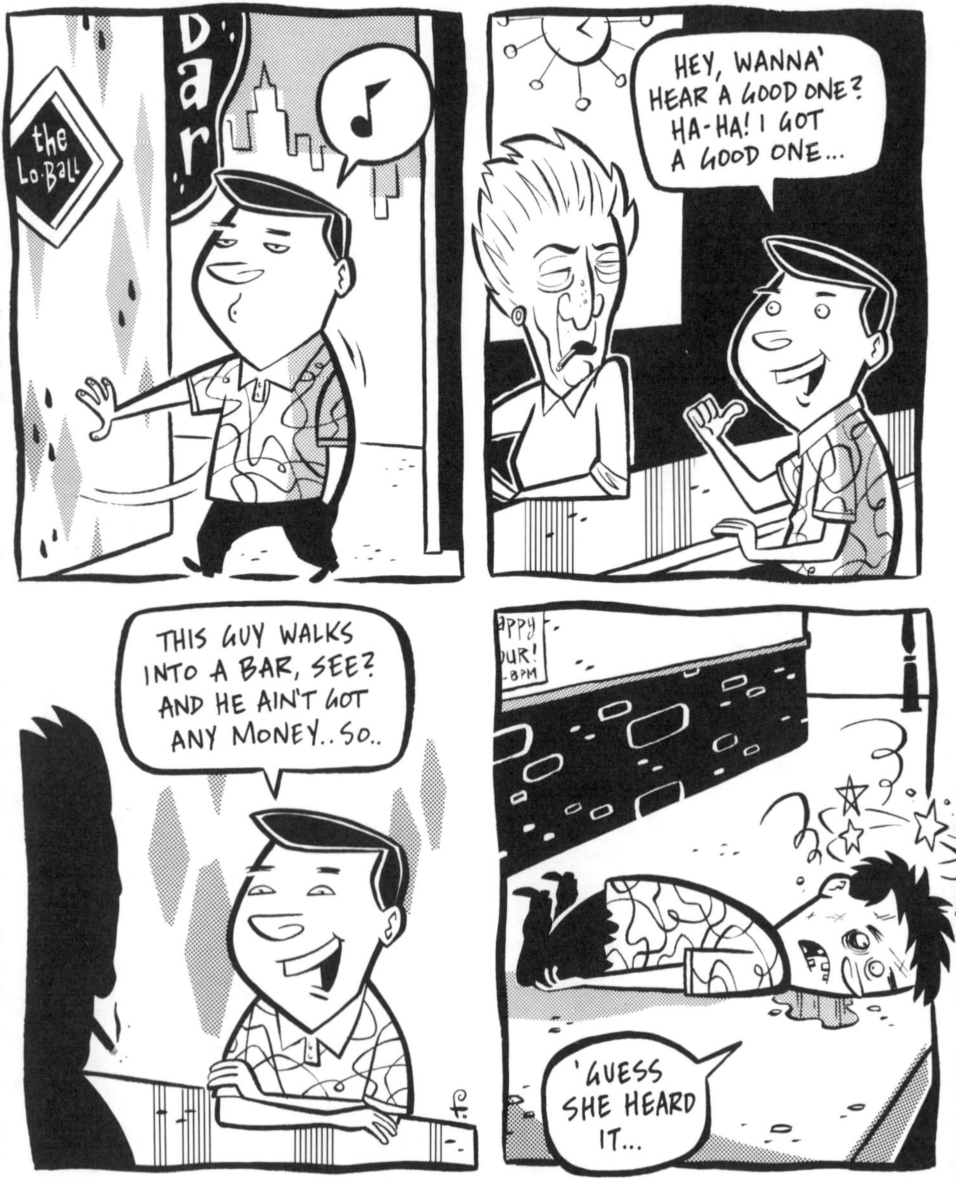
the Lo-Ball
bar
HEY, WANNA' HEAR A GOOD ONE? HA-HA! I GOT A GOOD ONE...
THIS GUY WALKS INTO A BAR, SEE? AND HE AIN'T GOT ANY MONEY.. SO..
'GUESS SHE HEARD IT...

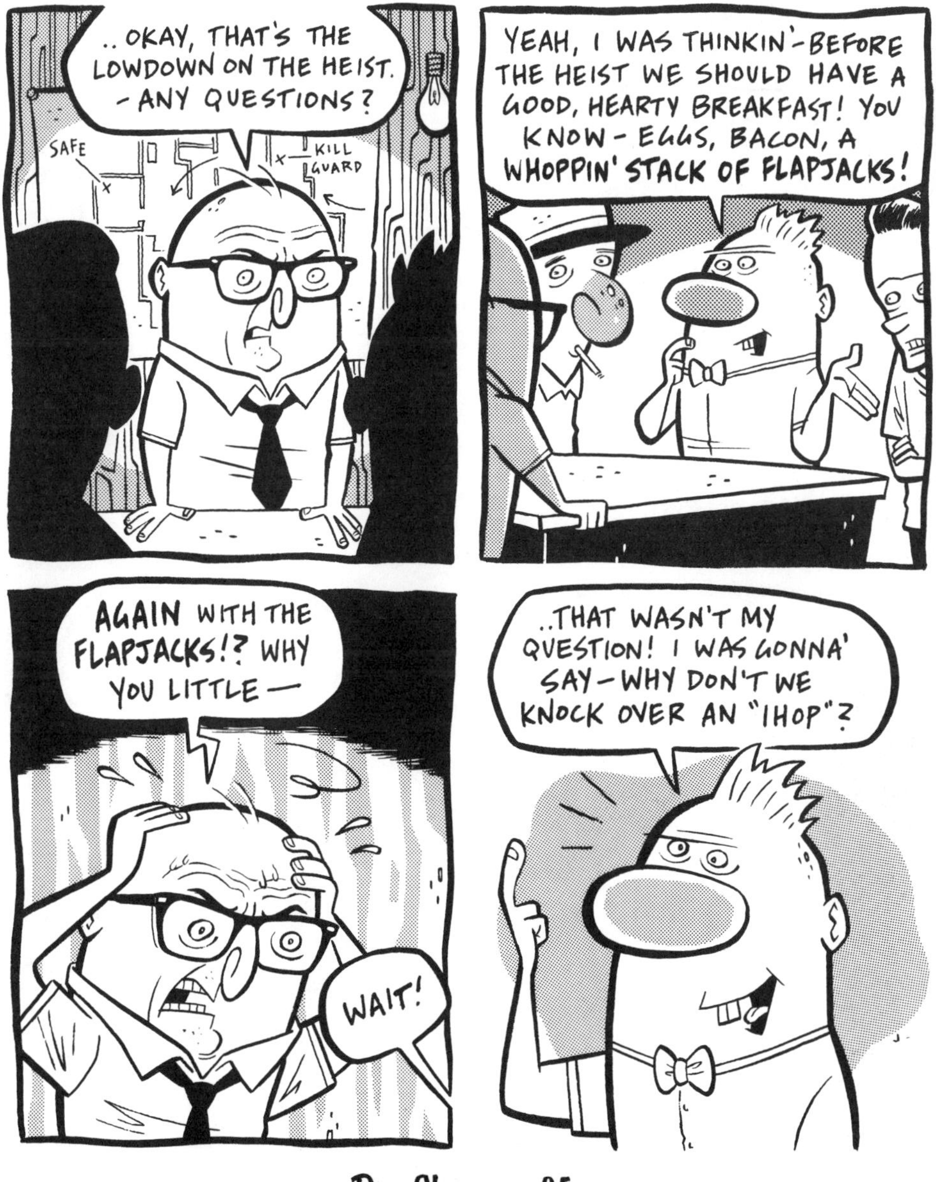
..OKAY, THAT'S THE LOWDOWN ON THE HEIST. -ANY QUESTIONS?
SAFE
KILL GUARD
YEAH, I WAS THINKIN'-BEFORE THE HEIST WE SHOULD HAVE A GOOD, HEARTY BREAKFAST! YOU KNOW- EGGS, BACON, A WHOPPIN' STACK OF FLAPJACKS!
AGAIN WITH THE FLAPJACKS!? WHY YOU LITTLE—
WAIT!
..THAT WASN'T MY QUESTION! I WAS GONNA' SAY-WHY DON'T WE KNOCK OVER AN "IHOP"?

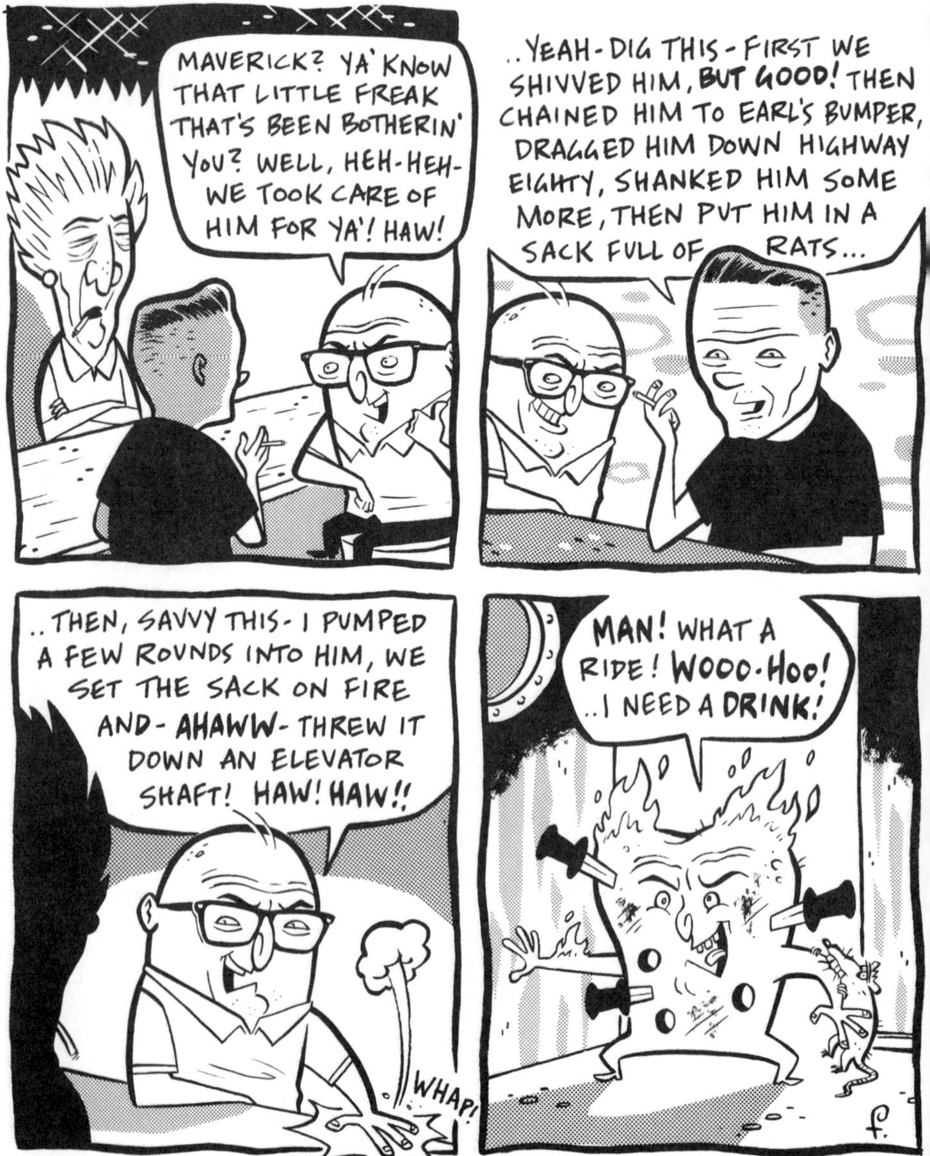
MAVERICK? YA' KNOW THAT LITTLE FREAK THAT'S BEEN BOTHERIN' YOU? WELL, HEH-HEH- WE TOOK CARE OF HIM FOR YA'! HAW!
..YEAH- DIG THIS- FIRST WE SHIVVED HIM, BUT GOOD! THEN CHAINED HIM TO EARL'S BUMPER, DRAGGED HIM DOWN HIGHWAY EIGHTY, SHANKED HIM SOME MORE, THEN PUT HIM IN A SACK FULL OF RATS...
..THEN, SAVVY THIS- I PUMPED A FEW ROUNDS INTO HIM, WE SET THE SACK ON FIRE AND- AHAWW- THREW IT DOWN AN ELEVATOR SHAFT! HAW! HAW!!
WHAP!
MAN! WHAT A RIDE! WOOO-HOO! ..I NEED A DRINK!
f.

..YEAH, I FINALLY GOT THAT APARTMENT IN VELVET'S BUILDING..

IT'S A FREAKIN' PALACE!

OH YEAH! I MEAN - BUILT-IN HOTPLATE, NO ROACHES - JUST SILVERFISH..THE WATER'S PRACTICALLY HOT! ..A FREAKIN' PALACE, I TELL YA'! WHA'? OH YEAH- VELVET PUT IN A GOOD WORD FOR ME...

..BUT, LIKE, IT AIN'T **ALL** GRAVY..SOMETIMES - OH CRAP! THERE'S THE DOOR! GOTTA' GO!

KONK KONK

CAN I BORROW A CUP OF HANDCUFFS?

Dry Shave • 97

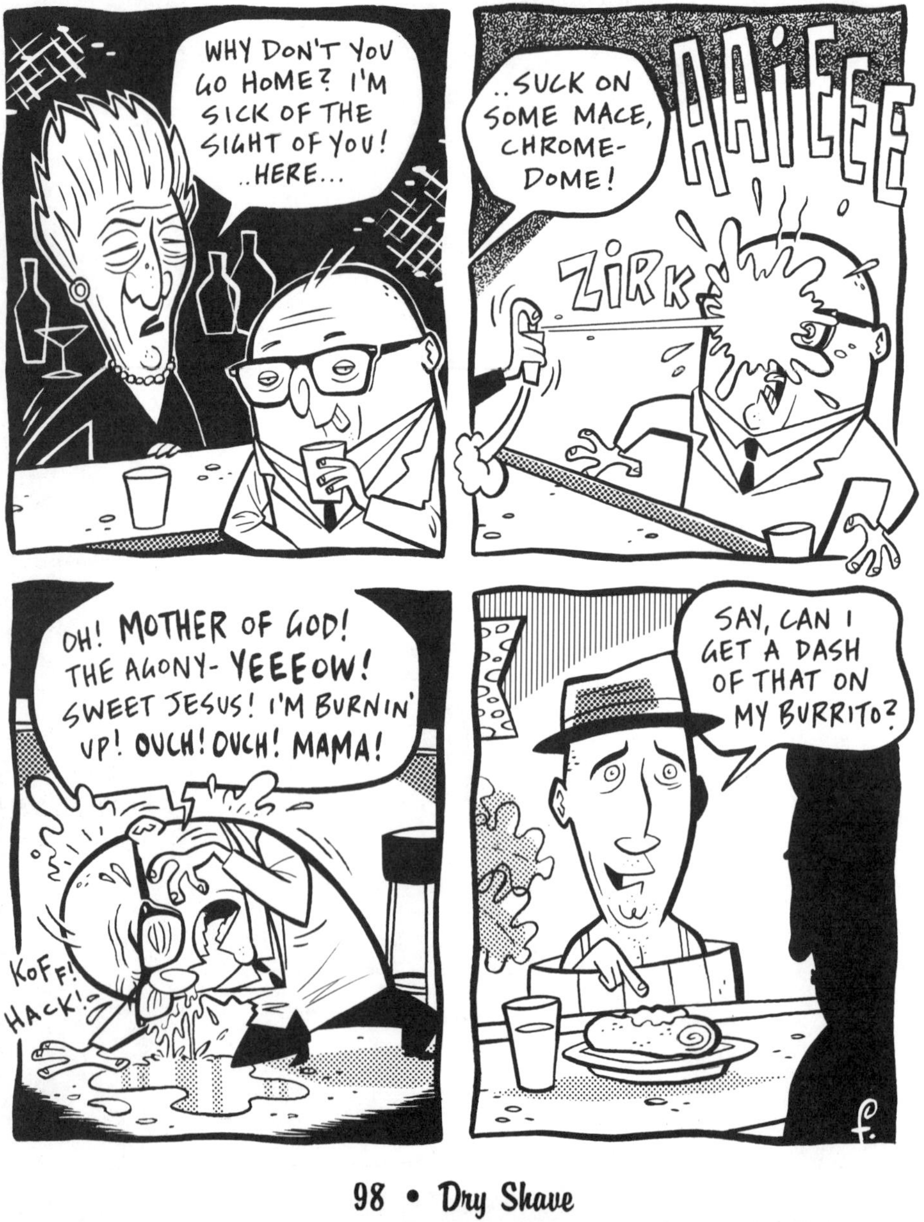
WHY DON'T YOU GO HOME? I'M SICK OF THE SIGHT OF YOU! ..HERE...
..SUCK ON SOME MACE, CHROME-DOME!
AAIEEE
ZIRK
OH! MOTHER OF GOD! THE AGONY- YEEEOW! SWEET JESUS! I'M BURNIN' UP! OUCH! OUCH! MAMA!
KOFF! HACK!
SAY, CAN I GET A DASH OF THAT ON MY BURRITO?

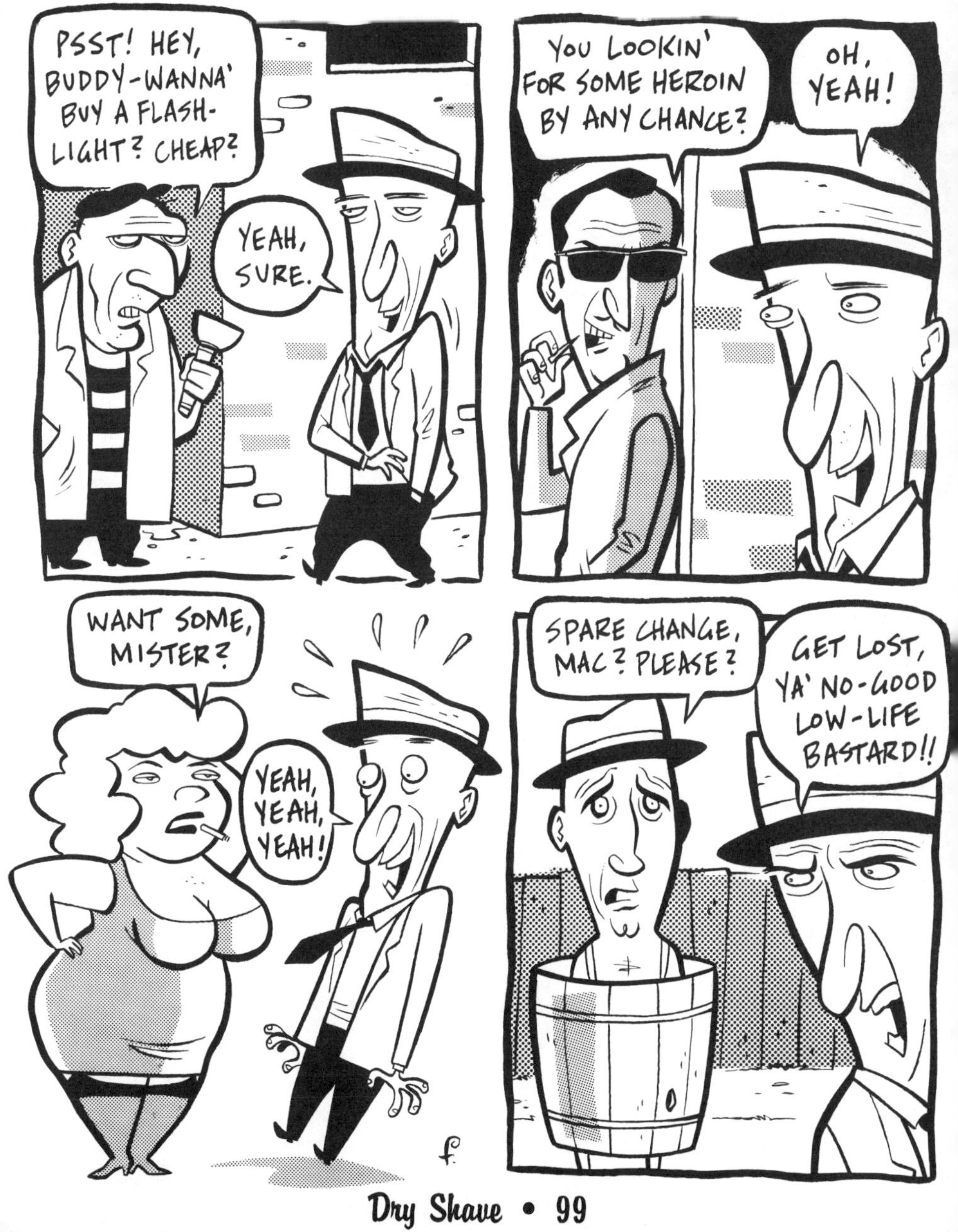
PSST! HEY, BUDDY-WANNA' BUY A FLASH-LIGHT? CHEAP?
YEAH, SURE.
YOU LOOKIN' FOR SOME HEROIN BY ANY CHANCE?
OH, YEAH!
WANT SOME, MISTER?
YEAH, YEAH, YEAH!
SPARE CHANGE, MAC? PLEASE?
GET LOST, YA' NO-GOOD LOW-LIFE BASTARD!!

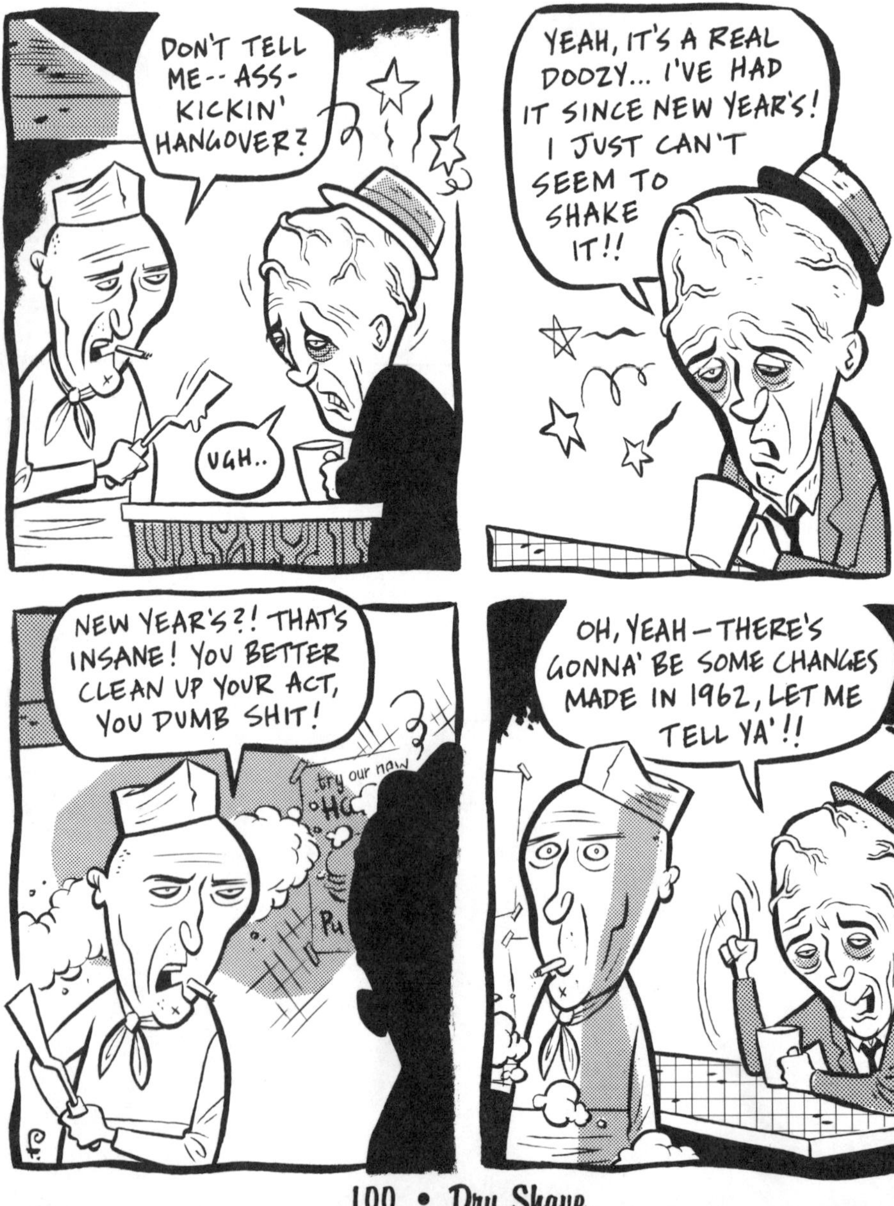
DON'T TELL ME-- ASS-KICKIN' HANGOVER?
UGH..
YEAH, IT'S A REAL DOOZY... I'VE HAD IT SINCE NEW YEAR'S! I JUST CAN'T SEEM TO SHAKE IT!!
NEW YEAR'S?! THAT'S INSANE! YOU BETTER CLEAN UP YOUR ACT, YOU DUMB SHIT!
try our new
OH, YEAH—THERE'S GONNA' BE SOME CHANGES MADE IN 1962, LET ME TELL YA'!!

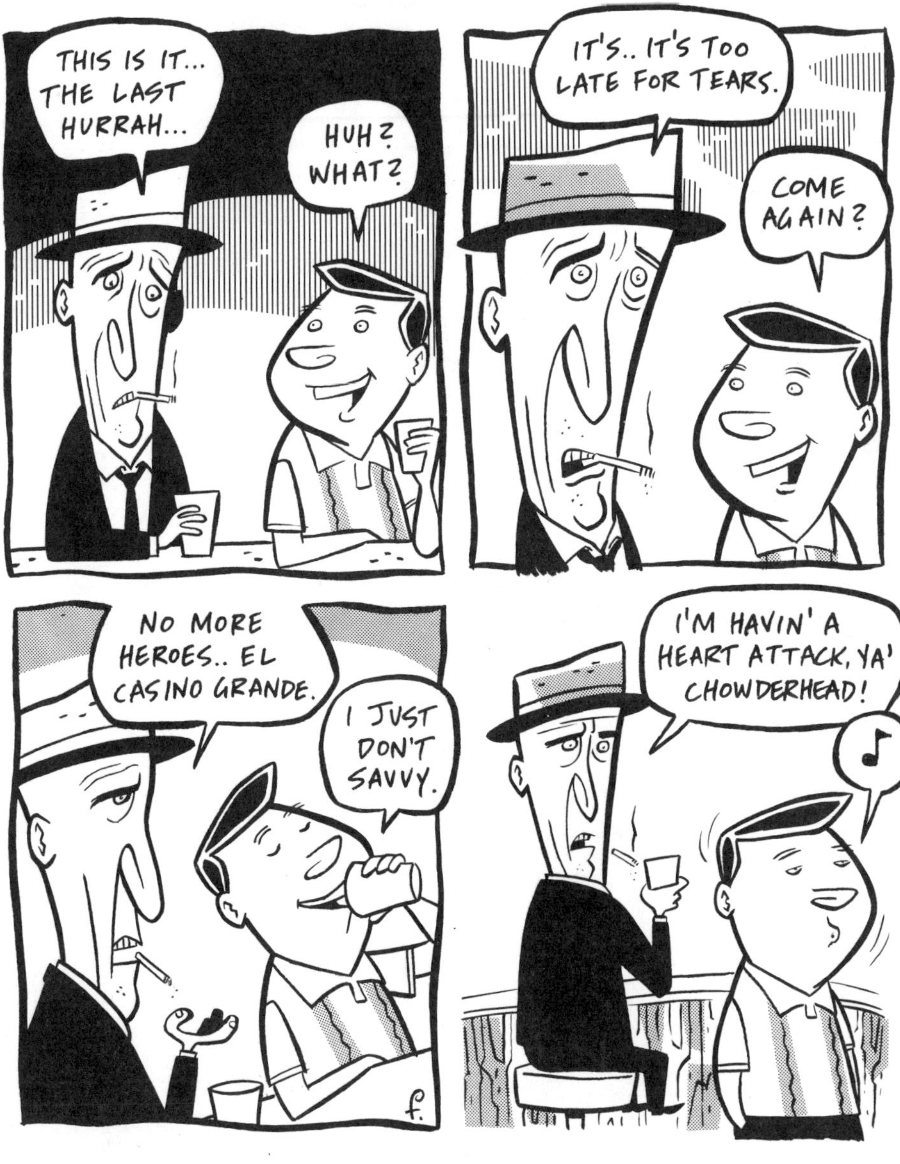
THIS IS IT... THE LAST HURRAH...
HUH? WHAT?
IT'S.. IT'S TOO LATE FOR TEARS.
COME AGAIN?
NO MORE HEROES.. EL CASINO GRANDE.
I JUST DON'T SAVVY.
I'M HAVIN' A HEART ATTACK, YA' CHOWDERHEAD!

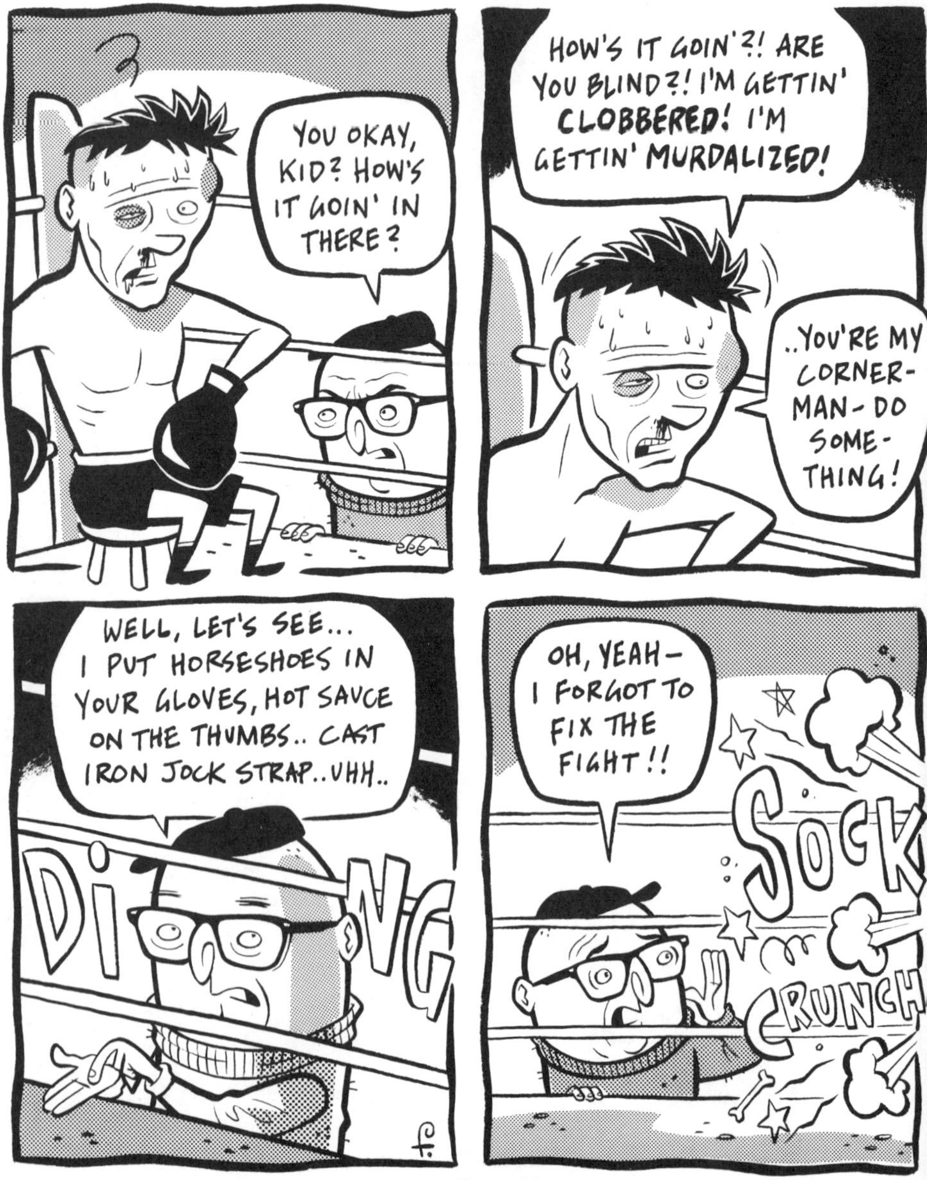
YOU OKAY, KID? HOW'S IT GOIN' IN THERE?
HOW'S IT GOIN'?! ARE YOU BLIND?! I'M GETTIN' CLOBBERED! I'M GETTIN' MURDALIZED!
..YOU'RE MY CORNER-MAN-DO SOME-THING!
WELL, LET'S SEE... I PUT HORSESHOES IN YOUR GLOVES, HOT SAUCE ON THE THUMBS.. CAST IRON JOCK STRAP..UHH..
DING
OH, YEAH- I FORGOT TO FIX THE FIGHT!!
SOCK
CRUNCH

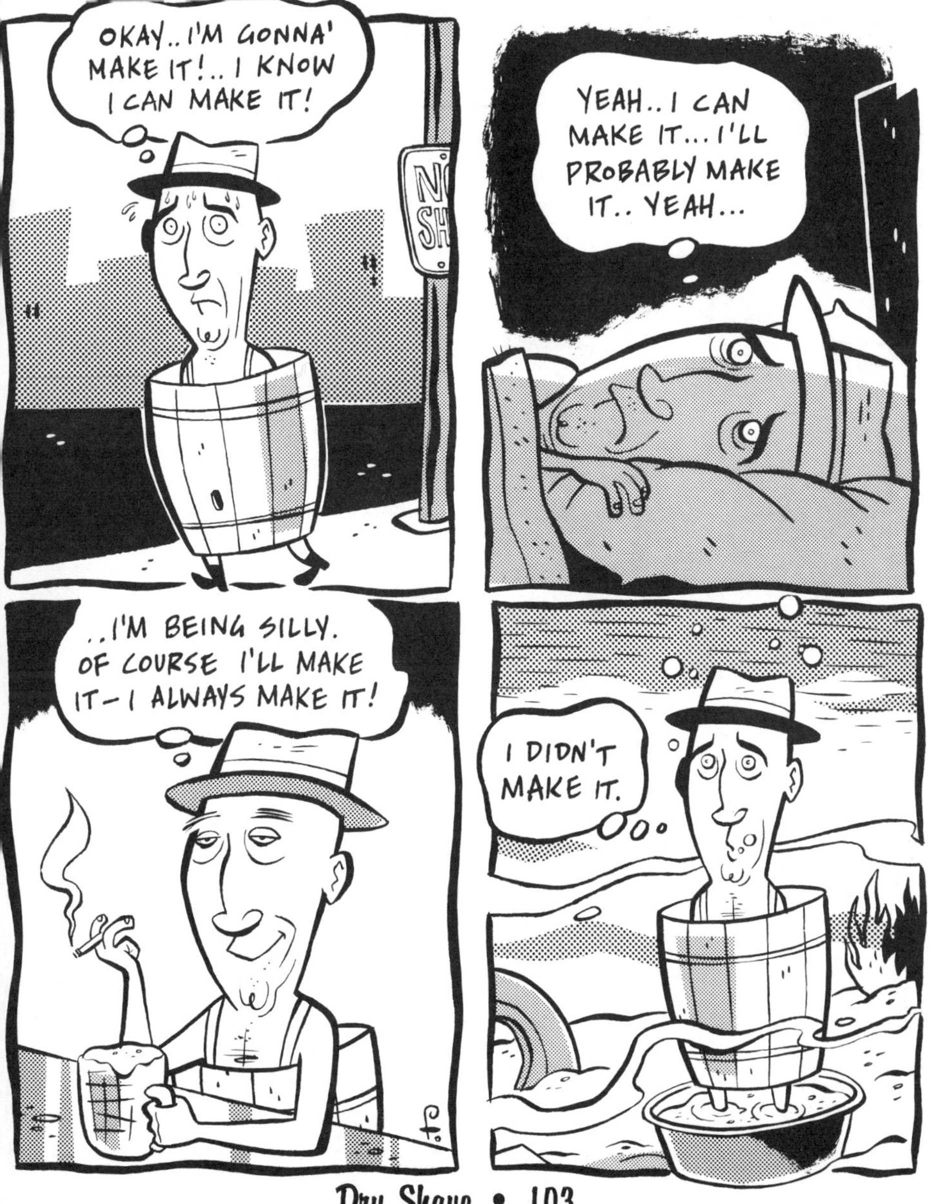
OKAY.. I'M GONNA' MAKE IT!.. I KNOW I CAN MAKE IT!
NO SH
YEAH.. I CAN MAKE IT... I'LL PROBABLY MAKE IT.. YEAH...
..I'M BEING SILLY. OF COURSE I'LL MAKE IT– I ALWAYS MAKE IT!
I DIDN'T MAKE IT.

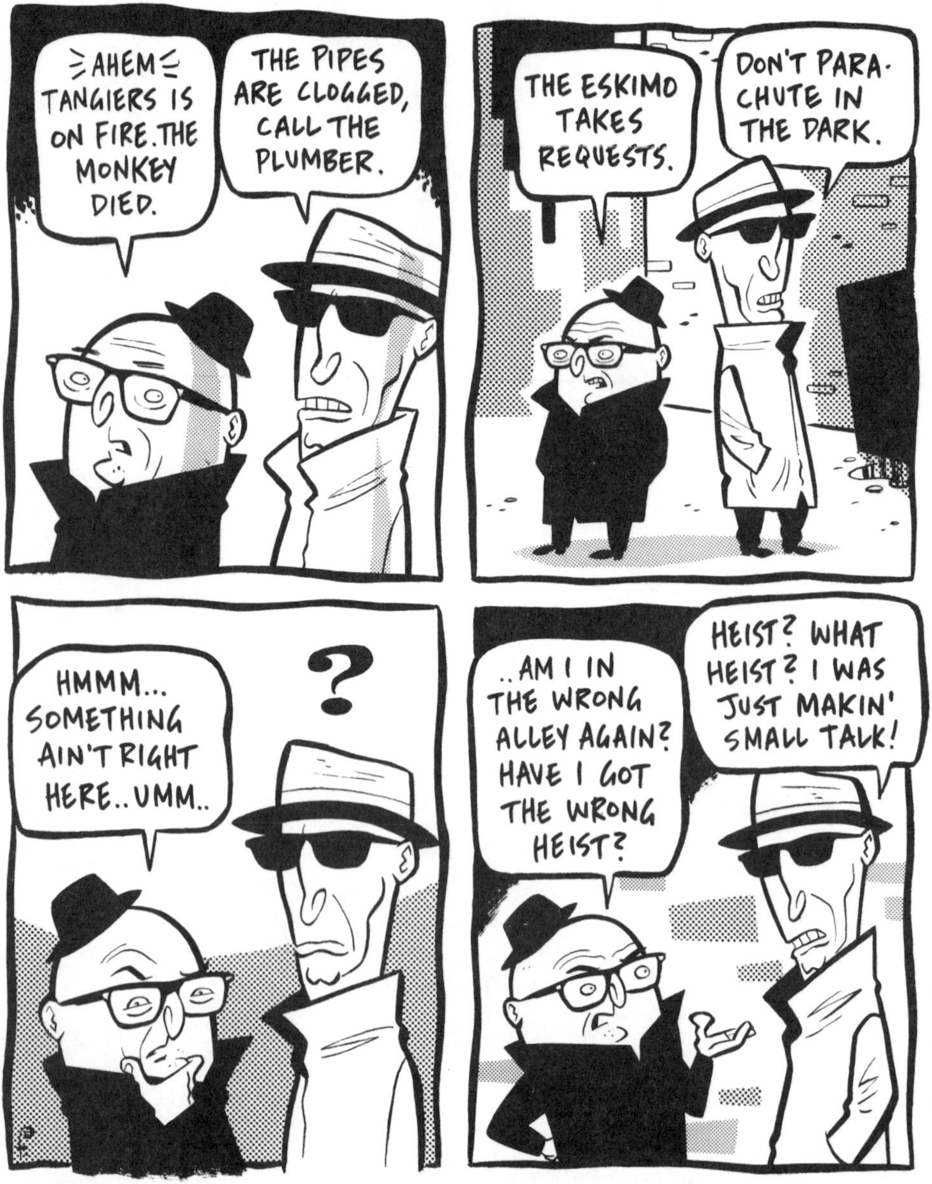

≥AHEM≤ TANGIERS IS ON FIRE. THE MONKEY DIED.
THE PIPES ARE CLOGGED, CALL THE PLUMBER.
THE ESKIMO TAKES REQUESTS.
DON'T PARA-CHUTE IN THE DARK.
HMMM... SOMETHING AIN'T RIGHT HERE.. UMM..
?
..AM I IN THE WRONG ALLEY AGAIN? HAVE I GOT THE WRONG HEIST?
HEIST? WHAT HEIST? I WAS JUST MAKIN' SMALL TALK!

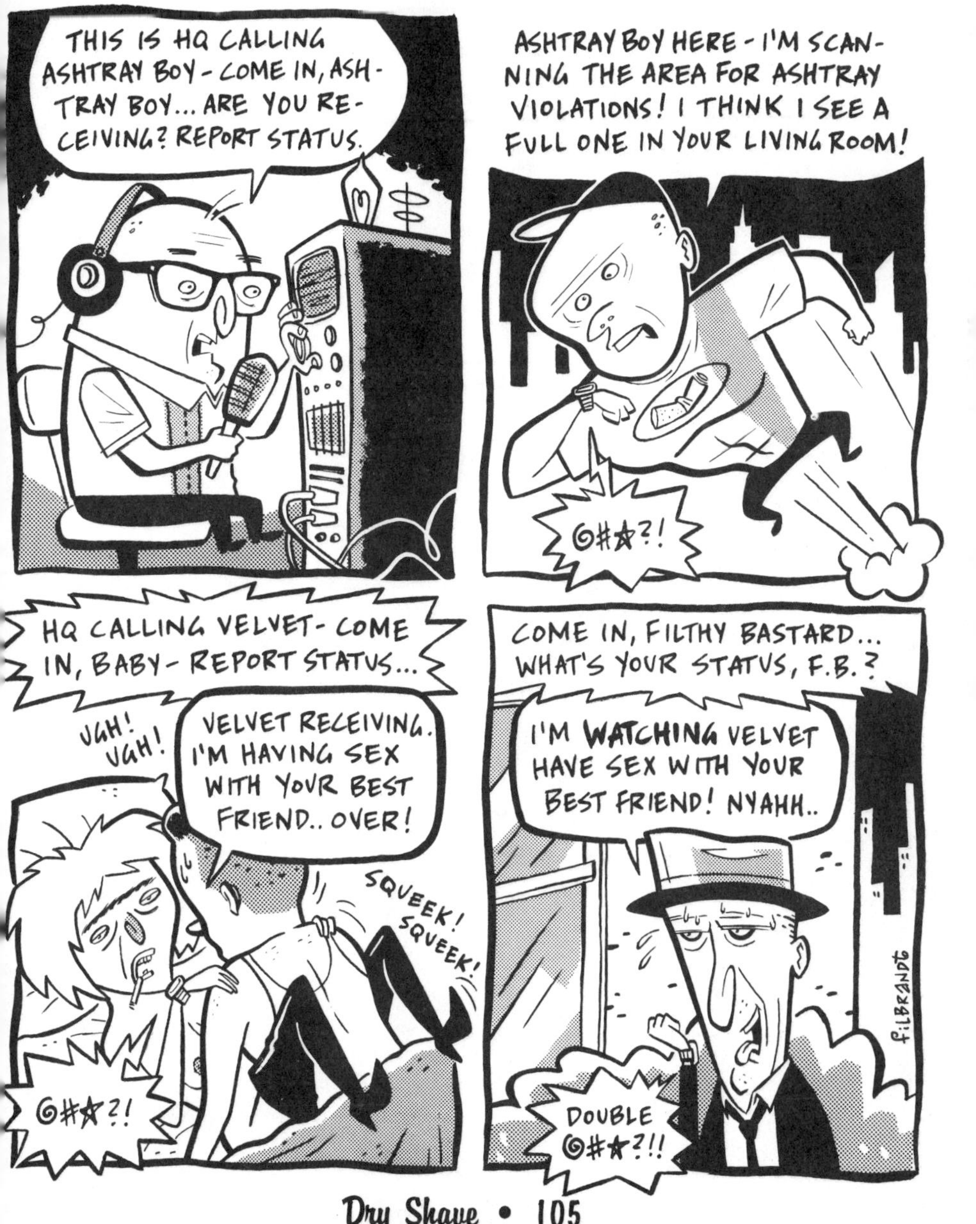
THIS IS HQ CALLING ASHTRAY BOY - COME IN, ASH-TRAY BOY... ARE YOU RE-CEIVING? REPORT STATUS.
ASHTRAY BOY HERE - I'M SCAN-NING THE AREA FOR ASHTRAY VIOLATIONS! I THINK I SEE A FULL ONE IN YOUR LIVING ROOM!
@#☆?!
HQ CALLING VELVET- COME IN, BABY- REPORT STATUS...
UGH! UGH!
VELVET RECEIVING. I'M HAVING SEX WITH YOUR BEST FRIEND.. OVER!
SQUEEK! SQUEEK!
@#☆?!
COME IN, FILTHY BASTARD... WHAT'S YOUR STATUS, F.B.?
I'M **WATCHING** VELVET HAVE SEX WITH YOUR BEST FRIEND! NYAHH..
DOUBLE @#☆?!!
FILBRANDT

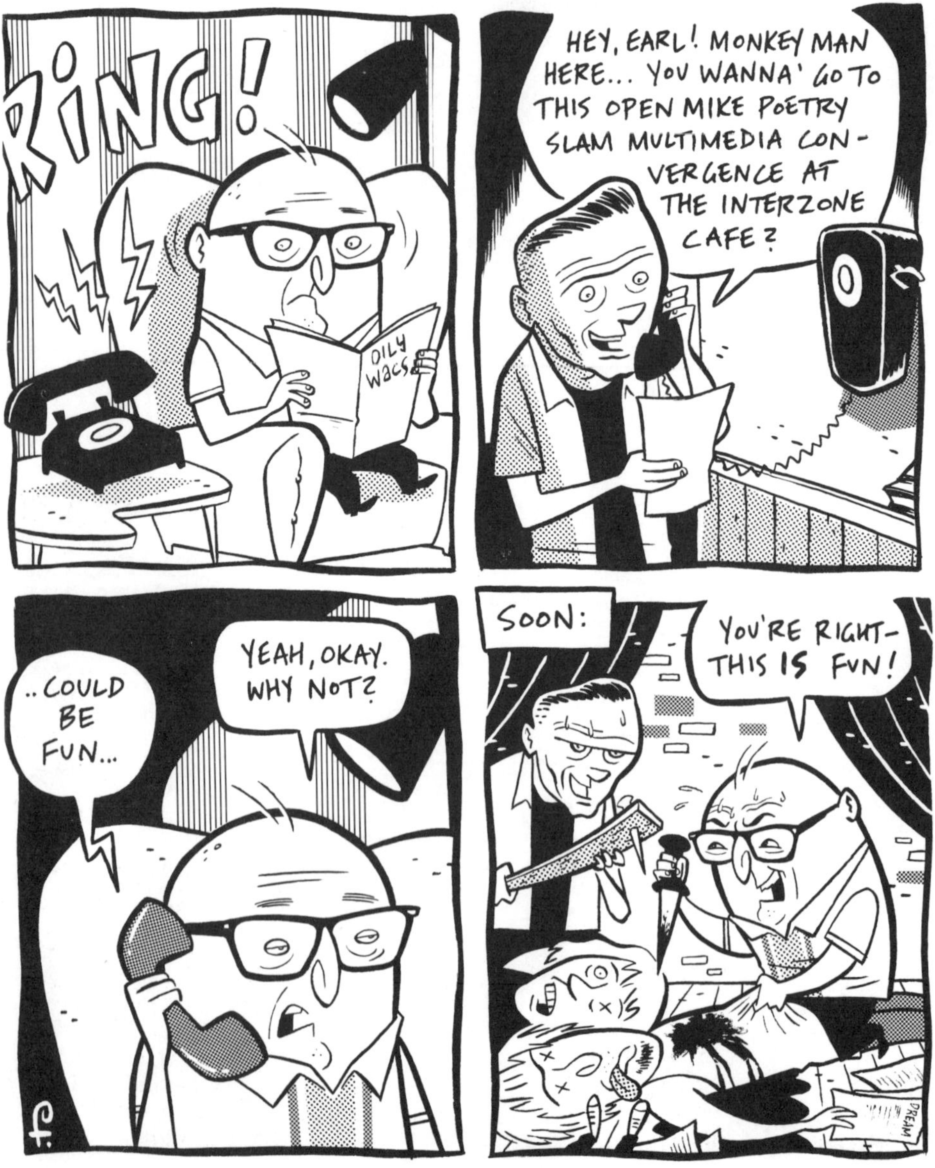
RING!
DILY WACS
HEY, EARL! MONKEY MAN HERE... YOU WANNA' GO TO THIS OPEN MIKE POETRY SLAM MULTIMEDIA CON-VERGENCE AT THE INTERZONE CAFE?
..COULD BE FUN...
YEAH, OKAY. WHY NOT?
SOON:
YOU'RE RIGHT- THIS IS FUN!
DREAM

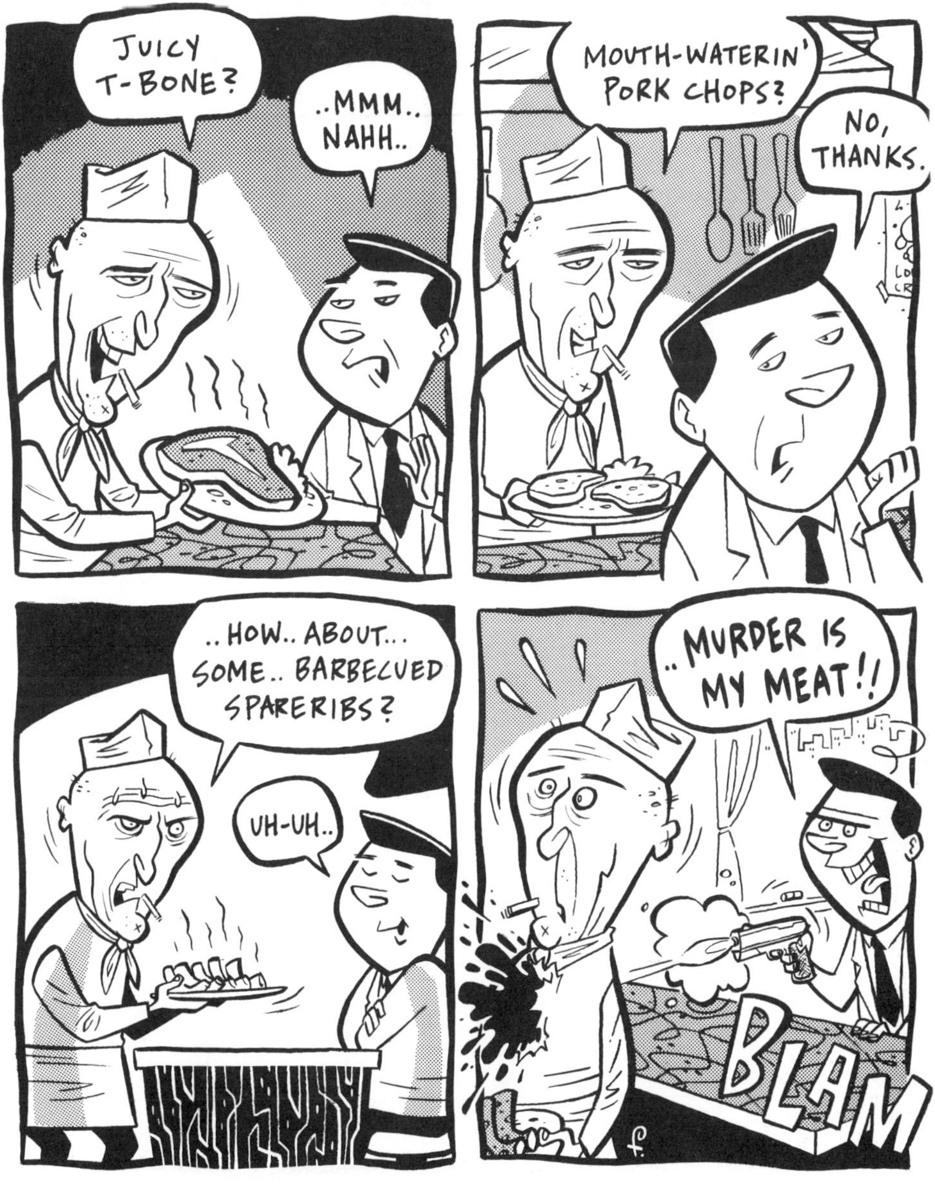
JUICY T-BONE?
..MMM.. NAHH..
MOUTH-WATERIN' PORK CHOPS?
NO, THANKS.
..HOW.. ABOUT... SOME.. BARBECUED SPARERIBS?
UH-UH..
..MURDER IS MY MEAT!!
BLAM

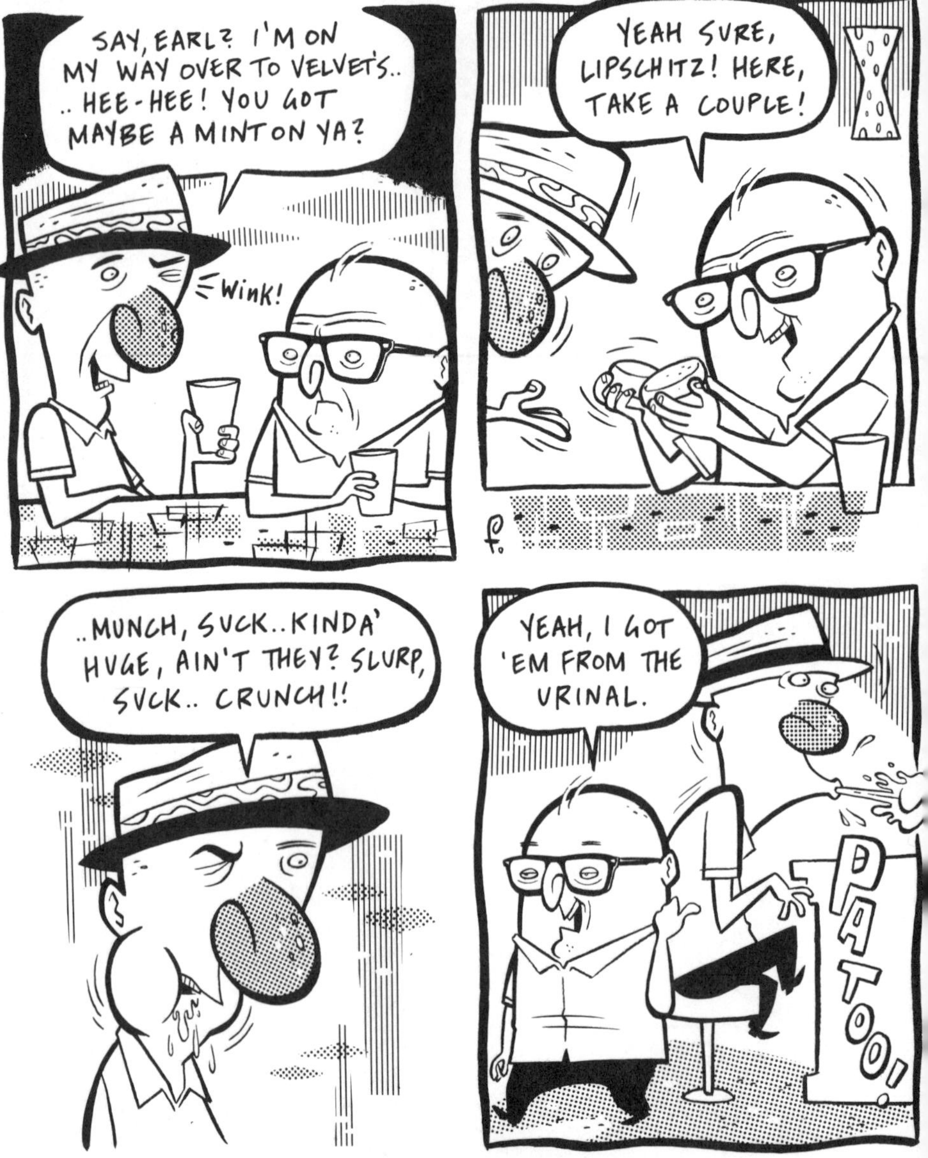
SAY, EARL? I'M ON MY WAY OVER TO VELVET'S.. .. HEE-HEE! YOU GOT MAYBE A MINT ON YA?
Wink!
YEAH SURE, LIPSCHITZ! HERE, TAKE A COUPLE!
..MUNCH, SUCK..KINDA' HUGE, AIN'T THEY? SLURP, SUCK.. CRUNCH!!
YEAH, I GOT 'EM FROM THE URINAL.
PATOO!

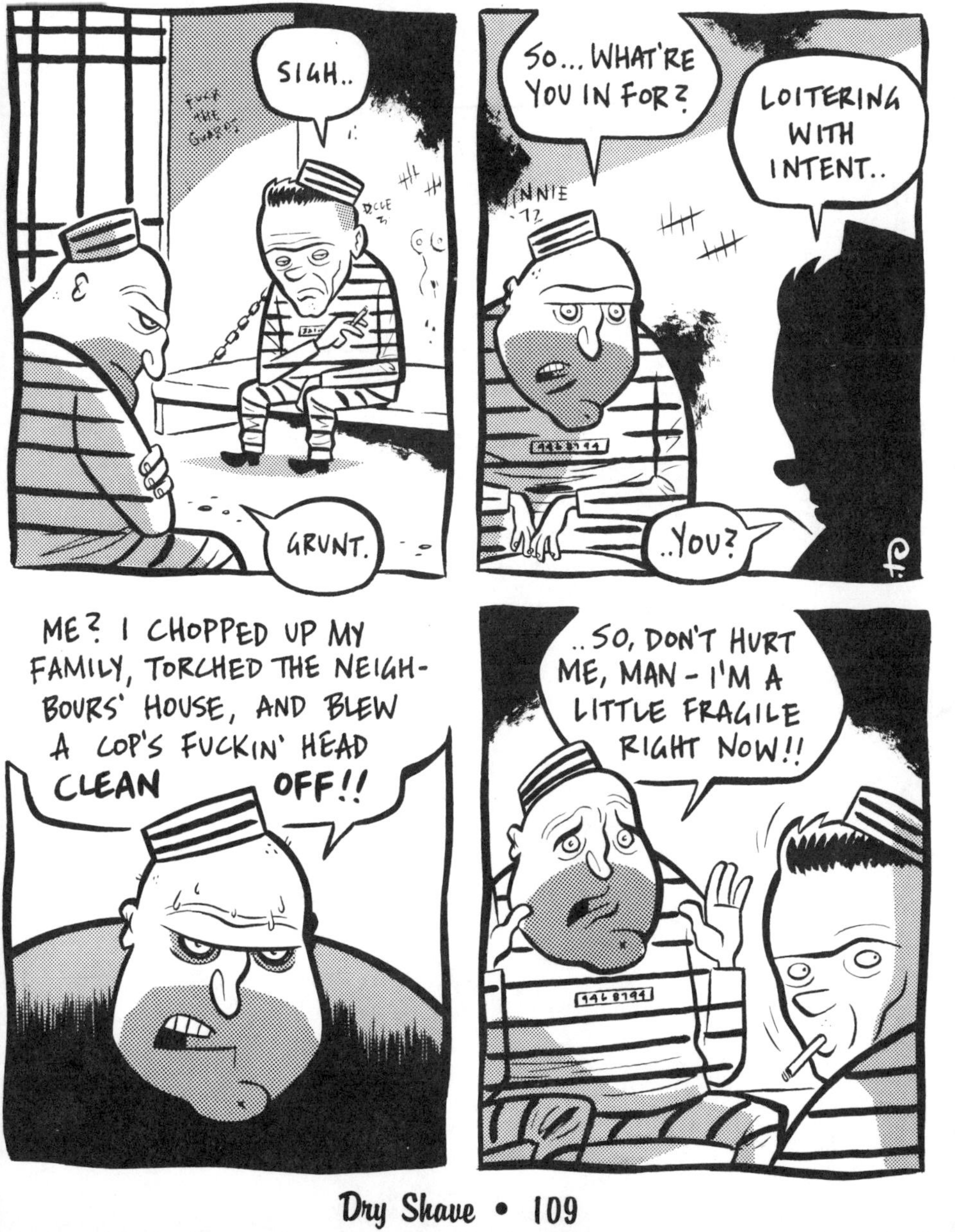
SIGH..
GRUNT.
SO... WHAT'RE YOU IN FOR?
LOITERING WITH INTENT..
..YOU?
ME? I CHOPPED UP MY FAMILY, TORCHED THE NEIGH-BOURS' HOUSE, AND BLEW A COP'S FUCKIN' HEAD CLEAN OFF!!
..SO, DON'T HURT ME, MAN - I'M A LITTLE FRAGILE RIGHT NOW!!

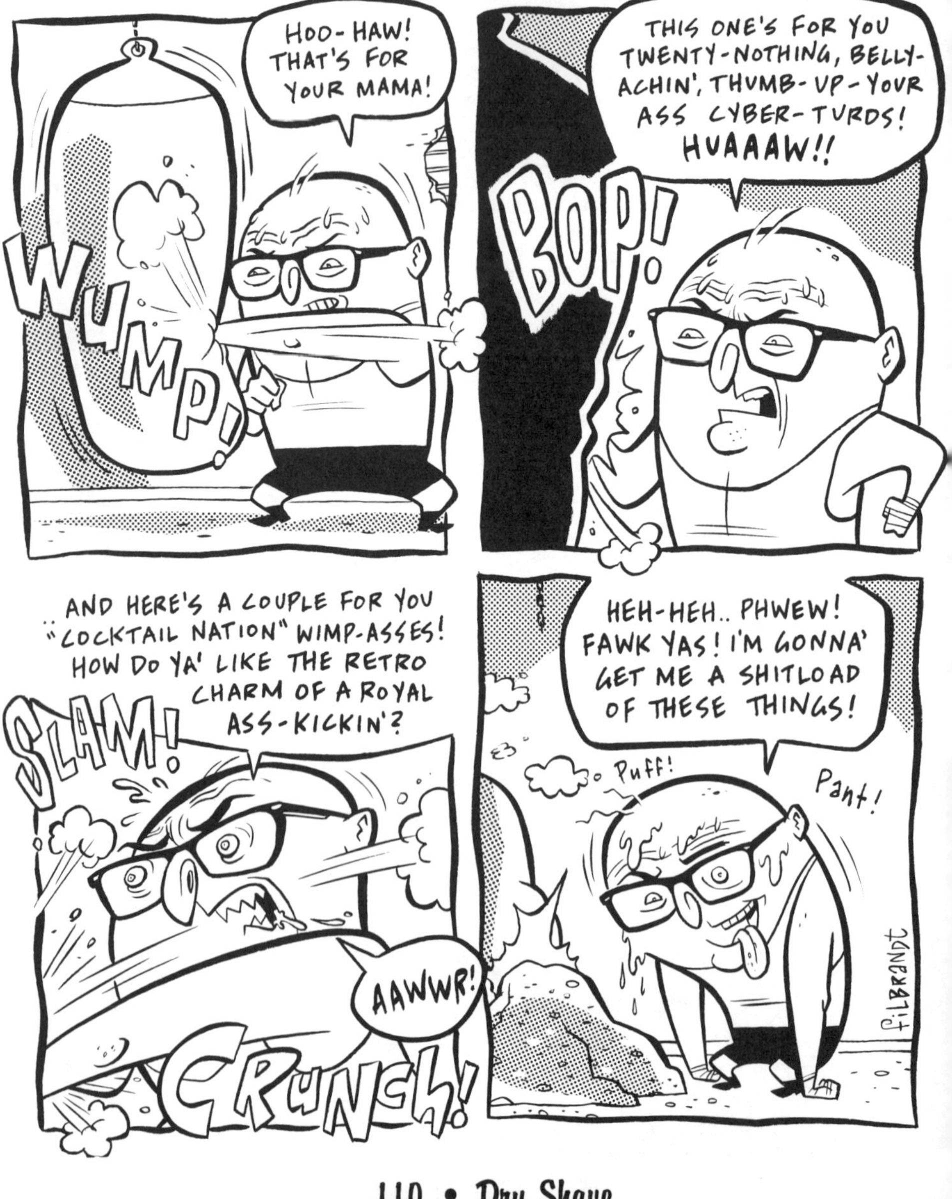
HOO-HAW! THAT'S FOR YOUR MAMA!
WUMP!
THIS ONE'S FOR YOU TWENTY-NOTHING, BELLY-ACHIN', THUMB-UP-YOUR ASS CYBER-TURDS! HUAAAW!!
BOP!
AND HERE'S A COUPLE FOR YOU "COCKTAIL NATION" WIMP-ASSES! HOW DO YA' LIKE THE RETRO CHARM OF A ROYAL ASS-KICKIN'?
SLAM!
AAWWR!
CRUNCH!
HEH-HEH.. PHWEW! FAWK YAS! I'M GONNA' GET ME A SHITLOAD OF THESE THINGS!
Puff!
Pant!
FILBRANDT

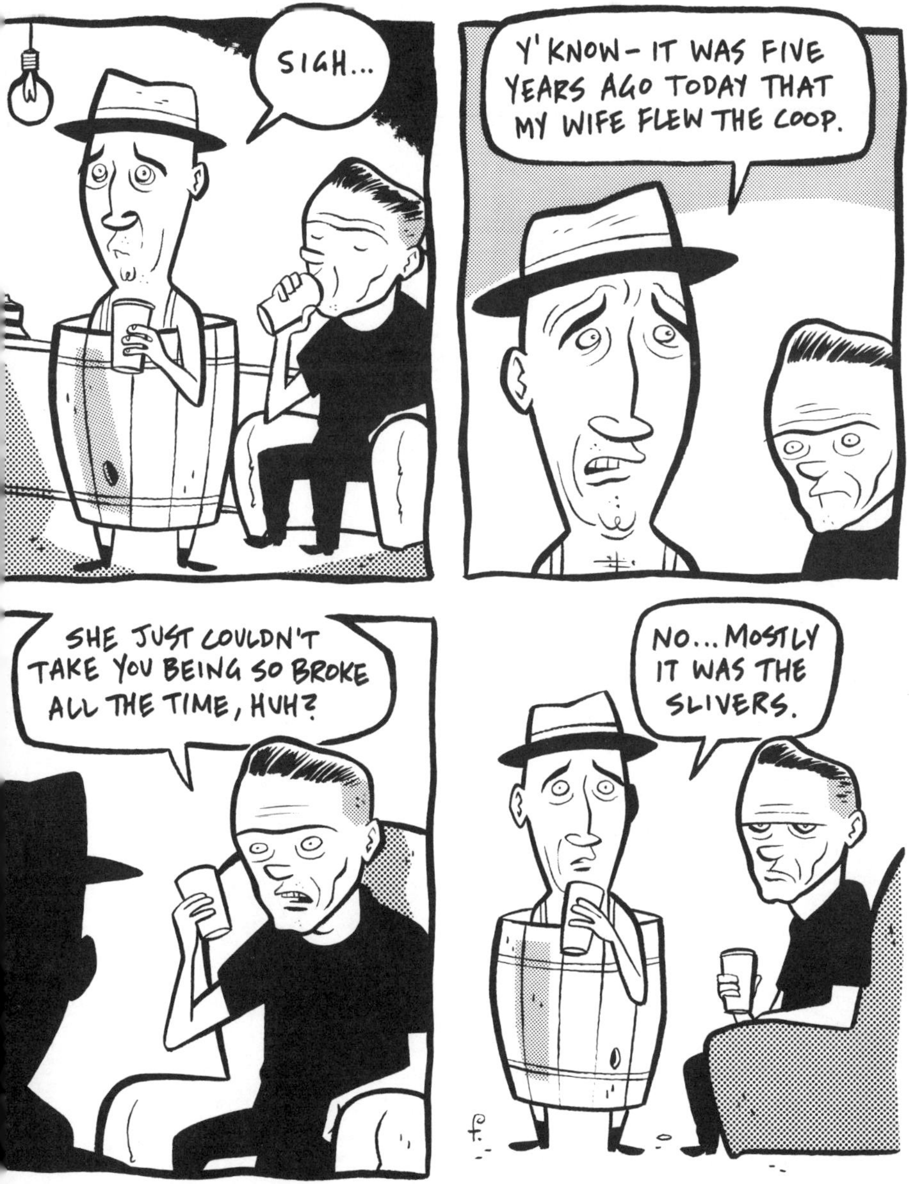
SIGH...
Y'KNOW- IT WAS FIVE YEARS AGO TODAY THAT MY WIFE FLEW THE COOP.
SHE JUST COULDN'T TAKE YOU BEING SO BROKE ALL THE TIME, HUH?
NO... MOSTLY IT WAS THE SLIVERS.

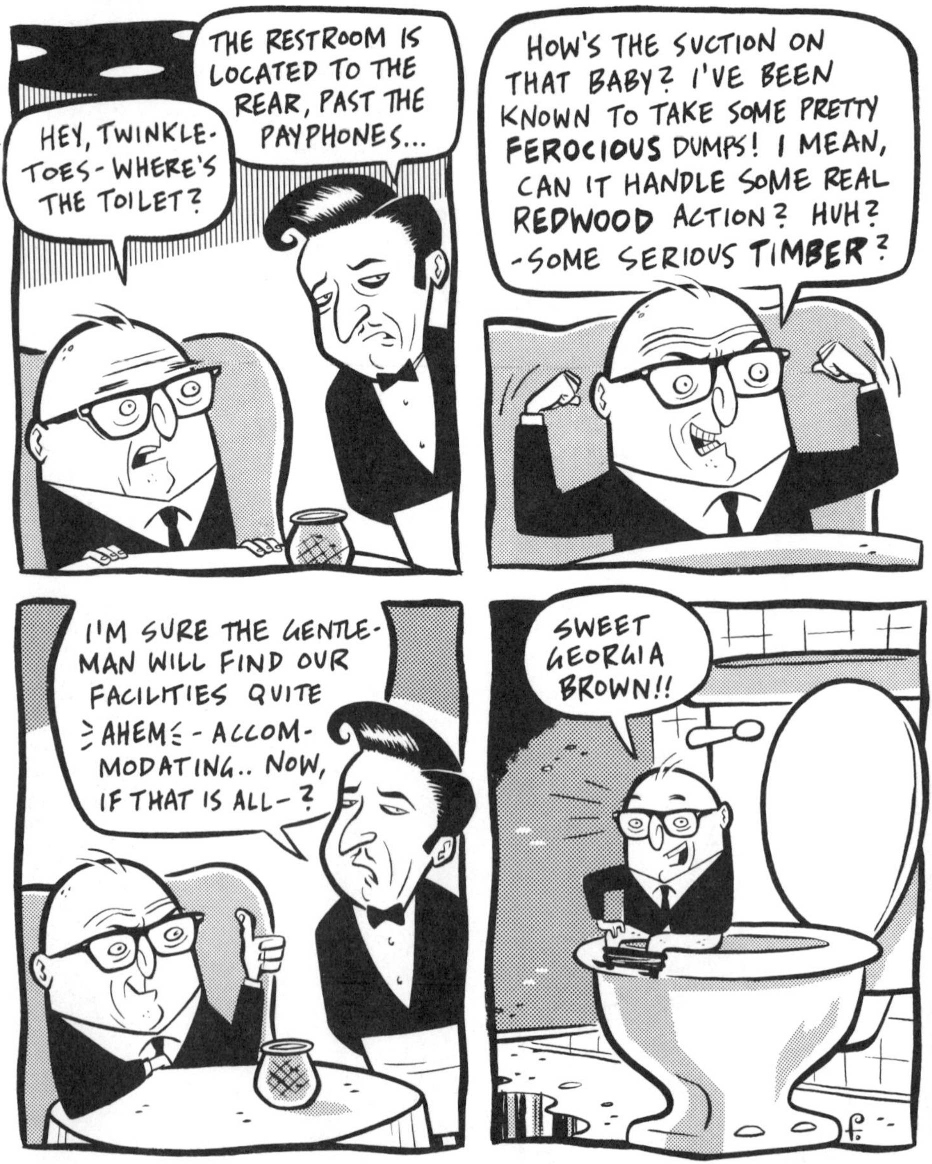
HEY, TWINKLE-TOES- WHERE'S THE TOILET?
THE RESTROOM IS LOCATED TO THE REAR, PAST THE PAYPHONES...
HOW'S THE SUCTION ON THAT BABY? I'VE BEEN KNOWN TO TAKE SOME PRETTY FEROCIOUS DUMPS! I MEAN, CAN IT HANDLE SOME REAL REDWOOD ACTION? HUH? -SOME SERIOUS TIMBER?
I'M SURE THE GENTLE-MAN WILL FIND OUR FACILITIES QUITE ≥AHEM≤ - ACCOM-MODATING.. NOW, IF THAT IS ALL-?
SWEET GEORGIA BROWN!!

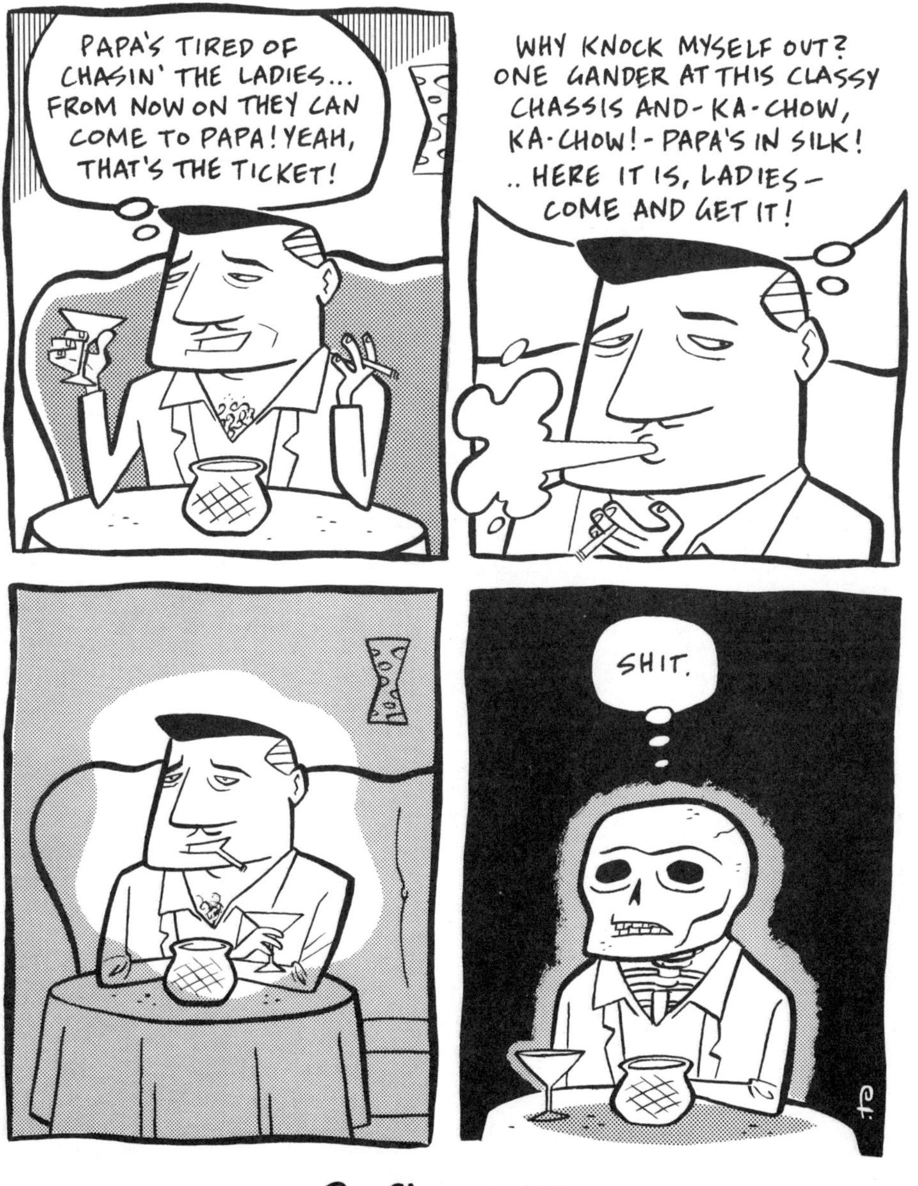
PAPA'S TIRED OF CHASIN' THE LADIES... FROM NOW ON THEY CAN COME TO PAPA! YEAH, THAT'S THE TICKET!
WHY KNOCK MYSELF OUT? ONE GANDER AT THIS CLASSY CHASSIS AND-KA-CHOW, KA-CHOW!-PAPA'S IN SILK! .. HERE IT IS, LADIES- COME AND GET IT!
SHIT.

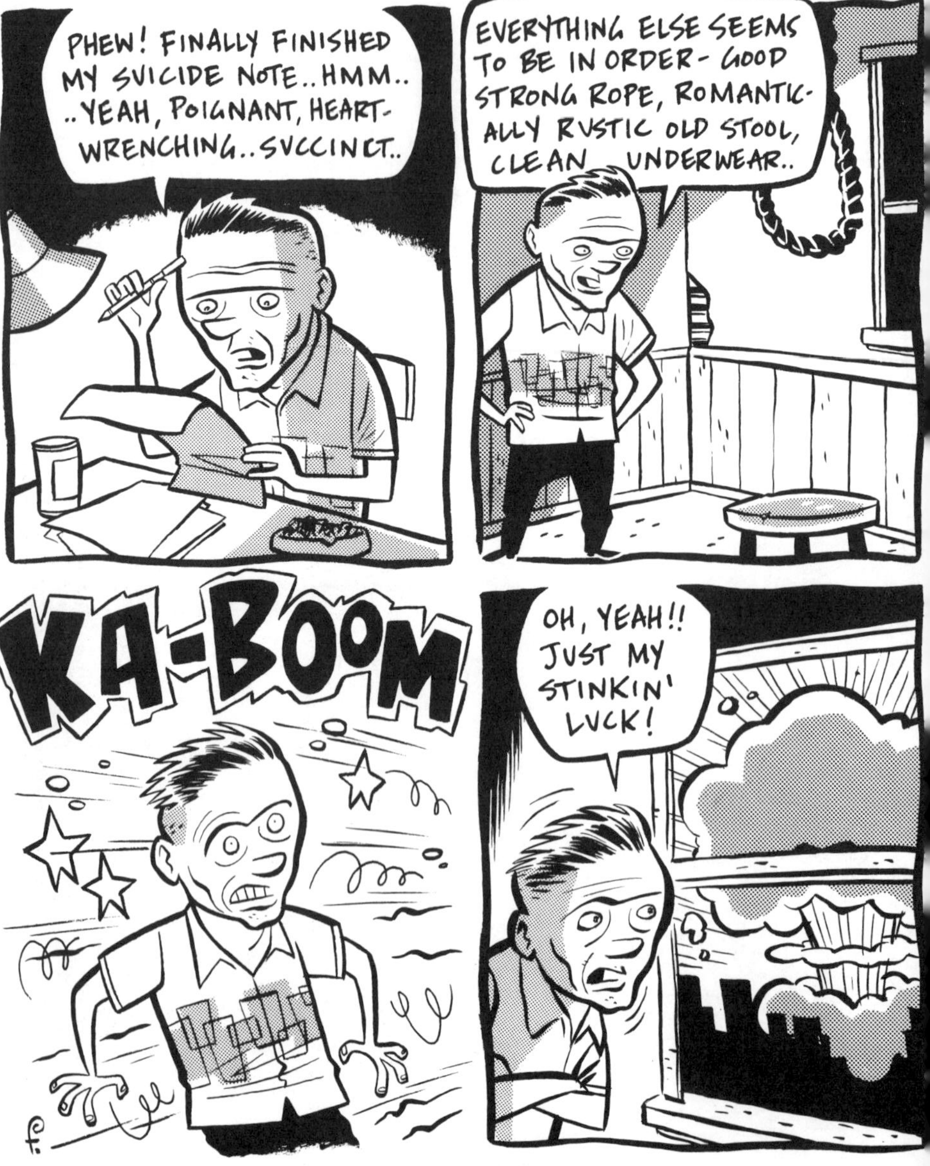
PHEW! FINALLY FINISHED MY SUICIDE NOTE..HMM.. ..YEAH, POIGNANT, HEART-WRENCHING..SUCCINCT..
EVERYTHING ELSE SEEMS TO BE IN ORDER- GOOD STRONG ROPE, ROMANTIC-ALLY RUSTIC OLD STOOL, CLEAN UNDERWEAR..
KA-BOOM
OH, YEAH!! JUST MY STINKIN' LUCK!

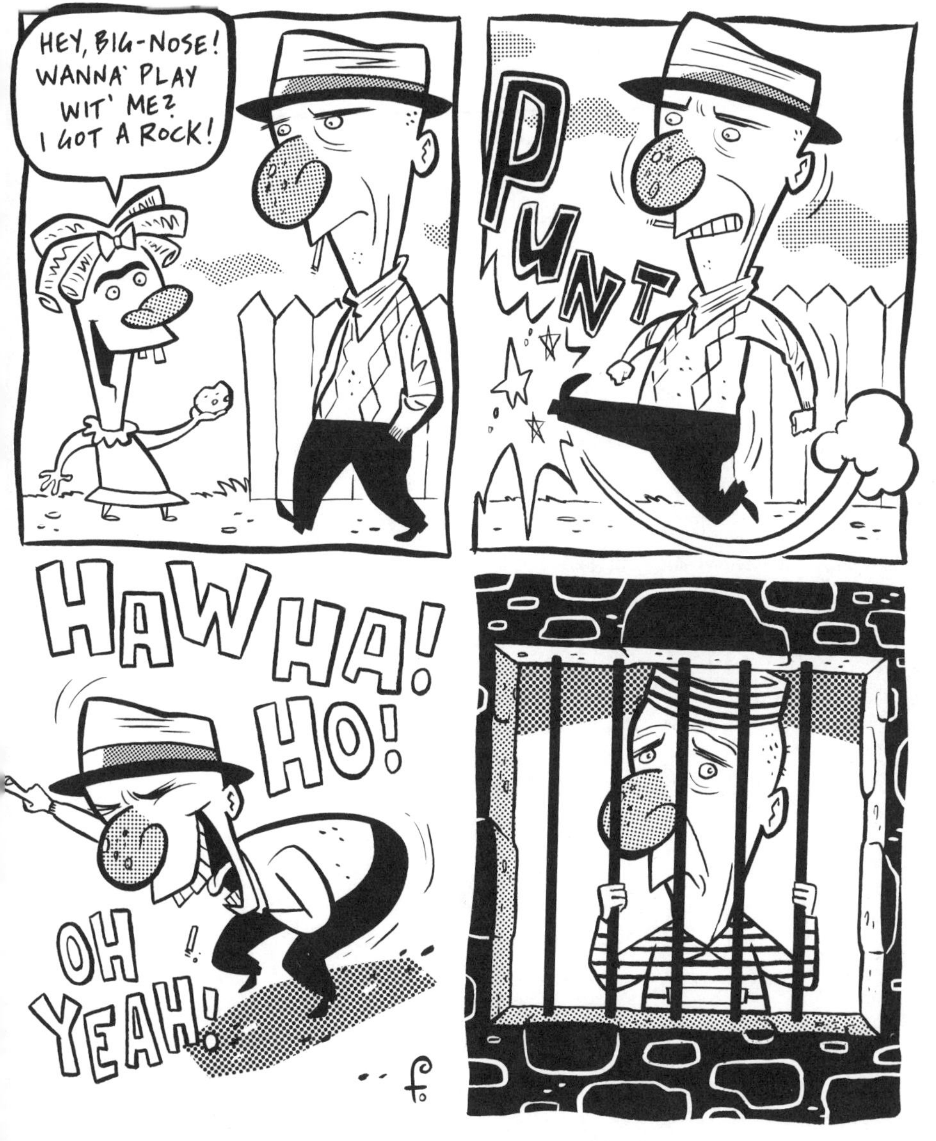
HEY, BIG-NOSE! WANNA' PLAY WIT' ME? I GOT A ROCK!
PUNT
HAW HA! HO!
OH YEAH!
f.

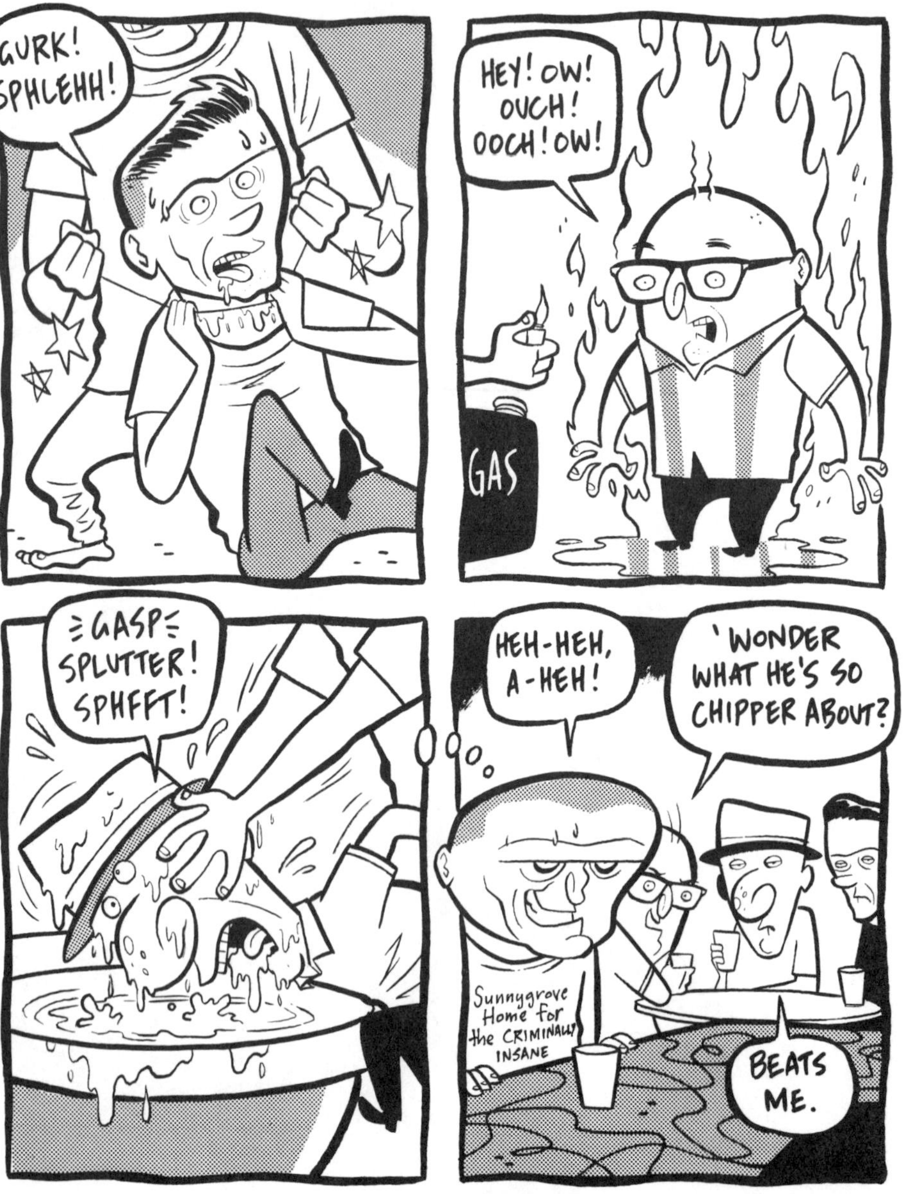
GURK! SPHLEHH!
HEY! OW! OUCH! OOCH! OW!
GAS
GASP SPLUTTER! SPHFFT!
HEH-HEH, A-HEH!
'WONDER WHAT HE'S SO CHIPPER ABOUT?
Sunnygrove Home for the CRIMINALLY INSANE
BEATS ME.

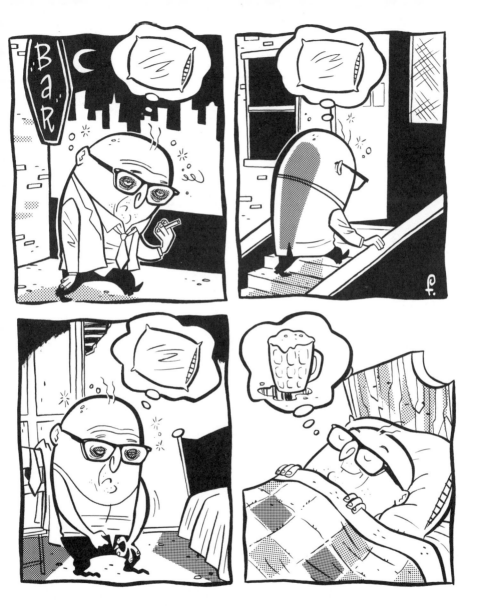

Dry Shave • 117

Publishing notable titles since 1991.

Anvil Press publishes contemporary fiction, poetry, drama and culturally explorative books.

For a free catalogue of Anvil Press titles, write to us at:

Anvil Press Publishers
#204-A 175 East Broadway
Vancouver, BC V5T 1W2
CANADA